Enterprise Exit Processes in Transition Economies

Edited by
Leszek Balcerowicz, Cheryl W. Gray, and Iraj Hoshi

Enterprise Exit Processes in Transition Economies

Downsizing, Workouts, and Liquidation

Edited by
Leszek Balcerowicz
Cheryl W. Gray
and Iraj Hoshi

CEU PRESS

Central European University Press
Budapest

ISBN 963 9116 07 6 Hardback
ISBN 963 9116 16 5 Paperback

Central European University Press
Október 6. utca 12.
H-1051 Budapest
Hungary

Distributed by
Plymbridge Distribution Ltd., Estover Road
Plymouth PL6 7PZ, United Kingdom
Distributed in the United States by
Cornell University Press Services, 750 Cascadilla Street, Ithaca,
New York 14851-0250, USA

Library of Congress Cataloging in Publication Data
A CIP catalog record for this book is available from the Library of Congress

Printed and bound in Great Britain by Biddles Ltd.
Guildford and King's Lynn.

Contents

Contributors

Contributors

Ewa Balcerowicz is co-founder and Vice-President of the Center for Social and Economic Research (CASE) in Warsaw, Poland. She is a full time researcher.

Leszek Balcerowicz, Poland's Deputy Prime Minister and Minister of Finance since November 1997, is a Professor of Economics at the Warsaw School of Economics.

Cheryl W. Gray is the Director of the Public Sector Group in the Poverty Reduction and Economic Management Network of the World Bank, Washington, D.C.

Irena Grosfeld is a Professor at the Departement et Laboratoire d'Economie Theorique et Appliquee, Centre National de la Recherche Scientifique in Paris, France.

Arnold Holle is an Investment Manager with Baring Private Equity Partners, London, United Kingdom.

Iraj Hoshi is a Principal Lecturer in Economics at Staffordshire University, Stoke-on-Trent, United Kingdom.

Jan Mladek served as Deputy Minister of Economy in the Czechoslovak Government in 1991-1992 and as an advisor to the Minister of Industry and Trade of the Czech Republic from 1992-1995. He is the founder and Director of the Czech Institute of Applied Economics in Prague and is engaged in full time research and ocnsultancy.

Nilan Nikolić is a doctoral student at the School of Slavonic and East European Studies, London University, United Kingdom.

Tamas Novak is a researcher at the Institute of World Economy of the Hungarian Academy of Sciences in Budapest, Hungary.

Jacek Rostowski has served as an economic advisor to the Polish Government as well as the authorities in Russia. He is the Chairman of the Economics Department and Professor of Economics at the Central European University, Budapest, Hungary.

Alison Sinclair is a consultant at Intelligent Financial Systems, London,

United Kingdom. She previously taught at Staffordshire University, United Kingdom, and Potsdam University, Germany.

Sabine Schlorke is an Investment Officer with the International Finance Corporation, Washington, D.C.

Miklos Szanyi is a Senior Research Fellow at the Institute of Economics of the Hungarian Academy of Sciences and an Assistant Professor of Economics at Budapest University of Economics.

List of tables and figures

Chapter 3

Chapter 4

Chapter 5

Chapter 7

Chapter 8

Chapter 9

1 Introduction and Overview

Ewa Balcerowicz, Leszek Balcerowicz, Cheryl W. Gray, and Iraj Hoshi

This book is about enterprise exit in the transition economies of Central Europe. What is "exit"? For our purposes it means the noncyclical movement of resources out of an organization into another organization or into unemployment. Exit goes far beyond bankruptcy to encompass a wide variety of processes that differ in several dimensions. First, exit processes differ in range. Exit can be as small as the sale of a few assets or as large as the complete closure of a company. Second, these processes differ in legal basis. Exit via the sale of assets or of parts of a firm as a going concern can be carried out under general civil or commercial codes, while exit via bankruptcy must generally follow detailed legal rules, which are laid out in special laws. We refer to special exit regimes as "classical" exit mechanisms and to those based on general laws as "nonclassical." Third, exit processes differ in motivation. Exit can be voluntary—the sale of surplus property to increase profitability—or involuntary—the result of severe financial distress. Finally, the driving force behind the various processes may differ. Owners and their agents may be in control, particularly when exit is voluntary. But when exit is involuntary, creditors are, more often than not, in the driver's seat.

Is privatization a form of exit? For the purposes of this book, we have not included privatization of an entire operating enterprise in the concept of exit, despite the fact that a key benefit of privatization—a change in control over assets—is also a key benefit of exit. We recognize, however, that much of the downsizing of enterprises that occurred in Central Europe in the early 1990s (as will be discussed in chapter 4) was in fact the partial privatization of parts of viable firms through sales or spinoffs to new owners.

Why are we concerned with exit? Because exit is critical to the functioning of all successful market economies. Without exit, an economy cannot have extensive entry, because new firms are often built with the assets of old firms. Exit, in the sense of a movement of resources across organizations, means that assets are changing hands and can be channelled to more competent management teams. In this way, less efficient organizations disappear and make room for more efficient ones. Furthermore, without the threat of exit and the existence of credible exit mechanisms, creditors—whether suppliers, banks, or the government—cannot influence corporate governance and impose financial discipline (hard budget constraints) on firms. New entry and hard budget constraints together foster the competition that is so essential in forcing resources to migrate to their best uses (allocative efficiency) and in forcing firms to lower their costs of production (technical efficiency and X-efficiency). Exit and entry also foster dynamic efficiency—the selection of appropriate technology over time to enhance productivity. In sum, exit as a threat helps to create proper incentives and enhance financial discipline in existing firms, and exit as a reality allows markets to select the most efficient enterprises as their agents of production. What would a world without exit look like? Socialism!

Developing credible and efficient exit mechanisms is particularly urgent—and particularly challenging—for transition economies. A fundamental change in mind-set is needed, unlike in established market economies. The long legacy of soft budget constraints must be changed, and reforms will be credible only if exit—long avoided under socialism—becomes an accepted reality. Furthermore, the extent of needed restructuring is far deeper in transition economies. When compared to firms in established market economies, socialist firms tended to be too large and often monopolistic. Rapid entry and exit are needed to diversify production and foster the growth of small- and medium-sized firms. In addition, socialist production was skewed toward heavy industry; thus, an economy-wide shift of resources is now needed toward lighter manufacturing and trade and services. From the perspective of individual firms, socialist firms typically had too many employees, were poorly managed, possessed outdated technology, and produced poor-quality products. Being in a seller's market, these firms paid little attention to marketing; having ready access to finance and subsidies, they lacked skills in accounting and financial planning. In many cases, fundamental changes are needed in most, if not all, aspects of enterprise organization, staffing, production, and management. Only financial discipline and competition will bring these changes about. Finally, the transition to capitalism requires a large-scale change from state to private ownership that most established market economies need not face. Exit via asset sales or spinoffs can stimulate ownership change by moving assets from state firms to new private companies.

Although exit is needed, some forms of exit, particularly the creditor-led classical ones, are far more difficult to implement in transition settings. The fresh memories of soft budget constraints undercut both the incentives of firms to accept exit as a real option and the willingness of creditors to use exit as a threat to force payment discipline. Distortions in relative prices, particularly in the early stages of reform before extensive price liberalization, may blur the distinction between viable and unviable firms. And the shortage of legal mechanisms and the weakness of institutions—whether legal institutions or supporting institutions, such as accounting services or banking supervision—make any implementation of classical exit mechanisms problematic.

The absence of classical exit does not mean, however, that exit does not occur during the early stages of transition. Indeed, exit mechanisms typically develop in a particular sequence in such environments. In the first phase, there is likely to be little classical exit, but there could still be an extensive exit of resources through asset sales and downsizing. Specialized exit mechanisms can be expected to develop only over time, as market-based incentives strengthen and institutions develop. This pattern is not unlike that commonly found in developing countries, which may suffer severe economic shocks from time to time but tend to lack the incentives and institutional mechanisms needed for significant exit through more classical channels. As a result, any exit that does occur is more likely to be through downsizing.

Causes and Types of Exit: A Framework for Analysis

We use a simple conceptual framework to identify the processes that affect the rate and forms of exit in a transition economy and to guide the individual chapters and general organization of this book. The framework starts with two variables: the ***inherited economic structure*** of a country and the ***economic shocks*** that hit the country's enterprises in the early stages of transition. The inherited economic structure includes, among other things, the extent of distortions in prices and production profiles (as compared to a market-based economy with similar endowments), the capability and credibility of socialist institutions, and the extent of the population's memory of market-based exit processes. Economic shocks (discussed in greater detail in chapter 3) can arise from radical changes in domestic policies or from exogenous changes in the international environment. The former typically include, for example, rapid cuts in credit or direct subsidies to enterprises and dramatic changes in both domestic relative prices and exchange rates as part of stabilization and liberalization programs. The latter may include rapid changes in commodity prices, in foreign demand for a country's exports, or in trading arrangements. For the transition economies of Central Europe, the demise of the trading regime of the Council for Mutual Economic Assistance (CMEA) was a major exogenous shock, coinciding in the early 1990s with recessions in Western and Eastern European trading partners.

The inherited economic structure and the extent of economic shocks that affect an economy together cause a certain amount of pressure for firms to exit. Given this ***pressure to exit,*** two factors influence the extent and form of actual exit: the government's policy response—in particular, the extent of ***financial accommodation*** it allows—and the ***processing capacity*** that exists for exit, given the specific legal and administrative framework in the country. Governments can rid enterprises of the pressure to exit, for example, by giving new subsidies or credit, providing tax relief through lower tax rates or the build up of tax arrears, or erecting new barriers to trade and competition. To the extent that governments adopt such accommodative policies, the pressure on firms to exit will decrease; to the extent that they resist financial accommodation, the pressure will remain. Among transition countries, the more progressive reformers are generally the ones that have offered less financial accommodation to firms in financial distress.

The mechanisms through which exit occurs will depend in part on the legal and administrative framework in the country: namely, the design of laws covering classical exit mechanisms (whether company or state enterprise liquidation laws, bankruptcy laws, or other special exit regimes like the Polish bank conciliation process discussed in chapter 7 or the Hungarian debtor consolidation scheme mentioned in chapter 6) and the administrative capacity of the courts and related professions (such as bailiffs, trustees, liquidators, and such supporting institutions as accountants, appraisers, investigators, securities regulators, or the press) to implement the law. Well-developed legal and administrative machinery makes classical exit easier, and an increased demand for exit helps propel institutional development.[1]

We differentiate types of exit along two dimensions: (1) who is in control of the process and (2) whether the exit mechanism is conducted under special legal and administrative regimes (classical exit) or under general laws, such as civil or commercial codes, that cover basic market functioning. Who controls the exit process is not necessarily the same as who formally initiates it; control refers to who has the primary power to dictate outcomes. In general, control is in the hands of either owners (often with managers as agents) or creditors. Exit controlled by owners includes downsizing (i.e., the sale of assets or, less frequently, of parts of a firm) and owner-led liquidation (of either private or state companies under general company law or state companies under special state enterprise law). Exit controlled by creditors includes workouts under general contract law, reorganizations under bankruptcy-type laws, and liquidation under bankruptcy law. The major difference between the first two (workouts and reorganizations) is typically who is bound by the process: workouts under contract law bind only direct parties to the negotiations, while reorganizations under bankruptcy-type laws (whether "bankruptcy" in Hungary, "settlement" in the Czech Republic, or "arrangement" or "conciliation" in Poland) bind all creditors if a certain proportion agree.

Whether owner-led or creditor-led, exit processes are generally carried out by agents (managers, trustees, or liquidators), who act on behalf of creditors. If the agents' own interests are incompatible with those of their principals (whether owners or creditors) and monitoring by principals is weak, outcomes may differ from what they would be in the absence of these principal–agent relationships. For example, if banks are repeatedly recapitalized, as they were in Hungary between 1991 and 1994, they are likely to lack the incentive to pursue debt collection vigorously.[2] Similarly, if the remuneration of bankruptcy trustees or liquidators is too low, as in the Czech Republic until recently (see chapter 5), or is unrelated to the speed or outcome of a bankruptcy, as in Hungary (see chapter 6), the process may be slow or inefficient. Such skewed incentives are particularly common in the early stages of transition and make it more likely, particularly given the weakness of monitoring, that the rates and the outcomes of exit will differ from those expected in stable market economies.

Design Issues in Classical Exit Mechanisms

Most of the country chapters in this book focus on the design and implementation of classical exit mechanisms. Below are some of the key issues in the design of these processes.

Trigger. Ideally, the eligibility of firms to enter classical exit mechanisms such as bankruptcy should be based on cash flow criteria (the inability to pay debts as they become due) rather than balance sheet insolvency. The latter is an inaccurate measure—given the severe distortions resulting from accounting standards and valuation of assets in many transition economies—and can lead to uncertainty, arbitrariness, and corruption in the choice of firms that enter the process. Hungary uses a cash flow trigger, while the Czech Republic relies on a balance sheet notion of insolvency.

Relief from creditors. Whether or not to allow debtor firms filing for formal reorganization some period of automatic relief from creditors (i.e., a moratorium on debt service and on creditors' power to foreclose on collateral) is a difficult issue. On the one hand, debtors in true financial distress may need such relief in order to survive long enough to formulate and negotiate a reorganization plan with creditors. On the other hand, the existence of such automatic relief invites filings from firms not in true financial distress just to save debt service costs. For example, Hungary's 1992 law granted automatic relief from creditors for three months, but such automatic relief was replaced in September 1993 by discretionary relief (dependent on a vote of creditors) in the belief that the former rule had invited too much abuse (a criticism also often levied against the well-known "Chapter 11" reorganization scheme in the U.S.). Perhaps the best advice is to allow some protection from creditors, but limit this period and give creditors recourse (such as the ability to void the protection and collect overdue debt service) if a filing is proven to be spurious.

Replacement of managers. Some classical workout processes (such as those in Hungary and Poland) allow incumbent managers to stay in power and formulate the initial reorganization plan. Such a provision is based on the belief that managers know the company's problems best and is supported by the fact that such leniency encourages firms to file earlier, before the problems have become insurmountable. In contrast, other processes (such as that in the United Kingdom) automatically remove incumbent management and replace it with a receiver or administrator who subsequently runs the company and decides on a workout plan. In transition economies, the former approach is arguably most reasonable. Managers are in short supply, and there are initially only a few trained receivers upon whom to draw. Incumbent management may indeed have a better sense of the company's problems, which may or may not—given the many internal and external shocks facing transition economies—be the fault of earlier management practices. Finally, the designation is not necessarily final. If incumbent management is clearly part of the problem, creditors should be free to disapprove the first plan and submit an alternative one that forces a replacement in management.

Range of possible actions. Although there are valid arguments to the contrary, we believe on balance that a bankruptcy law for a transition economy should provide as wide a range of options as possible. Not only is it useful to have a clear reorganization option (in lieu of straight liquidation), but within such a reorganization it should be possible to include financial terms (such as debt forgiveness, extensions of maturity, reductions in interest rates, and debt–equity swaps), governance terms (such as replacement of management or board members), and operational terms (such as changes in employment, investment, lines of business, or asset structure). It is important, however, that the reorganization route should not be mandatory. Firms with no hope of successful reorganization should go straight into liquidation.

Approval percentage. What percentage of creditors should have to approve a formal reorganization for it to be binding on dissenting creditors? A higher percentage provides more protection to creditors—and thus may indirectly reduce the cost of credit— but makes it harder to reach an agreement. Furthermore, a high approval percentage gives greater power and incentive to smaller creditors; this may activate them as monitors but can slow or endanger the process. As a general standard, a significant majority—somewhere around two-thirds of claims—is probably best. Fifty percent may be too low, because such a percentage disempowers too many creditors, and 100 percent is clearly too high. Indeed, a unanimous approval requirement removes the primary difference between formal reorganizations and contractual workout procedures altogether.

Time limits. It is very important to impose reasonable but strictly observed time limits on any judicial process. A debtor's ability to drag on a reorganization process indefinitely will undercut the threat of exit through which creditors can exert financial discipline. A sixty- to ninety-day rule for submitting reorganization plans, with similar time frames for negotiation and the submission of subsequent plans, is reasonable. Time limits of, say, two to three years can be imposed on liquidations.

Transfers to liquidation. The 1991 Hungarian bankruptcy law provided that reorganization cases would automatically revert to liquidation cases if creditors and the debtor failed to reach an agreement on a reorganization plan. While such a rule is quite strict and may inhibit some reorganization filings, it does provide an important impetus to be reasonable and results-oriented in reorganization negotiations. For such a rule to have the desired effect, however, the liquidation process must be efficient and effective.

Points of court involvement. For a formal reorganization or liquidation process to work efficiently, particularly in transition economies where judicial institutions are underdeveloped, it is important to minimize the points of court involvement. For example, after a case is approved to proceed (and a trustee or liquidator appointed if applicable), the judge need not be involved except to check progress, hear appeals or complaints about the process from involved parties, and approve the final dispositions of the cases. This is more or less the role of the judge in Hungary, and reorganizations have typically taken between six and twelve months (see chapter 6); this compares very favorably with court-led Czech proceedings that typically last two to three years (see chapter 5). To prevent fraud and asset-stripping, the debtor (in a reorganization) or liquidator (in a liquidation) should be required to submit regular—perhaps monthly—financial reports to the judge. The judge should not, however, be responsible for the day-to-day handling of the case.

Need for creditors' committees and trustees. In reorganization cases, both creditors' committees and trustees appointed to represent creditors can help oversee the process and offset the strong powers and control exercised by debtor management. They can also help monitor the actions of liquidators in liquidation cases. However, such committees and trustees will succeed at this task only if the creditors are motivated to make them work. To avoid slowing the process, trustees in particular should perhaps be optional rather than mandatory.

Priorities among existing claimholders. Having a clear and reasonable structure of priorities among claims to the bankrupt's assets is extremely important if a bankruptcy law is to work as desired. Secured creditors should have top priority to the secured property, and security interests need to be supported by a well-designed collateral law and registry. Other priority credits, behind those of secured creditors (with respect to the secured property) but ahead of general unsecured credits, might include the costs of the procedure, government liens (whether for tax, social security, customs, or rent arrears), wage arrears, and environmental costs. Next in line come the claims of general unsecured creditors (including secured creditors to the extent that their claims exceed the value of their security), followed by subordinated debt and finally by equity holders.

Priorities for new money. In the United States, loans made to a firm in "Chapter 11" reorganization have priority over pre-existing loans. Indeed, lending to these firms is considered highly attractive for this reason. Such a provision does not exist in the formal reorganization processes in either Hungary or Poland. While it is probably advisable, its importance should not be overstressed. In many cases, firms in financial distress need primarily to streamline and downsize. New borrowing may be of secondary importance, particularly if money can be raised through the sale of superfluous assets and if the reorganization process can be implemented rapidly.

Ability of liquidators to void prior transactions. Liquidators—overseen by judges—need the power to void transactions made up to one year prior to the liquidation filing, if they suspect the transactions are fraudulent. Although this provision is difficult to enforce in practice, given the paucity of transaction records (in part because insiders may be motivated to destroy records that might work against them), it is an important power and should be included in any bankruptcy law.

Remuneration of liquidators. Liquidators must face proper incentives and monitoring if they are to carry out their assigned tasks efficiently and effectively, but many bankruptcy regimes in developing and transition economies have just the opposite—counterproductive incentives and lax monitoring. If liquidators are paid a percentage of the gross revenues of the debtor firm before it is closed, for example, they will have an incentive to keep the firm in operation as long as possible. If liquidators are paid a set fee per month, they may have an incentive to drag the liquidation on for as long as possible. If allowed to hire consultants and experts to help them without limit or monitoring, liquidators may use the opportunity to hire friends and relatives and pay them out of the estate.

A proper incentive structure ties the remuneration of liquidators directly to the amount of proceeds earned upon sale of the debtor's assets. The percentage of proceeds going to the liquidator can be determined on a sliding scale, with the percentage slowly declining as the value of the debtor firm's assets rises. If liquidators need liquidity up front, a portion of their remuneration can be paid in advance, but the total amount paid should still be tied to the proceeds realized from the eventual sale, even if a partial refund of the prepaid amount is sometimes required.

Overview of Findings

The chapters in this book broadly follow the framework and issues outlined above. Together they provide a picture of the nature and magnitude of economic shocks and financial accommodation, the extent of downsizing (or nonclassical exit), and the design and usage of classical exit mechanisms in several of the most advanced reformers among transition economies—the Czech Republic, Hungary, and Poland.

In chapter 2, Iraj Hoshi sets the stage for a later discussion of classical creditor-led exit processes in transition countries by looking at the design of these processes in several advanced market economies. He concludes that the bankruptcy laws of the United States and France, particularly until the mid-1980s, were more sympathetic to debtors than regimes in the United Kingdom and Germany. All of these laws were reviewed and amended in the last decade. Although extensive convergence was expected, the laws in fact maintained significant differences in orientation.

The chapter's discussion of bankruptcy regimes in advanced market economies offers potential lessons for transition economies. The specific conditions in transition economies, in particular the enormous pressure for exit combined with weak institutional capacity for classical exit and widespread creditor passivity, suggest that certain models may be preferable to others. Because financial distress is so widespread in transition economies yet is partly the result of exogenous shocks, more debtor-friendly reorganization strategies should arguably be encouraged. However, careful attention to the design of classical exit mechanisms to create proper incentives for efficient restructuring is important. For example, some kind of automatic trigger, although probably not as strong as that described for Hungary in chapter 6, may be valuable in combating creditor passivity. Furthermore, a decentralized reorganization process is preferable to one with extensive court involvement. In addition, because classical exit is so difficult, downsizing—likely to be the major form of exit during the early stages of transition—should be encouraged. Governments should be wary about imposing restraints on asset sales, although some monitoring of such sales to prevent fraud, such as the kind of monitoring practiced in the early 1990s in the Czech Republic and Poland, may be needed.

Chapter 3 begins the discussion of exit mechanisms in transition economies by summarizing and attempting to quantify the extent and nature of shocks and policy accommodation in the Czech Republic,

Hungary, and Poland in the early 1990s. Jacek Rostowski and Milan Nikolić conclude that the shocks from the breakdown of CMEA trade and from subsidy reductions were more severe than other shocks, such as credit restrictions or the undervaluation of the exchange rate.

Accommodation existed in all three countries, but to a lesser extent than in many other transition economies; some accommodation is indeed unavoidable, but in general "less is better" from an economic perspective, as can be seen in the faster return to growth in countries with less accommodation. The forms of accommodation, however, differed among the three countries discussed in this chapter. Poland was the only one of the three to implement significant trade restrictions, while the allowance of an increase in bad debts was prominent in the Czech Republic, and Hungary's main forms of accommodation were a consistently large budget deficit and growing stocks of bad debts in the banking system. Excessive devaluation of the exchange rate was not an important form of accommodation in Poland or Hungary, although the exchange rate remained somewhat undervalued in the Czech Republic.

The most widespread form of exit to date in transition settings—downsizing by owners—is discussed in chapter 4. Time-series data from the early 1990s on output, employment, and labor productivity are presented by Ewa Balcerowicz, Iraj Hoshi, Jan Mládek, Tamás Novák, Alison Sinclair, and Miklós Szanyi for the largest 150–200 manufacturing enterprises in the Czech Republic, Hungary, and Poland. They show that enormous downsizing occurred in all three countries, particularly in the second year and subsequent years after stabilization. Hungary saw the largest declines in employment, a 47 percent cumulative decline on average over four years, while the Czech Republic and Poland saw cumulative declines of 32 and 33 percent over three and four years, respectively.[3] Employment tended to decline slower than sales (with a lag of at least one year) but eventually caught up, reversing the initial decline in labor productivity. Certainly in the Czech Republic and Poland, and probably also in Hungary, informal downsizing has been the most significant form of exit in transition to date.

Chapter 5, by Iraj Hoshi, Jan Mládek, and Alison Sinclair, begins the analysis of classical exit mechanisms in transition economies by focusing on the Czech Republic. The Czech government accommodated initial pressures to exit through various forms of debt relief and a postponement of the implementation of the 1991 bankruptcy law, but the use of the bankruptcy process in the Czech Republic has expanded rapidly in recent years. The chapter surveys Czech bankruptcy law and recent practice and discusses the results of a sample survey of thirty-one firms in liquidation and bankruptcy, with a view to highlighting the main features of these two types of exit. The chapter concludes that Czech bankruptcy law is too strict and not conducive to reorganization. Even as a liquidation mechanism, the Czech regime has some weak design features—in particular, its weak triggering mechanism, the excessive involvement of courts in all aspects of the process, and the weak incentive structure for liquidators and, until recently, trustees (administrators). Legal institutions are in their infancy in the Czech Republic, and little effort has been made to foster the growth of a well-functioning trustee or liquidator profession. Considering the significant accommodation to initial shocks, the poor design of the law, and the weak supporting institutions, it is not surprising that there were relatively few bankruptcies in the early years of the Czech transition.

In chapter 6, Cheryl W. Gray, Sabine Schlorke, and Miklós Szanyi take a detailed look at Hungary's bankruptcy experience in 1992 and 1993, unique in the transition setting because of its enormous size. Unlike the Czech Republic, Hungary witnessed an explosion in bankruptcy filings in 1992, the first year of the new law's implementation, in large measure due to the automatic trigger mechanism contained in the law. Using data obtained from a survey of 119 firms, the chapter concludes that the process was able roughly to separate viable from unviable firms and that reorganizations, unlike liquidations, were concluded surprisingly quickly. However, the effectiveness of the process was compromised by the banks' weak incentives for monitoring (caused in part by successive bank recapitalizations), by the law's skewed incentives for liquidators, and by the diversion of assets that may have occurred as a result. The liquidation process was particularly slow, and fraud was reputed to be quite widespread. The law was amended in 1993, and its use declined dramatically thereafter. Although the current law could be improved by changing the remuneration of liquidators and taking several other steps, it is in general quite well designed, and major improvement will come only through a strengthening of incentives and the capacity for creditor monitoring.

Because of their variety and complexity, exit mechanisms in Poland are covered in two chapters. Both chapters draw from a sample of 139 firms subject to Poland's Enterprise and Bank Restructuring Program (EBRP), adopted by parliament in February 1993. The EBRP recapitalized seven state-owned commercial banks and required these banks to take action to resolve problem loans. The banks could utilize a new and innovative temporary workout process adopted by Poland in 1993—the bank-led conciliation process—or could sell the debt on the secondary market, or turn to one of several existing classical exit mechanisms.

Chapter 7, by Cheryl W. Gray and Arnold Holle, focuses on three classical exit processes: two creditor-led mechanisms, bankruptcy and court-led reorganization (variously translated as "court conciliation," "settlement," or "arrangement" proceedings), and one owner-led mechanism, state enterprise liquidation under the law on state enterprises. Gray and Holle also look briefly at the experience and characteristics of firms that repaid their debt and firms whose debt was sold on the secondary market. The chapter concludes that Poland's classical exit processes work poorly in stimulating either restructuring or exit and in helping creditors recover debts.

Poland's bankruptcy legislation has major weaknesses in design and implementation, most notably the low priority given to secured creditors, the institutional weakness of the bankruptcy courts and related professions, and the difficulty that judges and trustees have in identifying and curbing fraudulent behavior. State enterprise liquidation is perhaps the most problematic of the classical processes. State enterprise liquidation is almost entirely controlled by debtors and is significantly slower than bankruptcy, even though firms entering this route were supposedly in better shape at the outset. Bank conciliation was available for three years and has now expired. It is time for Poland to shift its energies to improving classical processes, the fundamental tools for debt collection and corporate governance in any market economy.

In chapter 8, Cheryl W. Gray and Arnold Holle look in detail at the bank conciliation process in Poland that was in effect until early 1996. The design of this process had quite a lot in common with the Hungarian reorganization procedure, although the courts were less involved in the Polish process. Banks as major creditors were empowered to negotiate reorganization agreements with problem debtors that were binding on all creditors if creditors holding at least 50 percent of the company's debt agreed. These agreements could allow for debt write-offs, extensions of maturity, and debt–equity swaps, and were in theory based on reorganization plans that required companies to undertake operational restructuring. This chapter looks at the practical operation of the process in sixty-two Polish state enterprises indebted to nine major commercial banks. It concludes that the process was relatively well designed and was generally implemented as intended and in the time frame required. The main result appears to have been debt relief and some limited ownership change, but little actual privatization occurred. There is less evidence of major enterprise restructuring; operating profits declined slightly on average, and some other indicators of restructuring (such as changes in employment, wage levels, and management) lagged in the first two years of implementation.

Chapter 9 ends the discussion by revisiting the question of why exit matters. Irena Grosfeld discusses the links between exit mechanisms and other economic processes, including financial discipline (and the credibility of regime change), privatization, the restructuring of markets and individual firms, the allocation of management skills, and the development of financial systems. She emphasizes the importance of exit mechanisms, including liquidation processes, in unbundling assets and thereby stimulating changes in the structure of markets and production. The author concludes that the short-term negative impact of exit on employment is overshadowed by the more positive long-term effect—as assets move to better uses that generate greater efficiency, increased demand for labor, and higher productivity.

Taken together, the chapters outlined above point to several broad comparative conclusions with regard to the Czech Republic, Hungary, and Poland. Enterprises in all three countries began transition with major distortions in internal structure and sectoral composition, and they all suffered extensive shocks at the beginning of transition due to stabilization and liberalization processes and the collapse of traditional trading structures. Governments in all three countries adopted some accommodative policies to soothe the shocks, but the nature of the exact policies adopted differed significantly among the countries. Furthermore, the policies were not totally accommodative; thus, significant pressures for exit remained.

An extensive exit of resources from existing firms resulted almost immediately in all three settings. The major mode of exit was downsizing. There was relatively little classical exit through bankruptcy or other special exit regimes, particularly in the Czech Republic and to an even lesser extent in Poland. In the Czech Republic, the government gave clear priority to privatization and delayed the implementation of the 1991 bankruptcy law. When the law was finally implemented, it proved to be too restrictive to foster extensive restructuring, and its poor design has hampered institutional development, particularly of a well-trained trustee or liquidator profession.

Hungary is the only one of the three countries to have seen extensive exit via bankruptcy law early during transition. Hungary's law was simpler and better designed than those of the other two countries, particularly better than that of the Czech Republic, and the law included an automatic trigger that countered creditor passivity and led immediately to a massive wave of bankruptcy filings. The experience spurred extensive institutional development in the courts and the trustee profession, but the skewed incentives facing creditors—resulting in part from successive bank recapitalizations and the introduction of a second, poorly designed, albeit temporary, classical exit mechanism—prevented the process from working ideally. Many agency problems arose, as poor monitoring and creditor passivity gave extensive room to managers and liquidators to pursue interests that may have been divergent from those of creditors.

In Poland, a very complex classical legal framework with many intertwined elements has led to confusing and sometimes bizarre outcomes. Firms sometimes move from one exit mechanism to another, perhaps searching for the weakest path. An outdated bankruptcy law has been slow to spur institutional development in courts, and a new modern law is needed. An even worse process governing state enterprise liquidation under the state enterprise law has left bank and trade creditors virtually out of the picture altogether. The most positive element of the exit picture until early 1996 in Poland was an innovative and well-designed process called "bank conciliation" that was available for three years (1993–1996) as a debtor–creditor work-out mechanism. It was similar to Hungary's reorganization process in both design and initial outcomes, and some of its principles could usefully be incorporated into a redesigned judicial bankruptcy regime. On another positive note, Poland also paid significantly more attention than the Czech Republic or Hungary to creditor, particularly bank, incentives during the 1991–1994 period, and this attention promoted rapid change in the outlook and capacity of the banks. Poland still has some way to go, however, in developing good exit laws and institutions.

These experiences confirm the importance of both financial discipline and well-designed classical exit processes. They are not substitutes but rather complements in forcing financial discipline and restructuring in firms, as well as competitive selection among firms.

These experiences also hint at a second general theme: policymakers should arguably focus on improving traditional and broadly applicable exit and workout processes, rather than adding new ones for selected subsets of firms. Special alternatives for selected firms—whether bank conciliation in Poland, debtor consolidation in Hungary, or enterprise isolation programs elsewhere—tend to suffer from the same general problem: they lead firms to expect lenient treatment and thereby create a moral hazard that may stall further restructuring. In any case, traditional processes (formal and informal workout processes and bankruptcy) are needed. Judges need not be heavily involved in all aspects of these processes (and more decentralization to debtors, creditors, trustees, and liquidators is generally better), but some oversight by courts is definitely needed to protect against fraud and to insure due process in the treatment of all parties.

References

Baer, Herbert L. and Cheryl W. Gray. 1996. Debt as a control device in transitional economies: The experiences of Hungary and Poland. In *Corporate Governance in Central Europe and Russia,* edited by Roman Frydman, Cheryl W. Gray, and Andrzej Rapaczynski, Budapest: Central European University Press.

Notes

1. For the purposes of this book, the term "bankruptcy" law refers to a country's classical creditor-led exit mechanism; it virtually always covers creditor-led liquidation and might also include rules for creditor-led reorganization. This terminology may differ from that used in a specific country's laws. For example, Hungary uses the word "bankruptcy" to refer only to the reorganization section of its law.

The word "trustee" generally refers to a court-appointed party charged with overseeing a reorganization process, while "liquidator" refers to a court-appointed party charged with winding down a company and selling its assets in a liquidation proceeding. Some countries use "administrator" or "receiver" to cover these two terms, respectively.

2. Baer and Gray (1996).

3. Spinoffs and "spontaneous privatization" probably accounted for a significant amount of the downsizing in Hungary, more so than in the other countries.

2 Bankruptcy, Reorganization, and Liquidation in Mature Market Economies: Lessons for Economies in Transition

Iraj Hoshi

The Role and Design of Bankruptcy Regimes

Entry and exit are fundamental underpinnings of the competitive process in mature market economies. When a firm gets into financial difficulty in a developed financial market, distress will manifest itself in a lower share price and will set in motion a number of possible mechanisms.

First, a merger or takeover may be encouraged—or provoked—by the appearance of signs of financial distress and a lower share price. This is particularly true if other market participants consider the firm's financial problems a temporary phenomenon caused by inefficient production, or management systems, or an inappropriate output bundle. Through the takeover mechanism, the ownership of the distressed firm may pass on to new owners who can get the firm out of financial difficulty by producing the right bundle of goods more efficiently. The takeover process effectively facilitates the exit of excess or inefficient capacity.

Second, the distressed firm may embark on formal or informal negotiations with its creditors, with a view to working out a program of rehabilitation by rescheduling its debts and rearranging its financial status. Such programs usually involve restructuring the firm which may include downsizing and closing loss-making operations. Here, too, there will be some exit of resources from the industry.

Third, the financially distressed firm may face bankruptcy and, ultimately, liquidation, leading to the physical exit of the firm from the market. This process is most likely to occur when all other options are closed. If financial markets and the takeover mechanism performed efficiently, with all the relevant information available to all participants, the takeover mechanism would eliminate the need for a separate bankruptcy procedure. The value of any firm, even those in financial difficulties, would be transparent to market participants, and any firm could find a buyer at the right price. As soon as financial distress set in, one would expect a fall in the value of the firm and the appearance of some buyers on the scene. But the absence of fully efficient financial markets and the existence of asymmetric information between insiders (managers) and outsiders (claimants) require an additional system of checks and balances to protect the interests of a firm's creditors. These checks and balances are codified into bankruptcy laws and procedures, supplementing the existing property laws and helping their enforcement.

The process of exit, whatever form it takes, is set in motion by either the firm itself (usually on the managers) or by its creditors. Exits through downsizing, restructuring, mergers and take-overs—the flow of resources out of an activity or a firm—are generally planned and implemented by managers on behalf of the firm's owners. But the more drastic forms of exit—entering bankruptcy proceedings with the possibility of liquidation—are usually forced upon a firm by its creditors or by legal provisions aimed at protecting the interests of creditors.

The creditors of a financially distressed firm play the crucial role of monitoring its performance and imposing financial discipline, including the threat of bankruptcy, on it. In sharp contrast to the transitional economies of Central and Eastern Europe where *creditor passivity* has been identified as a major cause of the persistence of a quasi-soft-budget constraint regime, the creditors in a developed market economy have direct and strong incentives to insist on the implementation of the appropriate legal provisions when faced with a defaulting debtor. In a developed market economy, the creditors must respond to market signals relating to the debtor firm and act promptly—and aggressively—in their own interest for survival. Any sign of passivity will reflect badly on the creditors and may quickly undermine their position via the financial markets.[1]

The process of exit is also affected by the nature of bankruptcy laws and the associated incentives which influence the behavior of different agents (creditors, managers, owners, etc.). The availability of a bankruptcy procedure, and the threat of its imposition, is an important mechanism for bringing these agents under the discipline of market forces. Bankruptcy procedures regulate the way each group of claimants is recompensed without the claims of other groups being undermined. In the absence of these procedures, any sign of financial distress may result in a "creditors' rush," like a run on a bank, as each creditor tries to seize a part of the firm's assets and realize their claim. Bankruptcy laws ensure that the claims of *all* creditors are dealt with at the same time, in one place, and in an orderly fashion.

Furthermore, bankruptcy regulations establish a system of priority to settle the claims of different claimants. Known as the "absolute priority rule" (APR), the system generally starts with the claims of secured (senior) creditors with a lien on physical assets, followed by the government's tax and social security claims, then the unpaid wages of employees, the claims of unsecured (junior) creditors or bondholders, the claims of trade creditors, and finally the equity claims of the firm's shareholders (themselves divided into the holders of preference shares and ordinary shares). The importance of APR lies in the requirement that each category of claim, in the established order of priority, must be settled in full before the claims of the next class of creditors are attended to. The shareholders at the bottom of the priority pyramid receive something only if the claims of all other creditors are met in full. The observance or violation of APR has a major impact on the operation and implementation of bankruptcy laws and, as we shall see later, has been a source of controversy among bankruptcy scholars.

The operation of bankruptcy laws and procedures is closely related to the nature and level of information available to each of the stakeholders. The managers of modern corporations are in the unique position of using resources owned by other people on their behalf—"other people's money" as Merton Miller called it.[2] In this process, managers also borrow money to supplement internal funds and make investment and production decisions that influence the owners' net wealth. With the management's superior knowledge of the firm's true financial position and the asymmetric information between managers and creditors (existing and potential), it is always possible that the management may embark on imprudent investment decisions. In particular, if their position is threatened by a potential bankruptcy, the probability of desperate and risky investment decisions will increase, and thus the value of the firm will decrease. The limited liability form of organization—in comparison to individual proprietorship and partnership forms—allows the managers to make such risky decisions and grants them personal immunity from the consequences of these decisions. Moreover, in the presence of uncertainty and incomplete information, managers are able to hide the real position of the firm from its creditors for a considerable length of time. Bankruptcy laws therefore try to stipulate a number of mechanisms to ensure that all stakeholders are properly informed about the financial position of the firm. These laws stipulate the conditions under which the procedure is triggered and specify the person or body with the legal obligation to initiate the process.[3]

Given the managers' superior knowledge of the firm's position, most bankruptcy laws place the onus of declaration on them. Even though managers may to a greater or lesser extent be responsible for the plight of the company, they nonetheless are often in the best position to initiate the process.[4] Managers are the first to become aware of the firm's financial distress, and the interests of creditors will be better protected if managers are under legal obligation to set the bankruptcy process in motion. In the United Kingdom, for example, more than a thousand company directors have been disqualified for failing in their legal obligations to declare insolvency under the 1986 Insolvency Act.[5] Indeed, in the three European countries studied here, the management is legally responsible to file for bankruptcy within two to three weeks of insolvency or default on debt. In most countries, the creditors (or a specified group of them) are also entitled to trigger the procedure if the information available to them points in the direction of default or insolvency.

The bankruptcy procedure, once triggered, does not necessarily lead to the exit of the firm from the market. Liquidation is only one option facing the firm. In this case, the bankruptcy procedures specify the manner in which either the firm in the liquidation process is sold as a going concern, or its assets are disposed of piece by piece, in order to repay the claimants in accordance with APR. If a firm is to be liquidated, the observance of APR means that shareholders and managers will often receive little or nothing as the value of a firm's assets may fall short of the claims against the firm.

Alternatively, bankruptcy procedures may allow the management to choose reorganization. Reorganization or restructuring aims to rescue the firm from financial distress and salvage all or parts of it for the benefit of its stakeholders. Typically, reorganization involves a process of negotiation between debtors and creditors to establish a new arrangement for the settlement of claims—writing off some of the claims, injecting new capital, swapping equities for old claims, or exchanging bonds and other debts for new notes, bonds, or cash. In short, reorganization rewrites the debt contracts of different groups of claimants and creditors. Any negotiation aimed at rewriting debt contracts will confer a bargaining power on debtors from which they may benefit at the expense of creditors. This will amount to a violation of APR and, as many observers believe, may potentially undermine the basis of normal business practice, property rights, and rational economic calculations.

Insiders will have a strong incentive to prefer this option to liquidation and strict adherence to APR. But in addition to the insiders' self-interest, other considerations may encourage managers and creditors to opt for reorganization, including the desire to reduce the creditors' losses, protect jobs, retain productive capacity, or qualify for government subsidies. Moreover, the availability of reorganization as an option may discourage managers of a distressed firm from making high-risk investment decisions of the type to which we referred earlier. Any comparison of liquidation and reorganization should take into account the *total* costs and benefits of each option to the given society. To put this differently, bankruptcy laws should be designed to produce an optimum number of bankruptcies, preventing both premature and delayed liquidations. These laws should enable firms to survive if and only if their value as a going concern under existing management exceeds their liquidation value.

The legal rules concerning the choice between reorganization and liquidation vary significantly among market economies. Although debtor firms may have strong incentives to opt for formal, court-based reorganizations to try to resolve their financial difficulties and regain their health, legal provisions may not always support such a preference.[6]

The purpose of this chapter is to analyze the economic implications of bankruptcy procedures in Western market economies with a view to drawing appropriate lessons for transition economies. We will first discuss the bankruptcy procedures in four developed market economies, emphasizing the conditions under which financially distressed firms are reorganized or liquidated. Afterwards, we will focus on the relative efficacy of reorganization and liquidation processes. Finally, we will highlight the lessons that transition economies can learn from the experiences of established market economies, drawing attention to a number of important areas of concern with respect to the design and implementation of bankruptcy laws.

Bankruptcy Procedures in Developed Market Economies

We outline below the bankruptcy procedures in four established market economies: the United States, the United Kingdom, Germany, and

France. The relative positions and powers of creditors and debtors and thus the incentives of different economic agents in the process vary considerably in these countries.

United States

The emphasis of the bankruptcy procedures in the United States (and also in France, as we shall see shortly) is on the survival of the firm, saving jobs, and retaining the firm's productive capacities—thus the notion of "debtor-oriented" procedures.[7] This orientation is achieved by providing the firm in financial distress with breathing space to enable it, free from the pressure of claimants, to negotiate with its creditors to restructure its debts and find a way out of distress. The U.S. Bankruptcy Reform Act of 1978 and the supplementary legislation in 1994 allow the management of the firm to file for bankruptcy either under Chapter 7 (the liquidation option) or Chapter 11 (the reorganization option) of the act. If the latter course of action is chosen, the managers will receive temporary court protection from their creditors and will be given time to prepare a reorganization plan, which has to be submitted to the claimants for approval. During this period, referred to as "debtor-in-possession," the management remains in charge of the firm, protected by an automatic stay of claims against the company. The management is also able to raise new finances on preferential terms (i.e., as high priority claims). Moreover, firms in reorganization benefit from a number of explicit and implicit subsidies, mostly from the government.[8] The management has 120 days to prepare a reorganization plan—a period which may be, and often is, extended by the court—and a further two months to gain the approval of its creditors.[9] The law groups claimants into different classes according to the nature of their claims: secured creditors are treated as one class, unsecured bondholders another, small claimants another, shareholders another, and so on. The reorganization plan must be approved by the majority of creditors (representing two-thirds of claims) in each class of claimants.[10] The plan may and often does include certain restrictions on the management that are aimed at protecting the creditors from unjustified risky behavior by the management: for example, a threshold debt–asset ratio or market valuation beyond which automatic sanctions come into effect.

The reorganization option of the American bankruptcy code has proved to be very popular with firms in financial distress. The number of filings for court protection increased by sixfold between 1979 and 1989—from 3,042 in 1979 to 17,447 in 1989. Some observers attribute this massive increase to the enhanced protection of debtors and the opportunity to protract the existing managers' control over the firm's assets without imposing any of the costs on the management.[11] After all, if the firm fails in its attempt to regain its health, the expenses of reorganization fall on the creditors, with the managers and shareholders being no worse off than before. Others, however, have pointed out that the increased number of Chapter 11 filings, which have benefited creditors as well as debtors, should be seen in the context of the dramatic increase (forty-fivefold) in the number of bankruptcies in the post-war period.[12] We shall return to this issue later.

The American bankruptcy procedure also allows for privately arranged reorganizations (or work-outs) as another option for financially distressed firms and their creditors. Work-outs involve negotiations between debtors and creditors over a reorganization plan agreeable to all creditors and avoid a lengthy court-based litigation process. This type of reorganization is speedier and less costly than that under Chapter 11 and therefore offers the potential of benefiting all claimants. But this process lacks the court protection, the temporary stay of claims, the tax advantages, and the relatively cheaper credit available under formal reorganization procedures. A study by Gilson et al. (1990) of eighty large financially distressed firms engaged in private work-outs between 1978 and 1987 concluded that this method is more likely to succeed if (1) the distressed firm has more intangible assets (i.e., if there is a greater difference between the going-concern value of assets and their piecemeal values, which may be lost in a lengthy procedure or in liquidation); (2) it owes more to banks and financial institutions than to other businesses; and (3) there are fewer creditors to deal with. When the number of creditors is large, the chance of reaching an agreement, which has to be unanimous, diminshes.[13] In a more recent study, Franks and Torous (1994) compared the costs and benefits of work-outs and reorganizations for a sample of forty-five large firms going through the work-out procedure with thirty-seven firms completing the Chapter 11 reorganization. They conclude that, in comparison with Chapter 11 reorganizations, informal work-outs were quicker (eighteen months versus thirty months), and the recovery rates for creditors and equity holders were higher.

Despite the controversy and heated debate surrounding the 1978 Bankruptcy Reform Act, the 1994 amendments have left the essential features of this act, particularly the provisions for reorganization under Chapter 11, basically intact. Changes to the law have been relatively minor—strengthening the rights of certain creditors and authorizing the courts to speed up the litigation process.

United Kingdom

In the United Kingdom (and also in Germany) the emphasis of the bankruptcy procedure is on the protection of creditors' interest, the "creditor-oriented" procedures.[14] The most important feature of this orientation is that the management loses its unquestioned right to manage the firm's assets during the proceedings. The 1986 Insolvency Act obliges the management of a defaulting company to petition the court for bankruptcy.[15] It also allows the creditors to initiate the process.[16] The act offers the management and the creditors of an insolvent firm several options: liquidation, receivership, or administration: all of which involve the appointment of an insolvency practitioner to protect the interests of creditors. Under the liquidation option, the firm or any of the creditors may apply to the court for the appointment of a liquidator, whose sole task is to sell the assets of the firm in order to meet the claims of creditors according to APR. The receivership option, which is available only if there are secured creditors, is more complicated.[17] Any secured creditor with a fixed charge may appoint its own receiver who will take control of that charge (the asset used as security for that particular creditor). Here the receiver represents the interests of the appointor (the single creditor who appointed him). Alternatively, a secured creditor with a floating charge may appoint an administrative receiver to take control of all assets (except those with fixed charges) and be responsible to all creditors, albeit in some order of priority. Either type of receiver will have to decide on whether the firm should be maintained as a going concern or be wound up. A receiver cannot dispose of the asset over which he has been appointed if it affects the normal operation of the company, unless a decision is made to liquidate the company.

The receiver's behavior is influenced by the prevalent incentive mechanisms. Most often, the receiver prefers to liquidate the company in order to meet the claims of his "appointors". His lack of complete knowledge of the firm's potential and, more importantly, the fact that any of the other creditors can apply for the appointment of a liquidator at any time encourages the tendency toward liquidation. A receiver and a liquidator may be appointed at the same time. Furthermore, a receiver faces a potential conflict between the interests of the individual appointor and those of other creditors. The law has placed various restrictions on receivers in order to ensure that they will try to obtain the maximum possible proceeds from the disposal of assets and other activities.[18] This objective is further strengthened by the method of remuneration of receivers—usually 5 percent of the gross proceeds.

The 1986 act offered the management and creditors of companies in financial difficulty a new option—administration. Here, the creditors and the management petition the Companies Court for the appointment of an administrator to take charge of the company.[19] The administrator, who takes precedence over both the liquidator and the receiver, has three months to prepare a plan for reorganization, which has to be approved by more than 50 percent of the creditors. The court, too, can impose the plan on the creditors. With the administrator appointed, there is a stay of claims against the company while a reorganization plan is being prepared.

One important distinguishing feature of procedures in the United Kingdom is the fact that the reorganization plan is prepared by the administrator and not by the management, whose powers are greatly reduced during the administration period. Another distinctive feature of the British procedure is that secured creditors with a fixed or floating charge are able to block the appointment of the administrator by appointing their own receiver or liquidator. In other words, the administrator can only be appointed if the majority of the creditors are convinced that the appointment may serve a purpose. It was initially thought that the administration option would usher in a procedure similar to the Chapter 11 provisions of the American bankruptcy code. But, as Webb (1991) has pointed out, the limitations placed on the management and the emphasis on creditors' rights meant that the 1986 act "stopped a long way short of giving the U.K. the equivalent of Chapter 11." The creditor orientation of the British law has meant that there was no repeat of the American experience of an explosion in the number of filings for reorganization following the adoption of the new act. Although there were over 202,000 cases of company bankruptcies in the first ten years of implementation of the 1986 act, liquidations remained by far the most frequent outcome, accounting for 78 percent of all cases. This was followed by receiverships in 20 percent and administrations in just under 1 percent of cases.[20]

Finally, as in the United States, the 1986 act allows for the possibility of semiformal, privately arranged reorganizations, known as "workouts" or "schemes of arrangement". The court must, of course, approve arrangements agreed upon by the company and its creditors. The number of successful arrangements, though increasing recently, has remained very small—just under 1 percent of all bankruptcies between 1987 and 1996.[21]

Germany

The German insolvency procedures have always been creditor-oriented.[22] Until recently, German procedures were explicitly aimed at complementing the competitive process of natural selection by facilitating the elimination of weaker firms. In the last two decades, however, Germany has recognized that a higher survival rate for enterprises in financial difficulty may be beneficial in an economy with high unemployment. This recognition lies behind the new bankruptcy code, which will come into force in 1999.

In Germany at present, a company in default may follow either one of two separate legal provisions: the Bankruptcy Act, for the purpose of liquidation, or the Judicial Composition Proceedings, for the purpose of reorganization.[23] The firm or the unsecured creditors can initiate the bankruptcy procedures by petitioning the bankruptcy court. It is incumbent upon the management of the debtor firm to file a petition with the court within three weeks of ascertaining that the firm is insolvent.[24] The company's control and management is then transferred to a court-appointed trustee with the explicit objective of liquidating the company and realizing the value of its assets in order to meet the creditors' claims according to APR. The secured creditors may also petition for bankruptcy even though they generally operate outside the bankruptcy procedures and use the security in their charge to recoup their claim. In Germany, as a defensive mechanism against bankruptcies, most loans to companies are secured in order to enable creditors to recoup their loan independent of bankruptcy laws.

A particular feature of the German law is that the majority of bankruptcy proceedings, up to 76 percent according to Heiko Fialski's estimate, are not completed due to an inability to meet the procedural costs.[25] The court may dismiss the petition for bankruptcy on the grounds that procedural costs can not be covered.[26] If the bankruptcy petition is dismissed because of insufficient funds, the joint stock company will be dissolved in accordance with section 107.1.1 of KO.[27]

The debtor firm may, alternatively, petition the court under the Judicial Composition Proceedings (which date back to 1935) and propose a composition, or reorganization, plan. The composition plan must be approved by a simple majority of creditors, representing 75 percent of all claims. Under composition proceedings, the management remains in charge of the company even though they are subject to the monitoring and examining roles of a court-appointed trustee. As in bankruptcy cases, the composition petition may be dismissed if the available resources are insufficient to meet the procedural costs. Once a composition plan is confirmed by the court, no application for bankruptcy will be entertained.

The legal framework for composition, however, is highly restrictive. First, unlike American procedures, there is no stay of claims against secured creditors, who can still liquidate their security to recoup their claims against the firm.[28] Second, the firm must be able to offer all creditors 35 percent of their claims in cash as a minimum condition for a composition. Because of these restrictions, composition proceedings play a minor role in Germany. Only 1 percent of insolvencies are resolved through this option—a proportion very similar to that in the United Kingdom.[29] If the composition plan does not receive sufficient support, the liquidation procedure comes into force.

It is also possible, as in the United States and the United Kingdom, to arrange out-of-court compositions, which are not subject to the strict rules of normal compositions. In fact, given the difficulties of the composition procedure, a large number of insolvencies (according to some estimates as high as 20–30 percent) opt for out-of-court arrangements.[30]

There has been much discussion in recent years about reforming the German insolvency procedures. The Commission for Insolvency Law, appointed in 1978, produced proposals aiming at unifying the three insolvency procedures, including the separate act governing insolvency in the former GDR, into one law and at bringing the spirit of the German law somewhat closer to the American Chapter 11 provisions, thus encouraging more reorganizations. The new legislation was passed in 1994 and is due to take effect in 1999. Although the new code does not resolve the problems caused by the German practice of pledging nearly all assets to creditors, it will affect the operation of bankruptcy procedures in a number of important ways. It will bring liquidation and composition proceedings into a unified law, remove the ability of secured creditors to dispose of the secured assets during the liquidation or composition proceedings, create classes of creditors, introduce a three-month stay of claims, and enable the creditors to put forward composition plans of their own.[31] It is expected that these changes will improve the effectiveness of the process as a whole and facilitate the greater use of the composition option.

France

The current French bankruptcy procedure is based on laws passed in 1984 and 1985 and the amendments of June 1994.[32] Before the recent amendments, the law was strongly aimed at facilitating the rescue of financially distressed firms through reorganization. The social and political motives behind the law were transparent: under conditions of high unemployment, jobs and production capacities should be saved if at all possible. The 1994 amendments, however, were adopted in order to mitigate the strong debtor-orientation of the bankruptcy process, strengthen creditors' rights, and enhance the efficiency of the judicial restructuring process.

Under special procedures adopted in 1982, firms suffering from financial difficulties may obtain advice and support from counseling organizations at the national, regional, and departmental levels. The 1984 law also envisaged the appointment of a 'conciliator' by the Commercial Court who would assist the firm in raising new loans and in negotiating with creditors and suppliers in order to resolve its financial problems. In practice the conciliation procedures have not been used as widely as intended. They were last used successfully by the Paris Commercial Court to avert the bankruptcy of property firms hit by severe economic conditions in the early nineties.[33]

The bankruptcy procedure in France is set in motion by an application from the firm, the creditors, the public prosecutor's office, or court officials. The management is legally responsible for filing a bankruptcy petition with the Commercial Court within fifteen days of default on payment *(cessation des paiements)*.[34] The court may impose a range of legal sanctions against noncompliant managers, but, on the whole, the threat of sanctions is not very strong. Consequently, bankruptcies initiated by the management are exceptional.[35] Bankruptcy proceedings are often initiated by the firm's creditors, who only need to prove the firm's default on payment.

The 1985 law stipulated that the court, upon the verification of the bankruptcy claim, will issue a decree on judicial restructuring *(redressment judiciaire)*. The decree involves an observation period *(periode d' observation)* and the appointment of an administrator *(administrateur judiciaire)*. During the observation period, the administrator, whose powers are determined by the court, will assess the firm's economic and social conditions and the possibility of its recovery. The administrator, after the completion of an assessment of the conditions of the firm and negotiations with interested parties, may recommend rehabilitation, in which case he will prepare a continuation plan. The purpose of this plan is to create the necessary conditions for restructuring the firm which may involve downsizing its operations or changing the management structure if necessary, and renegotiating its debts, undertaking to pay some or all of the creditors within a specified time period. Alternatively, the administrator may decide that the firm has little chance of survival and should be liquidated, in which case a disposal plan will be prepared. This plan would involve finding a third party willing to take control of some or all of the firm's assets—but not its liabilities—for an agreed price.

The administrator has six months to prepare a plan for the court, a period which may be extended by a second period of six months (and a third in exceptional circumstances). Although there has been much discussion regarding the long duration of the observation period, and the 1994 amendments were expected to shorten this period, no significant changes have been made. Both the continuation plan and the disposal plan must be approved by the court. During the observation period, all proceedings initiated by the creditors against the firm are suspended along with any payment of pre-existing debts. Claims arising during the observation period will take priority.[36]

Finally, if the administrator cannot complete a continuation or disposal plan, the court will issue a judgment of judicial liquidation and appoint a liquidator (usually the representative of the creditors) to complete the sale of assets, at the highest obtainable price, and to distribute the proceeds among the creditors.

The procedures outlined above, in particular the compulsory observational phase, have a strong orientation toward the debtor firm and are likely to weaken the disciplinary nature of bankruptcy. The 1994 amendments removed the compulsory nature of the observation period, leaving it to the discretion of the court, which may now decide to initiate a judicial liquidation without going through that phase.[37] The change will, to some extent, strengthen the position of creditors and speed up the liquidation of firms with little chance of a successful continuation plan.

Unlike the American code, which requires the approval of the reorganization plan by a specified proportion of all classes of creditors, the French code empowers the courts to approve or reject the plan prepared by the administrator without requiring the creditors' majority approval. Of course, the administrator is required by the court to consult the firm's management, employee representatives, creditors, and other interested bodies and ask for their views on the continuation or disposal plan. But the ultimate decision is made by the court without requiring the approval of creditors. This aspect of the proceedings survived the 1994 amendments intact and is still a feature of the French bankruptcy procedures.

Recent Changes in Bankruptcy Codes

Bankruptcy codes have been the subject of much discussion and criticism in all four of the countries discussed above. The procedures in these countries have been amended in the last decade to resolve some of the prevailing problems. In the United Kingdom and Germany, criticism was aimed at the in-built creditor-orientation of the legislation and its bias against reorganization. In the United States and France, on the other hand, criticism was based on the debtor-orientation of the codes and the violation of creditors' rights associated with the reorganization process. The 1986 Insolvency Act in the United Kingdom and the 1994 Bankruptcy Law in Germany introduced or strengthened the possibility of reorganization and raised the chance of survival of distressed firms. The 1994 amendments in both the United States and France have gone some way to strengthen the position of creditors. These steps have been particularly aimed at speeding up the court proceedings and reducing litigation costs. While these two distinct types of bankruptcy procedures have moved somewhat closer to each other, they have retained their fundamental difference—the bias in favor of or against reorganization.

Is Reorganization Efficient?

An evaluation of the relative effectiveness of reorganization and liquidation options is crucial for any appraisal of the efficiency of bankruptcy procedures in a market economy. Whether or not reorganization is superior to liquidation depends on two important questions: first, what are the costs and benefits of reorganization and how do they compare with those of liquidation? Second, what is the impact of the distortion of market signals caused by the rewriting of debt contracts? It is important to emphasize that, at least in the United States, firms opting for liquidation are generally in a worse financial position than those filing for reorganization. In other words, reorganization is usually attempted by firms with some chance of survival, which could benefit all stakeholders.[38] Most of the research in this area is based on the American experience, where the reorganization procedure has been used most extensively. The literature concentrates on a number of important issues such as managerial behavior, the lengthy and costly process of bargaining and litigation, and the implications of the violation of APR.

Managerial Behavior under Financial Distress

Many observers have argued that the incentive mechanism associated with bankruptcy procedure encourages a high-risk strategy and opportunistic behavior by managers. Precisely because they remain in power during reorganization, managers may have a tendency to embark on riskier investment decisions, a tendency strengthened by the fact that they do not bear the ultimate costs of their decisions. If a firm is insolvent and is wound up, the shareholders and managers may receive very little or nothing upon liquidation. But if the managers embark on reorganization, there is some chance of the shareholders receiving something as a result of their increased bargaining position. However, even if the managers fail to turn the firm around and return it to health, they may not be much worse off than before. Thus Miller (1977) has compared the reorganization option to a "call option": the managers call on the option—to share in whatever benefits the reorganization creates—if their plans succeed but will not call on the option if their plans fail. The costs of reorganization, of course, are borne not by the managers but by the creditors. Stiglitz (1972) showed that if the possibility of bankruptcy is allowed, managers will have a tendency toward more risky borrowing.[39] Meckling (1977), Miller (1977), Moore (1977), and Bradley and Rosenzweig (1992) all argued that the protection offered by the American Chapter 11 results in higher levels of borrowing and greater risk-taking by firms in debt.[40] Moore and Meckling also pointed out that the cost of borrowing increases because creditors must be more careful in their lending policy, assess loan applications more thoroughly, and monitor the progress of their borrowers more frequently—these additional costs being passed on to borrowers.

It is of course correct to assume that managers have a personal interest in prolonging their reign and retaining control of the firm for as long as possible, and that they will use the Chapter 11 provision for this purpose if they have to. Many alternative theories of the firm also support this view. But it is incorrect to assume that managers have nothing to lose if their reorganization attempt fails. Reorganization is not a "call option" without any penalty. Managers, too, stand to lose in a bankruptcy, not only their jobs and the associated benefits but also their reputation—a point ignored by the proponents of a call option. In any market economy, there is a managerial labor market in which managers' performance is monitored and appropriate rewards or penalties determined. Gilson (1989, 1990) has shown that for a sample of 111 financially distressed firms, over 60 percent of the chief executive officers and members of the board of directors involved in either bankruptcy or private restructuring lose their jobs after the end of the proceedings. What is even more serious is that their chances of being appointed to other directorships also decline. These results severely undermine the argument that managers have nothing to lose when they embark on a Chapter 11 filing.

Cost of Reorganization

The reorganization procedure is obviously lengthy and costly, factors which should be taken into consideration when evaluating the relative efficiency of this option. The cost of reorganization, however, should not be seen in isolation. It should rather be compared with the costs of liquidation—something that has not been seriously attempted in the literature. The estimates for the time spent in reorganization vary between 1.4 years to 2.8 years depending on the particular sample analyzed in the various studies.[41] The length of the process is not only due to bargaining between creditors and debtors. Other legal claims against the company (for example, the possibility of exposure to toxic wastes or unsafe pharmaceutical products) account for many lengthy litigations.[42]

The estimates of the direct costs of reorganization—including the fees of lawyers, trustees, administrators, and consultants—vary widely in different studies.[43] Measured as a proportion of the market value of the firm in the year prior to the bankruptcy filing, these estimates vary from 2.8 percent to 4.6 percent. Measured as a proportion of the liquidation value of the firm, estimates vary from 3.4 percent to 7.5 percent. Although at first glance these costs seem rather high, it should be pointed out, as White (1984) has shown, that direct costs as a proportion of the amount received by creditors are less in reorganization than in straight liquidation.[44]

Violation of APR

The reorganization or restructuring plan negotiated between managers and creditors reflects the bargaining power of the debtors and some junior creditors and is manifested in alterations to the original terms of the contract, possibly in favor of these groups at the expense of other claimants. The alteration to the original terms of the contract, or the violation of APR, has been the focus of the contribution made by economists to this debate. Most of the research, however, is based on individual case studies and small sample investigations. Studies by Franks and Torous (1989), Eberhart et al. (1990), Weiss (1990), and Eberhart and Sweeney (1992), based on samples of between twenty-seven and thirty-seven firms filing for bankruptcy, all showed that the absolute priority rule was violated in the majority of cases. But there is less consensus about the magnitude and the method of measurement of the cost of this violation on the particular class(es) of creditors most affected by it. The amount received by shareholders in excess of what they would have received under APR varies between 1 percent and 7.6 percent according to different studies (with the more recent studies indicating smaller deviations).[45]

Success Rate

The successful adoption of a reorganization plan, i.e., the completion of the reorganization process, is one of the important areas of debate. First, it should be pointed out that the often quoted view that the bulk of firms in reorganization end up in liquidation is not based on comprehensive bankruptcy records,[46] since the data on the overall success rate of firms filing for reorganization is "virtually non-existent."[47] Second, the proponents of this view disregard the varying survival rates of firms of different sizes and activities. The available empirical evidence paints a more optimistic picture for this procedure, suggesting that the success rate is much higher, especially for larger firms. The success rate for listed companies filing for reorganization varies in different studies, ranging from 40 percent to 60 percent to 95 percent, and in the case of "megabankruptcies" (firms with assets in excess of $100 million) as high as 96 percent.[48]

An Assessment

The arguments outlined above fall short of a comprehensive assessment of the relative costs and benefits of reorganization versus liquidation. The critics of reorganization have put a particularly heavy emphasis on the potential negative impacts of this option on the efficient operation of the legal process without paying much attention to the magnitudes involved, alternatives available, or the potential benefits of reorganization. Beginning with the issue of management behavior under limited liability conditions, we have already pointed out the weakness of the argument that managers have little to lose in reorganization or bankruptcy. Moreover, it is sometimes ignored that the limited liability form of organization—blamed for excessive risk-taking by managers—is one of the most dynamic and efficient organizational innovations of the last century. The existence of external sources of finance, and firms and individuals who provide the financing, have facilitated the long-term growth of the corporate sector and the economy and guaranteed the efficient operation of joint-stock companies. Bondholders and other creditors (especially institutional creditors) have made managers less insular and more responsive to market signals. These bondholders and creditors engage in the collection and analysis of information and impose discipline on managers. In the absence of bondholders and creditors, firms will be nearly closed to outside scrutiny, with shareholders in danger of being manipulated by the managers. As Gilson (1990) and Wruck (1990) have demonstrated, when financial distress sets in, nonequity claimants take an active interest in corporate governance and put pressure on managers to find a solution, a pressure that might not materialize from equity holders.[49]

Second, regarding the violation of APR, there is no reason to believe that the unequal treatment of different claimants under reorganization, small as it is, creates significant market distortions or undermines the property rights system. In a bankruptcy, creditors will lose out to varying degrees depending on how secure their claims are. The amount of loss, which is part and parcel of business risk, will vary from case to case depending on the value of claims and the value of assets (either their liquidation value or their value as a going concern). There is no systematic, large-scale study of the magnitude of the costs of reorganization and those who suffer most.[50] The essential point is that if some of the claimants wish to form coalitions with other stakeholders that may be more beneficial to some and less to others, they are legally entitled to do so. The senior claimants may appreciate the value of managers' knowledge of the firm and their ability to preserve the firm's value and be prepared to strike a deal with them that offers the shareholders something in excess of that warranted by the strict application of APR. As Baird and Jackson (1988) have pointed out, the recontracting associated with the reorganization plan is at the discretion of the senior claimants who may "convey an interest in [the assets of the firm] to anyone they please."[51] The gains by equity holders are "because the senior creditor has concluded that doing so is in its interest."[52] There is nothing intrinsically inefficient about this recontracting process. Moreover, it should be remembered that, as many bankruptcy cases show, the creditors can (and often do) impose certain restrictive conditions on the firm and its managers that prevent them from excessively risky or opportunistic behavior. Reorganization plans have, for example, stipulated a threshold debt–asset ratio, above which managers cannot borrow on secured terms; threshold market capitalization levels, below which certain corrective mechanisms will automatically come into force; maximum allowable administrative expenses; and restrictions on asset disposals and investments.[53]

Finally, in any assessment of reorganization, the wider social costs and benefits of bankruptcy should be taken into account. A reorganization that prevents premature liquidation will lead to the preservation of jobs and productive capacities that may otherwise disappear forever.[54] What is crucial for the economy is that firms with a chance of survival should not go bankrupt prematurely. The optimum rate of bankruptcy is one that involves the least cost to society as a whole and results in the preservation of firms over a longer time period than that dictated by short-term financial considerations.

Reorganization is aimed at raising the value of a firm in financial distress above its liquidation value and may potentially benefit most of those concerned. The fact that a considerable number of firms (especially large ones) embarking on reorganization succeed is an indication of the positive value of this provision. Therefore, we may say that firms opt for reorganization not solely (or even primarily) for opportunistic reasons but also because of the following: (1) they believe they are in temporary financial difficulty and a short respite will allow them to return to health; (2) their liquidation value is (or may be) less than their value as a going concern; and (3) the post-reorganization situation may be more beneficial to most of the stakeholders. However, the reorganization option also involves costs, and every attempt should be made to reduce these costs. Any change in the legal process should concentrate on developing new or improved methods of rehabilitation for firms in *temporary* financial difficulty. Possible changes should aim at reducing the litigation time and costs and speeding up the financial restructuring of distressed firms while observing APR as closely as possible.[55]

Bankruptcy Procedures and Economies in Transition

What lessons can the East European economies in transition draw from the bankruptcy procedures of developed market economies? What are the options facing these reforming economies, and how can the experience of other countries help them choose the appropriate option? In the past seven years, most East European economies, particularly the Czech Republic, Hungary, and Poland, have adopted new bankruptcy laws and procedures or revived their old ones, while other countries in Eastern Europe are still pondering over the particular details they wish to include in their bankruptcy codes. Bankruptcy laws in the Czech Republic, Hungary, and Poland are examined in detail in other chapters. Our discussion of the bankruptcy procedures in the four mature market economies and the relative efficacy of reorganization and liquidation highlights a number of important areas that are of particular relevance in deciding on the appropriate legal framework for the bankruptcy procedure in economies in transition.

Causes of Financial Distress

The decision on which bankruptcy option (reorganization or liquidation) a firm should choose depends crucially on why the firm has run into financial difficulty. In an established market economy, the responsibility for financial distress lies with the firm and its management, but for East European firms, the position is more complicated. In the early stages of transition, the reason for the insolvency of a large number of firms was not simply that they were either inefficient or that they produced the wrong bundle of goods.[56] External shocks and government policies applied to the inherited industrial structure also resulted in financial distress. The restrictive macroeconomic policy, particularly the establishment of real positive interest rates, the liberalization of foreign trade, and the collapse of CMEA markets, resulted in financial difficulties for a large number of firms for which their management could not be held directly responsible. The necessary adjustments in the method of production, the deployment of resources, and the choice of output bundle or marketing, were not easy for many of these firms and could not be achieved with sufficient speed. The uncertainty about future ownership and the method of ownership-transformation combined with the inability to raise sufficient funds for new investment compounded the problem. Had firms been able to raise funds on financial markets, alter their production technology and product mix, and find new markets, many would have been able to sort out their problems.

In market economies, the number of firms in financial distress is relatively small, with the number of those going bankrupt even smaller. (In the United States, corporate failures in the 1970s and 1980s ranged between 1 percent and 2.5 percent of all firms.)[57] In transitional economies, however, the number of financially distressed firms is very large, constituting the majority of large and medium-size firms in some of these economies.[58] The liquidation or exit of these firms is not a minor issue, that is, simply a by-product of the competitive process and natural selection. Given the magnitudes involved, a potentially explosive situation could be created if all such firms were allowed or forced to go into liquidation. At stake is a massive productive capacity that could be lost forever as a result of these firms' exit. Moreover, the financing of unemployment benefits to redundant workers puts additional pressure on the state budget, with adverse implications for macroeconomic policy. Neither implication is economically or socially desirable, and neither may be acceptable to the citizens of these emerging democracies with their newly acquired voting rights.

The social, political, and economic costs of a large-scale liquidation of enterprises means that reorganization should be seriously considered and strongly encouraged as an alternative.[59] Naturally, reorganization would involve negotiations between the enterprise, government agencies, banks, and other creditors, and these could be lengthy and costly. However, given the particular ownership structure and the mechanism of credit allocation under socialism, it is possible to devise reorganization arrangements that involve less cost and fewer market distortions than the current practice. The state in transition economies is often the most senior claimant (with tax and social security arrears) as well as the most junior stakeholder (being the ultimate owner or part-owner) of enterprises. Moreover, as the owner (or part-owner) of commercial banks and other firms, the state is also among both secured and junior creditors. The unique position occupied by the government creates new opportunities for informal reorganization, which may be utilized to achieve the twin objective of enterprise restructuring and improving the balance sheets. The redistribution and distortion resulting from the violation of APR will be relatively small—the state may lose in one capacity but will gain in another. With government acting in several capacities, the number of claimants involved in any negotiation may be relatively small, and the chance of reaching a settlement may be higher. Most observers have supported reorganization procedures involving debt–equity swaps combined with appropriate incentives for enterprises and banks, such as writing off the interest on senior debts of enterprises, bank recapitalization, or rescheduling of other debts.[60] The bank-led enterprise restructuring program in Poland (discussed in chapter 7) is a good example of an innovative reorganization option specifically designed for transition economies. The important point here is the recognition of the fact that simplified work-out procedures, reflecting the specific conditions of each country, are needed to encourage and speed up the economic and financial restructuring of distressed firms.

The Design of Bankruptcy Laws

Encouragement and support for reorganization should not detract policy makers from the formulation of effective bankruptcy legislation dealing with both liquidation and reorganization. Efficient bankruptcy laws should in principle result in the exit of those firms whose resources could be deployed more effectively elsewhere. To this end, bankruptcy legislation should deter managers (or creditors) from applying for reorganization in order to prolong their incumbency when the firm has little chance of survival. But at the same time, the laws should also prevent premature liquidation—the disappearance of those firms which can be successfully reorganized. The design of bankruptcy law is particularly important because of the enhanced potential for opportunistic behavior by managers during the transition period. The incentive mechanisms (explicit or implicit in bankruptcy legislation) influencing different agents also have important implications for the effectiveness of the overall process. Based on the experience of developed market economies and the particular features of the transition process, the following major issues have to be taken into account in the design of effective bankruptcy laws.[61]

Declaration

The process of transition has created a fertile ground for opportunistic and self-interested behavior by enterprise managers, which must be taken seriously by policymakers and legislators. The managers of firms in financial distress wish to prolong their tenure by enlisting the support of government agencies (such as their founding bodies), banks, and suppliers and by lobbying the government for financial assistance. In some cases, as in Poland, financial difficulties were accommodated by simply allowing their debt to the state (taxes and social security arrears) or banks to rise. In other cases, as in the Czech Republic, the same was achieved by allowing their debt to other enterprises and banks to increase.

Bankruptcy procedures may involve effective mechanisms to prevent this situation and to impose a discipline on such managers. The legal obligation to declare insolvency or default on debt payment is the first step in this process. It can be backed up by other sanctions against the managers of insolvent or defaulting firms, ranging from financial penalties and dismissals to the appointment of a trustee or liquidator empowered to annul previous suspicious transactions. The Hungarian experience, whereby some 3,500 cases of bankruptcy were filed in April 1992 alone (when the ninety-day grace period stipulated by the new bankruptcy law came to an end), shows the potency of the "obligation to declare" provision.[62] The penalties associated with the declaration requirement, as pointed out in Mitchell (1990), guard against imprudent decisions by managers facing financial distress.

Protection of Creditors' Interest

Reorganization or liquidation should be overseen by outside specialists (judges, liquidators, administrators, or insolvency practitioners) in order to ensure that the interests of all creditors are protected and that they are treated equally. An essential element of the design of the law is the obligation to provide information on the firm's financial position, through reliable means, to all creditors. A related issue is the choice of the proportion of creditors needed for the conclusion of a reorganization agreement. In some countries, such as Hungary, reorganization was possible only with the unanimous agreement of all creditors.[63] In others, such as Poland, support of 50 percent is sufficient for reorganization. While in the Hungarian case, reorganization was very difficult (thus the need to lower the threshold), in the Polish case, the interest of minority creditors may be in danger of being violated. The creation of separate classes of creditors (as in the American legal provisions) combined with the majority approval seems to be a sensible compromise. Such a provision will prevent debtors from reaching private agreements with some creditors at the expense of others. This provision will also ensure that reorganizations involving accommodation between enterprises and banks (such as the bank conciliation process in Poland) are not carried out without the support of the majority of creditors.

The Role of Managers during Reorganization

An important question that should be addressed by the bankruptcy law is the following: who should be in charge of the company once bankruptcy proceedings have been initiated? As already mentioned, the bankruptcy procedures in some countries leave the existing managers in charge, particularly during reorganization, because of their superior knowledge of the firm and its potential. Given the shortage of alternative management personnel, insolvency practitioners and other experts in transition economies, this seems to be a sensible model for them as well. But, in order to prevent managers from taking advantage of their position as "debtors in charge," the procedure should impose a time-limit on the managers for preparation of a reorganization plan, which includes the provision that after the expiry of this time, the creditors should be able to propose their plan. Furthermore, provisions may be made for the automatic conversion of reorganization to liquidation, should the debtor and creditors fail to reach an agreement within the given time period. These mechanisms, together, may produce the right incentive package for managers and encourage them to speedily reach an agreement with creditors.

Absolute Priority Rule

The establishment of a system of priority is essential for the efficient operation of the bankruptcy process. Of equal importance are the installation, or strengthening, of a system of secured credits, the formulation of laws regulating collateralization, and the establishment of a national register of assets used as collateral in order to prevent fraudulent use of the same asset as collateral against several loans (in Poland, the law on the setting-up of a collaterals register was only passed in December 1996, coming into effect fully in January 1998).[64] These would allow banks and other creditors to provide secured loans to firms at reduced costs and enable the distressed firms to borrow new funds to facilitate the reorganization process, as these loans will have priority over pre-bankruptcy loans.

Incentives for Liquidators and Administrators

Once the liquidation of a company (either as a whole or by a piecemeal sale of assets) becomes inevitable and outside supervisors are appointed to oversee the process, it is important that an appropriate incentive mechanism is devised for them. The remuneration of outside supervisors and their conditions of service are particularly important. On the one hand, they should have an incentive to complete the process as quickly as possible. On the other hand, they should have an interest in maximizing the liquidation value of the firm. The incentive package, therefore, should include a fixed sum augmented by a proportion of the recovered value of assets. In the Czech Republic, for example, until the new amendments to the bankruptcy law (March 1996), very few lawyers were willing to be appointed as administrators because of the very poor reward for the job. At the same time, if the liquidators are paid too generously, their incentive to complete cases quickly will be weakened.

In addition to the remuneration package, the appointees should be held liable for their actions in order to prevent fraudulent disposal of the assets. The threat of legal action by creditors who suffer losses will impose some discipline on the liquidator or administrator. Of course, this procedure will be effective only if the appointee has deposited a bond or has a professional indemnity—neither of which are in place in most transition economies. The professionalization of court-appointed agents is one way of overcoming these shortcomings—with their professional organization being made responsible for their training, insurance, and regulation.

Creditor Passivity

The existence of bankruptcy laws will not, in themselves, ensure their application. Laws can only be applied if creditors have an incentive to pursue the debtors and demand the satisfaction of their claims. As Mitchell (1993) shows, creditor passivity has been one of the main reasons for the relatively small number of bankruptcies and has prevented a faster restructuring of enterprises. In many countries, the passivity of banks as the main creditors of financially distressed enterprises is particularly important and should be highlighted (see, for example, Mitchell 1993 and Buch 1994). In many cases, banks prefer to wait and retain some chance of recovering their claims rather than push the debtor into bankruptcy and receive nothing or very little. In some cases, banks may expect that the value of debtors' assets will rise in the future and some of the debts will be honored. More importantly, the writing-off of loans will reduce the value of the bank's assets, which is not in the interest of banks' managers in the preprivatization period. In some transitional economies, banks expect that enterprise debts will in the end be written off by the government and the banks will be recapitalized, thus their preference for waiting rather than embarking on the bankruptcy process. Case studies of financially distressed enterprises confirm the reluctance of banks to embark on lengthy bankruptcy proceedings.[65]

The main reason for the passivity of banks in transitional economies has been the fact that most of them are still fully or partially state-owned and face little competition from domestic or foreign private banks.[66] Newly established private banks, able to compete with state owned banks, will take a long time to appear on the scene. The privatization of banks has proceeded very slowly, and the state has remained a large shareholder in most semi privatized banks. The incentive to impose financial discipline on the debtors will remain at best weak until the emergence of a competitive banking sector and functioning financial markets. In the meantime, it is up to the state to use its moral position and voting power to enforce some discipline on bank managers, making them responsible for their lending policy. Any reorganization, encouraged by the state, must take into account the incentive structure not only of the enterprise managers but also the bank managers. They too should be subject to strict performance criteria with the threat of financial penalties and loss of employment for poor performance combined with rewards for good performance.

Mergers

In addition to reorganization, a financially distressed firm may be encouraged to merge with a healthy company in the same industry. Again, many Eastern European governments are in the unique position of being able to influence—if not exercise direct control over—the decision-making process in many firms. In such cases, the implications of mergers for the competitive process would have to be weighed against the consequences of bankruptcy and liquidation. As Miller (1977) and Peele and Wilson (1989) have shown, mergers may provide an efficient and viable alternative to liquidation, provided the antimonopoly rules are relaxed, or interpreted more favorably, in order to preserve all or most of the distressed firm.

References

Abel, I., and K. Gatsios. 1993. The economics of bankruptcy and the transition to a market economy. Discussion Paper no. 878 (December). London: Centre for Economic Policy Research.

Aghion, P., O. Hart, and J. Moore. 1992. The economics of bankruptcy reform. *Journal of Law, Economics and Organization* 8, no. 3: 523–46.

Akerloff, G. A. and P. M. Roemer. 1993. Looting: The economic underworld of bankruptcy for profit. *Brookings Papers on Economic Activity,* no. 2: 1–75.

Altman, E. I. 1984. A further empirical investigation of the bankruptcy cost question. *Journal of Finance* 39, no. 4 (September): 1067–89.

Ang, J., J. H. Chua, and J. J. McConnell. 1982. The administrative costs of corporate bankruptcy: A note. *Journal of Finance* 37, no. 1 (December): 219–26.

Baird, D. G. 1991. The initiation problem in bankruptcy. *International Review of Law and Economics* 11: 223–32.

Baird, D. G., and T. H. Jackson. 1988. Bargaining after the fall and the contours of the absolute priority rule. *University of Chicago Law Review* 55: 738–89.

Begg, D., and R. Portes. 1993. Enterprise debt and financial restructuring in Central and Eastern Europe. *European Economic Review* 37, no. 2–3: 396–408.

Bhandari, J. S. and L. A. Weiss. 1993. The increasing bankruptcy filing rate: An historical analysis. *American Bankruptcy Law Journal* 67: 1–15.

Bradley, M. and M. Rosenzweig. 1992. The untenable case for Chapter 11. *Yale Law Journal* 101 (March): 1043–95.

Buch, C.M. 1994. Dealing with bad debt: Lessons from Eastern Europe. Working Paper no. 642 (April). Kiel: Kiel Institute of World Economics.

Campana, M. J. and D. Legeais. 1994. Le nouvel article 40 de la Loi du 25 janvier 1985(The new article 40 of the Law of January 25, 1985). *Les Petites Affiches* 110, September 14.

Capek, A. and P. Mertlik. 1996. Organizational change and financial restructuring in Czech manufacturing enterprises 1990–95. Prague: Czech National Bank, Institute of Economics. Mimeographed.

Chartier, Y. 1989. Droit des Affaires, t.3. Enterprises en difficulté – Prevention, redressment, liquidation (Business Law, Vol. 3.

Enterprises in distress – Prevention, restructuring liquidation). Paris. Presses Universitaires du France..

Credot, F. J. 1994. Les grandes lignes de la reforme du droit des entreprises en difficulté (The broad outline of the reform of the law on enterprises in difficulty). *Les Petites Affiches* 110, September 14.

Department of Trade and Industry. 1997. *Insolvencies in the First Quarter 1997*. P/97/314. London. 2 May.

Derrida, F., P. Gode, and J. P. Sortais. 1991. *Redressement et liquidations judiciaires des entreprises* (*Restructuring and Judicial Liquidation of Enterprises*). Paris: Dalloz.

Derrida, F. and J. P. Sortais. 1994. La reforme du droit des entreprises en difficulté (premier aperçu) (The reform of the law on enterprises in difficulty – a first glimpse). *Revue Dalloz*, 6 October.

Easterbrook, F. H. 1990. Is corporate bankruptcy efficient? *Journal of Financial Economics* 27 (October): 411–7.

Eberhart, A.C., W. T. Moore, and R. L. Roenfeldt. 1990. Security pricing and deviations from the absolute priority rule in bankruptcy proceedings. *Journal of Finance* 45 (December): 1457–60.

Eberhart, A. C., and R. J. Sweeney. 1992. Does the bond market predict bankruptcy settlements? *Journal of Finance* 47, no. 3 (July): 943–80.

Fialski, H. 1994. Insolvency law in the Federal Republic of Germany: Organisation for Economic Cooperation and Development 1994: 21–32.

Franks, J. R., and W. N. Torous. 1989. An empirical investigation of U.S. firms in reorganization. *Journal of Finance* 44 (July): 747–69.

Franks, J. R., and W. N. Torous. 1992. Lessons from a comparison of US and UK insolvency codes. *Oxford Review of Economic Policy* 8, no. 3: 70–82.

Franks, J. R., and W. N. Torous. 1994. A comparison of financial recontracting in distressed exchanges and Chapter 11 reorganization. *Journal of Financial Economics* 35, no. 3 (June): 349–70.

Gilson, S. C. 1989. Management turnover and financial distress. *Journal of Financial Economics* 25 (December): 241–62.

Gilson, S. C. 1990. Bankruptcy, boards, banks, and blockholders: Evidence on changes in corporate ownership and control when firms default. *Journal of Financial Economics* 27, no. 2 (October): 355–87.

Gilson, S. C., K. John, and L. H. P. Lange. 1990. Troubled debt restructurings: An empirical study of private reorganization of firms in default. *Journal of Financial Economics* 27, no. 2 (October): 315–53.

Gray, C. W. 1993. Evolving legal framework for private sector development in Central and Eastern Europe. Discussion Paper no. 209. Washington, D.C.: World Bank.

Gray, C. W. 1994. Some common misconceptions about bankruptcy and conciliation in Hungary and Poland. Paper presented at Enterprise Exit Project Workshop, October 14–16, 1994, in Prague.

Guffey, D. M. and T. W. Moore. 1991. Direct bankruptcy costs: Evidence from the trucking industry. *Financial Review* 26, no. 2 (May): 223–35.

Hoshi, I., J. Mládek, and A. Sinclair. 1995. Enterprise behaviour and the process of exit: Case studies of four Czech firms. Paper presented at the Enterprise Exit Project Workshop, March 7-9, 1995, in Stoke on Trent,U.K.

Hudson, J. 1990. Comment on The corporate bankruptcy decision, by Michelle J. White. *Journal of Economic Perspectives* 4, no. 1 (Winter): 209–11.

Ickes, B. W., and R. Ryterman. 1993. Roadblock to economic reform: Inter-enterprise debt and the transition to markets. Working Paper no. 61. College Park, Md.:Center for Institutional Reform and Informal Sector (IRIS).

James, C. 1991. The losses realized in bank failures. *Journal of Finance,* 46, no. 4 (September): 1223–42.

Jensen, M. (1992). Corporate Control and Politics of Finance. In *Bankruptcy and Distressed Restructuring*, edited by E. Altman. New York: Irwin.

Klasmeyer, B., and B. M. Kubler. 1994. Bankruptcy and insolvency. In *Business Transactions in Germany,* edited by D. Campbell, C. Campbell, and B. Ruster. Vol. 1. Albany: Michael Bender.

Kornai, J. 1993. The evolution of financial discipline under the postsocialist system. *Kyklos* 46, fasc. 3: 315–36.

Lafont, H. 1994. The French bankruptcy system. Organisation for Economic Cooperation and Development 1994: 15–20.

LoPucki, L. M. 1983. The debtor in full control: Systems failure under Chapter 11 of the bankruptcy code? *American Bankruptcy Law Journal* 57: 99–126.

LoPucki, L. M., and Whitford 1991. Venue choice and forum shopping in the bankruptcy reorganization of large, publicly held companies. *Wisconsin Law Review,* no. 1: 11–63.

Meckling, W. H. 1974. Financial markets, default, and bankruptcy: The role of the state. *Law and Contemporary Problems* 41, no. 4: 13–39.

Miller, M. H. 1977. The wealth transfers of bankruptcy: Some illustrative examples. *Law and Contemporary Problems* 41, no. 4: 39-47.

Mitchell, J. 1990. The economics of bankruptcy in reforming socialist economies. Final report delivered to the National Council for Soviet and East European Research, October, in Ithaca, N.Y. Mimeographed.

Mitchell, J. 1993. Creditor passivity and bankruptcy: Implications for economic reform. Chap. 7 in *Capital Markets and Financial Integration*, edited by C. Meyer and X. Vives. Cambridge: Cambridge University Press.

Mizsei, K. 1993. Bankruptcy and the post-communist economies of East Central Europe. New York: Institute for East West Studies.

Moore, J. H. 1977. Foreword to *Law and Contemporary Problems* 41, no. 4: 1-10.

Morse, D. and W. Shaw. 1988. Investing in bankrupt firms. *Journal of Finance* 43, no. 5 (December): 1193–1206.

Organisation for Economic Cooperation and Development (OECD). 1994. *Corporate Bankruptcy and Reorganization Procedures in OECD and Central and Eastern European Countries*. Paris: Organisation for Economic Cooperation and Development.

Otter, K. 1988. *Insolvency practice: A practitioner's perspective*. London: Cork Gully.

Peele, M. J. and N. Wilson. 1989. The liquidation/merger alternative. *Managerial Decision Economics* 10, no. 3 (September): 209-22.

Rajak, H. 1994. The challenges of commercial reorganizations in insolvency: Empirical evidence from England. In *Current Developments in International and Comparative Corporate Insolvency Law*, edited by J. Ziegel. Oxford: Clarendon.

Rostowski, J. 1993. The inter-enterprise debt explosion in the former Soviet Union: Causes, consequences, curses. Discussion Paper no. 142. London: London School of Economics, Centre for Economic Performance.

Rubin, H. P. 1993. Growing a legal system, with special reference to the post-communist economies. Working Paper no. 63. College Park, Md .:Center for Institutional Reform and Informal Sector.

Saint-Alary-Houin, C. 1994. La reforme des plans de redressement(The reform of restructuring programs). *Les Petites Affiches* 110, September 14.

Simeon, Moquet, Borde and Associates. 1987. *Doing Business in France.* Albany: Michael Bender.

Stiglitz, J. 1972. Some aspects of the pure theory of corporate finance: Bankruptcies and take-overs. *Bell Journal of Economics and Management Science* 3 (August): 458–82.

Swain, C. H. 1994. United States bankruptcy-reorganization laws. Organisation for Economic Cooperation and Development 1994: 53–79.

Warren, E. 1991. A theory of absolute priority. *Annual Survey of American Law* 9, no.16: 9-48.

Van Wijnbergen, S. 1994. On the role of banks in enterprise restructuring: The Polish example. CEPR Discussion Paper no. 898. London: London School of Economics, Centre for Economic Policy Research.

Webb, D. C. 1987. The importance of incomplete information in explaining the existence of costly bankruptcy. *Economica* 54 (August): 279–88.

Webb, D. C. 1991. An empirical evaluation of insolvency procedures in the United Kingdom: Does the 1986 Insolvency Act satisfy the creditors' bargain? *Oxford Economic Papers* 43 (January): 139–57.

Weiss, L. A. 1990. Bankruptcy resolution: Direct costs and violation of priority of claims. *Journal of Financial Economics* 27 no. 2 (October): 285–314.

White, M. J. 1984. A bankruptcy liquidation and reorganization. Chap. 37 in *Handbook of Modern Finance,* edited by D. Logue. 2nd. ed. Boston: Warren, Gorham & Lamont.

White, M. J. 1989. The corporate bankruptcy decision. *Journal of Economic Perspectives* 3, no. 2 (spring): 129–51.

Wooldridge, F. H. 1987. *Administration Procedure.* Bristol: Jordans.

Wruck, K. H. 1990. Financial distress, reorganization, and organizational efficiency. *Journal of Financial Economics* 27 (October): 419–44

Notes

I am grateful to Cheryl Gray, Irena Grosfeld, Jacek Rostowski and John Wittaker for their helpful comments and suggestions on an earlier version of this chapter and to Sophie Bourguignon for her assistance with the section on recent changes in the French bankruptcy legislation.

1. For a discussion of causes and implications of creditor passivity in transition economies, see Mitchell (1993).

2. Miller (1977), 40. A more modern version of this concept is put forward in Akerloff and Roemer's (1993) notion of "bankruptcy for profit."

3. For a discussion of the importance of incomplete information and its implications for the cost of bankruptcy, see Webb (1987).

4. Baird has reminded us of the eighteenth-century English law under which noncooperating debtors in bankruptcy cases were hanged, whereas cooperating debtors received 5 percent of the value of recovered assets! See Baird (1991), 225.

5. Franks and Torous (1992), 75.

6. It is also possible to engage in informally arranged restructuring (work-outs) and avoid the lengthier formal procedures. This procedure will be discussed later.

7. For detailed discussion of the American bankruptcy code, see White (1984), Franks and Torous (1989), and White (1989).

8. These include the carrying forward of tax losses from previous years, debt forgiveness, termination of under-funded pension plans and their subsidization by the state, nonpayment of interest on credits during the period of preparing a reorganization plan, and the possibility of abandoning unprofitable contracts without a penalty. These subsidies, as White has pointed out, largely accrue to creditors and not to the equity holders—as the legislators may have intended. See White (1984), 37.24–37.26.

9. Although the debtor has extensive rights during the reorganization period, these rights are not at the expense of creditors whose interests are also protected by the code. Creditors usually set up a creditors' committee which has "rights of discovery" and, if necessary, can ask the court to appoint a trustee to supervise the work of management.

10. This is often referred to as the "unanimous consent procedure" (UCP). If the plan is not approved by all classes of creditors, an alternative procedure, called "cram-down," may be embarked on. Under

cram-down, a modified version of the reorganization plan is approved by the court and provisions are made for the fair and equitable treatment of the dissenting classes of creditors under the court's supervision.

11. See Bradley and Rosenzweig (1992), 1090.

12. The total number of bankruptcies (individuals and businesses) increased from about 20,000 in the early 1950s to about 900,000 in the late 1980s. See Bhandari and Weiss (1993), 1

13. Under Chapter 11 provisions, it is also possible to have a prepackaged procedure combining private restructuring and Chapter 11 court protection. Here, a privately negotiated restructuring plan is filed with the court at the same time as the bankruptcy application under Chapter 11. However, successful filings of this type are very rare; see Gilson et al. (1990), 324–5.

14. For a detailed discussion of bankruptcy procedures in the United Kingdom, see Otter (1988); Wooldridge (1987); Franks and Torous (1992); and Rajak (1994). In British legal terminology "bankruptcy" applies to individuals and "insolvency" to companies. Here, in the interest of simplicity and consistency with the terminology used in other countries, this distinction is ignored.

15. Default on payment, which may trigger the bankruptcy process, should be distinguished from the common practice of "late payment" of suppliers of goods and services. A creditor who has not been paid on time may serve a "statutory demand" notice on the debtor, who then has three weeks to comply with this demand. This notice is usually taken seriously by directors and, if at all possible, the creditor is paid. Default on payment after the deadline expires enables the creditor to petition the court to wind up the company by appointing a liquidator or a receiver. The directors are personally required to petition the court if they know, or should reasonably have known, that the company is insolvent. Although the acid test of insolvency is the inability to pay debts as they fall due, in practice this concept is less than straightforward. The debtor company, and even the courts, take the view that as long as the expected value of assets (including expected profits) exceeds the expected liabilities over a reasonable time period, the company is solvent.

16. Some creditors, especially financial institutions, however, secure their loans and establish procedures (in agreement with the debtor) that can automatically trigger the bankruptcy process and the appointment of a receiver without having to petition the court.

17. Under British law, there are two types of secured creditors: those with fixed charges and those with floating charges. A fixed charge is a

fixed asset, usually an immovable object, which is used as security for a loan. Any alteration to the use of the fixed charge by the company must be with the approval of the creditor. A floating charge is an unspecified asset used as security with the creditor, but the company retains its freedom to change the use of the said asset. If the company gets into financial difficulty, specified by certain criteria, a floating charge will become a fixed charge, and the creditor may appoint a representative (the receiver) to take control of it.

18. The receiver is personally liable for events after his appointment. Other creditors, for example, may file law suits against the receiver if they feel that their interests have been damaged by the activities of the receiver—thus the tendency to opt for liquidation as the safest option. For an example of this type of lawsuit, see Franks and Torous (1992), 73.

19. The petition for administration is usually dealt with very quickly: one day in 25 percent of the cases and less than a week in 50 percent of the cases on average. See Rajak (1994), 207.

20. These figures are based on Rajak's study (1994) of insolvencies from 1987 to 1990 and the data published by the Department of Trade and Industry (1997) for 1991–6. The share of administrations in total decreased slightly in the second subperiod (from 1.2 percent to 0.7 percent).

21. See Rajak (1994) and Department of Trade and Industry (1997). The share of voluntary arrangements in all bankruptcies increased from 0.3 percent between 1987 and 1990 to nearly 1 percent between 1991 and 1996—surpassing even the number of administrations (1,442 compared to 1,029). It should be remembered that even though the number of both administrations and voluntary arrangements is very small, these processes usually involve very large companies. In the United Kingdom, large companies in financial distress may also benefit from another informal procedure, known as the "London approach," which was devised by the Bank of England in the 1970s. This procedure, which is not part of the insolvency laws, seeks unanimous approval of all creditors to restructure the firm's finances without publicity (to avoid an adverse effect on the market). The London approach has been credited with rescuing some 160 companies in the past seven years (a small number compared to 111,700 liquidations, though much more important in terms of size). Many observers now believe that this approach is preferable to, and less costly than, the administration procedure of the

insolvency act or even the American Chapter 11 procedure. See *The Economist,* 1 March 1997.

22. For a detailed discussion of German bankruptcy laws, see Fialski (1994); Klasmeyer and Kubler (1994).

23. These two acts are *Konkursordnung* (usually referred to as *KO*) and *Vergleichsordnung* (usually referred to as *VerglO*). The territories of the former GDR (the five *Länder* and East Berlin) are subject to different insolvency procedures known as the General Enforcement Act (*Gesamtvollstreckungsordnug*, or *GesO*), which were passed as transitional measures in 1990. For more details, see Klasmeyer and Kubler (1994), 17-133 to 17-146.

24. This is defined as either an "inability to pay debts or overindebtedness," meaning that liabilities exceed the value of assets. See *Ibid.*, p.p. 17–23.

25. Fialski (1994), 23; Klasmeyer and Kubler (1994), 17. This is in sharp contrast to the British law which enables the court to deal with such firms using public funds. If the firm's assets are insufficient to cover the cost of the liquidator or receiver and procedural costs, the court appoints an "official receiver", who is a civil servant, to wind up the company and establish whether or not any of the directors have infringed the relevant laws, in which case the receiver would initiate the relevant legal process.

26. However, if the creditors are willing to pay the procedural costs, in advance, the bankruptcy petition will be heard.

27. Klasmeyer and Kubler (1994), 17.

28. The court may, of course, prevent such asset disposals.

29. Klasmeyer and Kubler (1994), 17; Fialski (1994), 27.

30. Klasmeyer and Kubler, 17.

31. For a discussion of the proposed new bankruptcy procedures, see Fialski (1994); *The Economist,* 21 May 1994.

32. For details of the French bankruptcy laws and procedures, see Simeon et al. (1987); Chartier (1989); Derrida et al. (1991); Lafont (1994); Credot (1994); Saint-Alary-Houin (1994). For the 1994 amendments (Law no. 94-475 of June 10, 1994), see Campana and Legeais (1994); *Journal Officiel,* June 11, 1994.

33. Apart from the official conciliation procedure, the courts have also appointed, on an *ad hoc* basis, guardians to advise financially distressed firms before they enter bankruptcy proceedings. See Lafont (1994), 18–9.

34. In the case of agricultural organizations or private noncommercial legal entities, the petition is filed with the Civil Court.

35. Chartier (1989), 174. This is in sharp contrast to the British practice where noncompliant managers face strong sanctions.

36. The priority of prebankruptcy secured creditors was somewhat unclear until the 1994 amendments, which gave these claims priority over claims arising after the initiation of the bankruptcy proceedings. See Campana and Legeais (1994).

37. Even under the 1985 law, judges had the discretion of reducing the compulsory observational phase to a symbolic minimum, e.g., pronouncing the liquidation of a manifestly unviable firm on the same day as the decree on judicial restructuring. See Derrida and Sortais (1994), 274.

38. White (1984), 37.

39. Stiglitz (1972), 461, 480.

40. Bradley and Rosenzweig showed that the average debt–asset ratio of firms filing for bankruptcy had increased after 1978, indicating the managers' increased borrowing tendency after the 1978 Bankruptcy Reform Act. However, a later study of the causes of consumer and corporate bankruptcies since the Second World War has shown that the increased incidence of bankruptcies has been due to the reduction in the debt-servicing capacity of the debtors and not to the adoption of the 1978 code. See Bradley and Rosenzweig (1992), 1095; Bhandari and Weiss (1993), 12.

41. The time spent in reorganization was 1.4 years for a sample of twenty-six firms in White (1984); 2.1 years for a sample of thirty firms in Eberhart et al. (1990); 2.4 years for a sample of thirty firms in Weiss (1990); 2.5 years for a sample of thirty-seven firms in Franks and Torous (1994); and 2.8 years for a different sample of twenty-six firms in Franks and Torous (1989).

42. For a discussion of this issue, see Eastbrook (1990), 416.

43. As for the indirect costs (opportunity costs) of bankruptcy (i.e., lost sales and profit, tarnished image, loss of reputation, loss of skilled employees, etc.), despite few rough attempts such as Altman (1984), which related to the period before the new bankruptcy code, no serious progress has been made. Altman estimated the indirect costs for a sample of eighteen firms filing for bankruptcy between 1972 and 1978 to be about 10 percent. See *Ibid.*, 1077.

44. These estimates are, respectively, from: Weiss (1990), 290, based on a sample of thirty-seven firms; Altman (1984), tables I and II,

1074–75, for a sample of eighteen firms; White (1984), 37, for sixty-four firms; and Ang, Chua, and McConnell (1982), 223, for eighty-six firms. Industry-specific studies have resulted in higher direct costs than those for mixed samples: 9.12 percent in Guffey and Moore (1991), for sixteen firms in the trucking industry; and 10 percent in James (1991), for 412 bank failures. See also White (1984), tables 37.4 and 37.5, 37.45.

45. See Eberhart et al. (1990), 1464; Eberhart and Sweeney (1992), 944; Franks and Torous (1994), 363. In a typical reorganization, shareholders often receive new securities and creditors receive a varying combination of securities, cash, bonds, or notes. The estimates for the deviation from APR have to be treated with caution as they are based on inaccurate—and sometimes inappropriate—methods of valuation of the new assets. The complications of comparing new securities with the old ones and other problems of measuring the extent of deviation are discussed in Franks and Torous (1989), 754–8; Weiss (1990), 292–3.

46. For example, an article entitled "When Firms Go Bust," *The Economist,* 1 August 1992, estimated the success rate of firms in reorganization at 20 percent. Similarly, in an OECD report, Swain (1994) maintains that the success rate was between 10 percent and 27 percent; the basis of calculations in both studies is unclear.

47. Warren (1991), 15.

48. These estimates are based on samples ranging from sixty-four to 162 firms. See White (1984), 37.40-37.41; Morse and Shaw (1988), 1198; Gilson et al. (1990), 321; LoPucki and Whitford (1991), 41, fn. 105. LoPucki (1983) was the first study that identified the much higher success rate for larger firms.

49. Wruck even argues that it is more efficient to be highly leveraged because the creditors will have a stronger incentive to monitor the managers and press them for restructuring in the face of financial distress. Wruck (1990), 433.

50. Some studies (Franks and Torous [1989], 755-7; Weiss [1990], 294-6) identify the junior creditors as the main losers. Others such as Eberhart and Sweeney (1992) maintain that bondholders (a subset of junior creditors) benefit from the violation of APR—albeit only a little—at the expense of senior creditors.

51. Baird and Jackson (1988), 743.

52. *Ibid.*, 743. Furthermore, it has been observed by some bankruptcy scholars that the 1978 Bankruptcy Code was largely what the creditors had wished for and that this code was aimed at meeting their requirement. See Easterbrook (1990), 413.

53. For more examples of restrictions imposed by creditors on the management, see Gilson (1990), 367.

54. Hudson (1990), 210–1.

55. For an innovative example of such new proposals, see Aghion, Hart, and Moore (1992).

56. For a detailed discussion of financial distress and indebtedness, see Begg and Portes (1993); Ickes and Ryterman (1993); Kornai (1993).

57. See Bhandari and Weiss (1993), 14.

58. For the extent and magnitude of indebtedness, see Mizsei (1993), 50–4; Kornai (1993); Mitchell (1993); Rostowski (1993); Buch (1994).

59. The support for reorganization procedures has been expressed by many scholars including, among others, Abel and Gatsios (1993); Gray (1993); Mizsei (1993).

60. For a discussion of some reorganization options, see Aghion, Hart, and Moore (1992); Van Wijnbergen (1994).

61. For a detailed discussion of the importance of the design of bankruptcy procedures, see Gray (1994), 13–8.

62. The Hungarian trigger mechanism was rather narrowly defined (ninety-day arrears to any creditor) in order to encourage indebted firms to find a solution for their financial problems (see chapter 6 for details). The situation in the Czech Republic and Poland is very different. In the Czech Republic, until June 1996, the bankruptcy law did not require the managers to file for bankruptcy on default, thus creating incentives for opportunistic behavior without any penalties. In Poland, despite the legal requirement, many managers have failed to declare their conditions and, so far, none have been prosecuted.

63. This was later changed to 50 percent (by number of creditors) and 67 percent (by the value of their claims).

64. For an example of multiple collateralization, see the case study of Cottex Hronov, in Hashi, Mládek, and Sinclair (1995). For a more general comment, see *The Economist,* 16 April 1994. In Poland, the law on the establishment of a register of collaterals was passed only in 1997.

65. For case studies of the bank–enterprise relationship, highlighting the banks' willingness to push their debtors into bankruptcy, particularly in the earlier phase of transition, see Capek and Mertlik (1996) and Hashi, Mládek, and Sinclair (1995).

66. For a discussion of the interaction between the banking system and the bankruptcy process, see Van Wijnbergen (1994).

3 Macroeconomic Shocks and Policy Responses During Transition: A Cross-Country Comparison

Jacek Rostowski and Milan Nikolić

Enterprises in post-communist economies have been subject to a wide range of shocks as the old economic order has been swept away. This chapter has two aims: first, to attempt to measure the size of the shocks affecting the fast reformers of the Visegrad group (the Czech Republic, Hungary, Poland, and Slovakia), with some reference to slower reformers, such as Bulgaria and Romania; and second, to assess the policy responses of these governments by classifying the policies as either adaptive or accommodative and gauging their importance. It has been claimed that among the most important of the shocks have been:

1. the elimination of soft budget constraints, resulting from the liberalization of prices, the elimination of soft credit (in the form of loans granted on either a noncommercial basis or at significantly negative real interest rates), and the drastic reduction of budgetary subsidies to enterprises;

2. foreign trade shocks, resulting from the disappearance of export markets and the shift to world prices in convertible currencies for raw materials and energy;

3. overdevaluation, as trade was liberalized and currencies sharply devalued to maintain the competitiveness of domestic producers.[1]

In the words of two eminent observers (Grosfeld and Roland 1996): 27.

> In a matter of days and weeks, Polish enterprises, subject to the simultaneous shocks of price liberalization, trade liberalization, and fiscal stabilization in January 1990, plunged from a shortage

economy characterized by a sellers' market into a buyers' market where firms must compete to sell their products. Similar changes took place in Czechoslovakia in early 1991, even though fiscal stabilization was less an issue due to more balanced initial macroeconomic conditions. Even though price liberalization proceeded more gradually in Hungary, price and trade liberalization accelerated substantially between 1989 and 1991. Last but not least, the CMEA breakdown constituted a price liberalization at the level of the whole region.

Credit Shocks in Post-Communist Economies

One measure of the elimination of soft budget constraints is the change in the stock of real credit to nongovernmental sectors that accompanied the transition. Under normal conditions, this is the indicator relevant for enterprise liquidity (together with the enterprise's own cash and trade credit, the latter of which is dealt with below). When firms repay principal and interest to banks, the sums concerned do not disappear as a source of liquidity. Instead, they are normally re-lent to some other borrowers. The real stock of credit does not need to increase continuously to maintain production! As a result, the breakdown of debt service payments into interest and principal by nonfinancial businesses does not matter; it is the stock measures of real bank and trade credit and the firm's own cash (including deposits) that determine liquidity.

Does this change if a large part of any increase in nominal credit is due to capitalized, although unpaid, interest? There is clearly a microeconomic problem if the economy's credit fund is not circulating, i.e., if most borrowers are bankrupt. Such a situation is often dealt with by maintaining a positive real flow of new credit to borrowers from the central bank. To the extent it is never repaid, such credit is a quasi-fiscal deficit paid for through inflation and should be thought of as a transfer payment or subsidy to borrowers, rather than a form of liquidity (although it does temporarily add to their liquidity). Furthermore, inflation caused by such new credit can often be sufficiently high to reduce the stock of real credit.

Thus, the purpose of tables 3.1 and 3.2 is to show what happened to real bank credit, rather than what happened to quasi-fiscal transfers to borrowers. If the "credit fund" of the economy is circulating, it can be thought of as a valid measure of liquidity, although any additional liquidity generated by quasi-fiscal transfers will be missed. Also, it is far more difficult to get reliable figures for quasi-fiscal transfers; one needs detailed information on the actual interest rates charged (often on a monthly basis) the amount of debt, and the rates of inflation.

In Czechoslovakia, the stock of real bank credit fell by 14 percent in 1990 and by 28 percent in the first half of 1991, followed by an increase of 5 percent in the second half of 1991 and of 1.5 percent in the first half of 1992. Thus, the overall effect was far from insignificant. In Slovakia, credit was noticeably tighter than in the Czech Republic, and from 1991 in both countries credit to state enterprises was significantly tighter than total credit. Particularly striking is the sharp fall (31 percent) in credit in Slovakia in 1990, even before the reforms began and at a time when credit was far less affected in the Czech Republic (8 percent). In Hungary, there has been little contraction in credit to businesses, whereas in Poland the reduction in real credit to firms has been by far the steepest among the four countries.

Table 3.1
Stock of Real Bank Credit to Enterprises (PPI deflated)

	Czechoslovakia	Czech Republic		Slovakia	
		total	SOE	total	SOE
12/1989	100	100	100	100	100
12/1990	86	92	89	69	70
06/1991	62	71	64	57	56
12/1991	65	69	63	60	56
06/1992	66	69	57	64	55
12/1992	–	70	–	60	–
12/1993	–	67	–	56	–
12/1994	–	73	–	51	–

Source: Author's calculations based on Svejnar (1993) and official statistics provided in the *Statistical Bulletin—Poland, Czech Republic, Slovakia, Hungary* (Quarterly).

The relationship between output and real credit is tenuous in all four countries. Between the beginning of 1989 and the end of 1993 in Hungary, real credit to enterprises actually increased marginally, whereas industrial output fell by 30 percent. In Poland between 1985 and 1988, real credit to enterprises fell by over 23 percent, while industrial output increased by 13.6 percent. During 1989 real credit to enterprises and industrial production developed as depicted in table 3.2. Thus, the index of the ratio of real credit to industrial output changed as follows during the year: 100, 100, 83, 47, 40 (first quarter, 1990). In the following eleven quarters (to the end of 1993), real credit to enterprises increased by over 70 percent, while industrial production grew by a mere 3 percent, increasing the ratio of real credit to industrial production back to 67. Then during the four quarters of 1994, industrial production increased by 12 percent while real credit fell by 4 percent. Thus in the medium term, from 1985 to 1994, there seems to be remarkably little relationship between the levels of industrial output and real credit to enterprises in Poland, with output often changing in the opposite direction as changes in real credit. Indeed, the correlation coefficient on quarterly data is both small and negative (-0.1797).[2]

Table 3.2
Stock of Real Bank Credit to Enterprises (PPI deflated)

	Poland		**Hungary**
	Real Credit	Industrial Output	Real Credit
Q1/1989	100	100	100
Q2/1989	96	96	98
Q3/1989	70	85	107
Q4/1989	43	91	103
Q1/1990	28	70	98
Q2/1990	41	66	93
Q3/1990	48	69	102
Q4/1990	49	76	96
Q2/1991	47	58	95
Q4/1991	53	60	99
Q4/1992	50	68	100
Q4/1993	48	73	108
Q4/1994	46	83	-

Sources: Commander and Coricelli (1992) and official statistics provided in the *Statistical Bulletin—Poland, Czech Republic, Slovakia, Hungary* (Quarterly).

Neverthless, Calvo and Coricelli (1993) claim that a relationship can be found on cross-sectional data when comparing the last quarter of 1989 and the first quarter of 1990, with a relatively low coefficient of about 0.2. They stress that the fall in interenterprise credit (IEC) that accompanied the stabilization in the first quarter of 1990 in Poland contributed to the discrepancy between the fall in real credit and the fall in output. The increase in real IEC in the last quarter of 1989 helped to offset the fall in real bank credit, whereas the fall in real IEC augmented the fall in real bank credit in the first quarter of 1990 (see table 3.3). However, what Calvo and Coricelli fail to take into account is that had this fall in real IEC not happened, the tightening in real bank credit might not have affected either output or inflation at the beginning of 1990, as industrial output fell by far less than real credit to enterprises. In the absence of the final tightening of real bank credit in the first quarter of 1990, IEC might have continued expanding in a bubble of the kind analyzed in Rostowski 1993, undermining stabilization. Indeed, this is what seems to have happened in Russia in the first half of 1992, when radical policy makers led by the then Deputy Prime Minister Yegor Gaidar tried to embark on a stabilization program.

Table 3.3
Interenterprise Credit in Poland

Q1 1989	100
Q2 1989	109
Q3 1989	92
Q4 1989	123
Q1 1990	73

Source: Rostowski (1993).

However weak the empirical relationship between real credit and industrial output was, there can be little doubt that a fundamental change in the availability of credit occurred at the beginning of 1990 in Poland and Slovakia and at the beginning of 1991 in the Czech Republic.[3] The change in the credit-allocation regime in Hungary may have been more gradual, yet it was equally as effective (as discussed below). This change was central to the change in the macroeconomic regime that occurred in these countries. It has been called a shift from "systemically bad" to "systemically good" credit (Rostowski 1995). Systemically bad credit was provided by the state-owned banking system without any assumption that it would ever be repaid. Also, in countries with high and accelerating rates of inflation (Poland until 1990 and Ukraine until 1994), this systemically bad credit was easily obtainable, bore significantly negative real interest rates, and constituted a major proportion of the quasi-fiscal deficit. As a result, the credit functioned as a mechanism by which the borrowers (mainly state enterprises and farms but also private farmers in Poland) received a significant proportion of the revenue from the inflation tax as a subsidy (Layard and Richter 1994).

For credit to become systemically good, banks had to learn to allocate credit on a commercial basis. For banks to have the incentive to acquire the skills needed to start allocating credit commercially, credit had to stop bearing significantly negative real interest rates, and it had to stop being easily available. Putting the conditions for systemically good credit in place was, however, tantamount to eliminating the subsidy borrowers had received through their access to a significant proportion of revenues from the inflation tax.[4] Since this subsidy was related in various ways to the output of enterprises, it is not surprising that output also fell when the subsidy was reduced.[5]

Thus the association between the introduction of a new "good credit" regime and a sharp fall in industrial output is not in doubt. What is doubtful is any direct quantitative relationship between real credit and industrial output and, perhaps more importantly, the policy implication that there was an alternative policy that could have avoided the fall in real credit in these countries, while at the same time preventing high inflation.[6]

Fiscal Adjustment and its Impact on State-Owned Enterprises

In all three Central European countries, budgetary subsidies were reduced sharply, as shown in table 3.4. The largest reduction in subsidies (but from the highest level) occurred in Czechoslovakia, which remained the country with the highest level of subsidies. The removal of subsidies is significant not only because it increases the hardness of budget constraints, but also because to some measure it indicates the extent of price liberalization. Thus it is no accident that subsidy reduction was by far the largest in Czechoslovakia. The relatively low level of subsidies in Hungary reflects its relatively high share of free prices in 1986, while the low level in Poland was due partly to freer prices and partly to greater shortages (i.e., unfunded price control).

Schaffer (1995), using data from the Central Statistical Office on 37,720 Polish firms for 1991 and 11,719 Czech firms for 1992, concluded the following: "The pattern for the two countries is very similar: about 85-90% of all firms . . . and 75-90% of total revenues, are in firms receiving virtually no subsidies (i.e. firms where subsidies make up 1%

Table 3.4
Fiscal Adjustment (Percentage of GDP)

	Poland			Hungary			Czechoslovakia		
	A	B	C	A	B	C	A	B	C
Subsidies	16.2	5.0	-11.2	15.6	5.6	-9.9	26.3	7.9	-18.5
of which: Subsidies to State Owned Enterprises	7.1	2.1	-5.0	9.8	3.3	-6.5	22.2	7.9	-14.3
Transfers[a]	9.9	19.7	9.9	13.7	24.4	10.7	11.8	16.3	4.4
Profit tax	11.1	5.8	- 5.3	10.5	4.0	-6.5	18.6	12.7	-5.8

Notes:
[a] to households
A = 1985–7; B = 1991–2; C = change
Source: Barbone and Marchetti (1994) and author's calculations.

or less of their total revenue) . . . already by the second year of the transition, most of the enterprise sector is budgetary subsidyfree." (p.124) Manufacturing firms in both countries received less than 10 percent of all subsidies, which accounted for less than 0.5 percent of their revenues. The transport sector received 35 to 40 forty percent of all subsidies in both countries. Mining in Poland received 37 percent of the subsidies in 1991, but coal prices were liberalized late that year, and these subsidies largely disappeared. In the Czech Republic, agriculture received 25 percent of subsidies. Although in general, subsidies were important for the strongly subsidized sectors, accounting for 5 percent to 18 percent of their revenues, their overall level was low and comparable to EU levels (see table 3.5).

These subsidy reductions have been similar in scale, if somewhat smaller, to the reductions in bank credit previously discussed (except in the case of Hungary). To the extent we accept that credit under the old system—be that central planning or market socialism—was systemically bad, then credit was effectively a form of subsidy, and therefore the

Table 3.5
Subsidies as a Percentage of GDP, 1993

Bulgaria	4.8
Czech Republic	4.4
Hungary	4.8
Poland	2.5
Slovakia	4.8
Romania	5.5

Source: Schaffer (1995) and World Economic Outlook, IMF, October 1994.

reduction in real credit is comparable to—and an addition to—the reduction in budgetary subsidies.[7] If we accept this approach, then the total initial magnitude of reductions in both bank lending and subsidies to enterprises and consumers was about 40 percent of GDP in Czechoslovakia and 33 percent (between mid-1989 and the first quarter of 1990) in Poland.[8] We have seen that the removal of subsidies in Hungary predominated and amounted to only about 6.5 percent of GDP.[9] The question then becomes: to what extent did remaining credit cease to have the characteristics of a subsidy under the new system? We return to this matter later in this chapter.

The CMEA and Soviet Import Trade shocks

Rosati (1993) distinguishes among three kinds of trade shock which affected the post-CMEA countries:

1. the terms of trade shock, resulting from the increase in the relative price of raw materials, particularly energy products, which had to be paid by importers (especially the Central European importers of Soviet primary exports);

2. that part of the Soviet import collapse that was due to the disintegration of CMEA through trade reduction and trade diversion;[10]

3. that part of the Soviet import collapse which was due to internal Soviet factors (recession, disintegration of the state, shortage of foreign currency, etc.).

The effects of these shocks account for a large proportion of the 1991 fall in GDP in Central and Eastern Europe, as seen in table 3.6.

Since real GDP is measured according to relative domestic prices, the approach based on the market exchange rate is preferred. On this basis, more than the entire 1991 fall in GDP is accounted for by trade shocks in Bulgaria and Hungary! In Czechoslovakia, slightly over half of the 1991 fall in GDP is due to trade shocks.[11] Almost all of the 1991 fall in Poland is due to such shocks; although it must be remembered that Poland had an 11.7 percent fall in GDP in 1990, which was only marginally due to trade effects, giving the lowest impact of trade shocks for

Table 3.6
The Impacts of Trade Shocks on GDP (in percentages)

	Bulgaria	Czechoslovakia	Hungary	Poland
GDP change	-25.7	-15.9	-10.2	-7.2
At market exchange rates				
effect (1)	–	–	-2.3	-0.2
effect (2)	-12.4	-3.1	-3.6	-3.1
effect (3)	-18.1	-5.4	-4.4	-3.2
GDP decline not due to trade shocks	-4.8	7.4	-0.2	0.7
At PPP exchange rates				
effect (1)	–	–	-1.3	-0.1
effect (2)	-3.5	-1.0	-2.1	-1.7
effect (3)	-5.1	-1.8	-2.5	-1.7
GDP decline not due to trade shocks	17.1	13.1	4.3	3.7

Source: Rosati (1993).

the 1990–91 period (over the period of two years, 12.4 percent of the fall in GDP is unexplained).

Dan Rodrik (1994) found the effect of trade shocks in Czechoslovakia and Hungary somewhat lower: 7.5 percent of GDP (versus 8.5 percent) and 7.8 percent (versus 10.2 percent), respectively. The effect for Poland was much weaker: 3.5 percent instead of 6.5 percent. However, Rodrik's work is flawed by his failure to account for the price equalization schemes that existed for CMEA trade, particularly important in Poland.

The Shock of Overdevaluation

Devaluations can have contractionary effects in the short run (Edwards 1986; Gylfasson and Schmid 1983). If this is so, then extreme overdevaluations could have sharply contractionary effects. One way of measuring the initial overdevaluation of the domestic currency is to look at the gap between PPP exchange rates and the fixed or floating exchange rates brought in at the beginning of the transition period when convertibility was introduced (see table 3.7).

As we can see from column 3 of table 3.7, Bulgaria and Czechoslovakia overdevalued quite significantly, relative to countries with similar GDPs per capita at PPP. Poland hardly overdevalued at all during the beginning of its reforms in 1990, compared to countries with similar per capita GDP at purchasing power parities, while Hungary

Table 3.7
Ratios of Purchasing Power Parity Rates (PPR) to Market Exchange Rates (MER), Annual Averages

	GDP per capita (MER)	GDP per capita (PPP)	PPP/MER
Bulgaria	**845**	**3000**	**3.550**
Mauritius	1933	3114	1.601
Panama	1919	3257	1.697
Thailand	1269	3476	2.739
Colombia	1219	3895	3.195
Turkey	1461	3973	2.719
Costa Rica	1807	4077	2.256
Poland	**1630**	**4200**	**2.560**
Argentina	1894	4499	2.375
Brazil	3270	4592	1.404
Mexico	2396	5186	2.164
Malaysia	2156	5289	2.453
Hungary	**3068**	**5400**	**1.760**
South Africa	2592	5451	2.103
Uruguay	2736	5565	2.034
Chile	1958	5603	2.862
Venezuela	2352	5770	2.453
Portugal	4413	6231	1.412
Czechoslovakia	**2063**	**6250**	**3.030**
Greece	5401	6904	1.278
Ireland	9273	8875	0.957
Cyprus	6394	9760	1.526
Spain	9601	10354	1.078
Israel	10256	10724	1.046

Data for 1989 are for nontransition countries, for 1990 for Poland, and for 1991 for the remaining transition economies.

Source: "Trends in International Distribution of Gross World Product", 1993, Department for Economics and Social Information and Policy Analysis, Statistical Division, National Account Statistics, Series X, No. 18, Special Issue,United Nations, New York; PlanEcon quoted in Rosati (1993) and author's calculations using the Polish official GDP deflator.

underdevalued (or maintained its currency overvalued) to quite a significant extent. This result for Poland holds only for the average of 1990 as a whole. With the nominal exchange rate constant and the purchasing power index (PPI) rising 192 percent during 1990, there must have been considerable overdevaluation at the very beginning of the year. However, when considering the results of economic policy in 1990, it is the average real exchange rate for the year that is likely to be more important.

Furthermore, it should be remembered that the PPI increased by 109 percent, or more than half of its total increase, in January 1990 alone.[12]

Accommodation via Bank Credit

In spite of the sharp fall in real credit to nongovernment sectors during 1989–90 in Poland, credit that was available continued initially to be provided by the banks in a highly inefficient manner. Pinto and van Wijnbergen (1994) found that from the third quarter of 1989 to the third quarter of 1991, there was a large and highly significant negative relationship between enterprise profits and bank credits. This result is strengthened when the enterprises in the sample are divided into profitable (AAA) and loss-making (A) subsamples (see table 3.8). In the authors' words: "Bank loans went to firms that were not doing well. . . . Banks played no role in corporate governance; they simply funded enterprise losses." Pinto and van Wijnbergen use the following equation to esimate the impact of credits on the two types of firms for two separate time periods. The results are shown in table 3.8.

$$(BB/EMPL)_{it} = a_1 + b_1 PRF_{it} + b_2 CC_{it} + e_{it} \quad (1)$$

BB = nominal bank borrowing deflated by PP; PRF = profit–sales ratio;
CC = cash constraint variable; EMPL = quarterly employment

Gomulka (1995) found similar results when he looked at the distibution of the stock of bank credit to enterprises at end of 1992, with the worst 10 percent of firms—responsible for some 12 percent of sales—accounting for approximately 60 percent of bank credit.

From the fourth quarter of 1991, the Kawalec–Sikora reforms of the governance of state-owned commercial banks (SOCBs) began. The banks were commercialized and provided with supervisory boards

Table 3.8
Changes in Bank Credit to Polish Firms

Firm type	Coefficient	1989 (3rd Quarter)–1991 (3rd Quarter)		1991 (4th Quarter)–1992 (2nd Quarter)	
AAA	b_1	-0.018	(-1.55)	0.025	(1.99)
	b_2	0.006	(1.76)	-0.003	(-0.82)
A	b_1	-0.037	(-5.60)	-0.007	(-1.56)
	b_2	-0.0004	(-0.63)	-0.00003	(-0.22)

Statistics in brackets: AAA-Profitable firms; A-Loss-making firms
Source: Pinto and van Wijnbergen (1994).

appointed by the Ministry of Finance. At the same time, work began on the preparation of the Enterprise and Bank Financial Restructuring Project and on the case-by-case privatization of banks. Pinto and Wijnbergen claim that taken together, the change in bank governance and the expectation of recapitalization and privatization seem to have fundamentally changed the incentives of bank management. The question remains, however, to what extent the change in the behavior of bank management depicted in table 3.8 was the result of the Kawalec–Sikora reforms, and to what extent it was simply the result of learning by doing (which takes time) in response to changes in the credit regime after January 1990. Interestingly, this change was not accompanied by a further fall in industrial output but, on the contrary, by the beginnings of recovery—even though it was accompanied by a further decline in real credit (see table 3.2). Pinto and van Wijnbergen also argue that even in 1990 (i.e., before bank governance reform), the perception of managers regarding the ease of obtaining bank credit was not at all related to their level of bank debt, suggesting that the passivity of banks resulted from a desire to prevent firm failures, rather than from a fear of exposing their bad debts to the public.

In the Czech Republic bank credit classified as "risky" (i.e., credits that are unrecoverable or doubtful according to the standard Anglo-Saxon classification) increased extremely fast (see table 3.9). It is unfortunately unclear to what extent this rise is a process of accumulation of risky credits, and to what extent it is one by which credits are revealed as risky. Dittus and Prowse (1994) show nonperforming loans in 1992 to be 28 percent of total credits in Hungary and 26 percent in Poland.[13] The equivalent figures for risky loans as a share of GDP are 12.6 percent and 5.5 percent compared to 17.3 percent in the Czech Republic.[14]

We have seen how the reform of bank governance in Poland may have changed the lending behavior of banks. A similar effect seems to have occurred in Hungary as a result of the introduction of the auto-

Table 3.9
Risky Bank Credit in the Czech Republic

	% of total Credit	**% of GDP**
end 1991	2.4	1.7
end 1992	19.0	13.7
end 1993	23.8	17.3

Source: Ministry of Industry and Trade of the Czech Republic, May 1994.

matic bankruptcy trigger. This effect may have been partially offset, however, by three successive recapitalizations of the state banks, which are believed by many observers to have introduced a severe moral hazard into the Hungarian banking system and cumulatively cost the state treasury the equivalent of 9 percent of GDP. Bank recapitalization in Poland was far less expensive (about 1.5 percent of GDP) and has not as yet resulted in a moral hazard.

Accommodation via Interenterprise Debt

It has been claimed that interenterprise debt (IED) expansion can be a means for enterprises to evade hard budget constraints and the effects of tightening macroeconomic policy, and that once a large stock of IED has been built up, "even sound policies such as tighter bank credit may have no effect" (Calvo and Coricelli 1995). Thus, IED in Russia in 1992 increased seven and a half times in real terms between December 1991 and June 1992, growing from 3.5 percent of GDP to 24.5 percent, while bank credit fell at the same time from 40 percent of GDP to 11.5 percent.[15] A number of other countries that have had severe difficulties stabilizing, such as Romania and Ukraine, have experienced similar IED surges (Khan and Clifton 1992). Nevertheless, it has been argued that for IED to be a mechanism of accommodation, some kind of multilateral clearing of IED must take place (Rostowski 1993). Furthermore, the experience of post-communist economies with IED has been varied. Thus, as we have already seen in table 3.3, IED fell 40 percent in Poland in real terms when macroeconomic stabilization was

Table 3.10
Enterprise End-Period Receivables as a Percentage of Annualized GDP

	1988	1989	1990	1991
Poland				
–total	–	–	–	27.8
–for G and S[a]	30.5	23.9	19.6	22.4
Hungary				
–for G and S[a]	36.4	33.3	33.5	33.1
Czechoslovakia				
–total	29.3	25.0	40.5	59.3

Note: [a] for goods and services.

Source: Fan and Schaffer (1993).

imposed. Interenterprise debt in Hungry has remained constant as the transition has progressed (see table 3.10).

In Czechoslovakia, on the other hand, there has been a significant accumulation of interenterprise debt. Not only did IED fail to increase in Poland and Hungary (unlike in Czechoslovakia) during the transition, but Polish and Hungarian data are well within the norm for Western countries. In Czechoslovakia the average payment period is about 3.5 months, which is the same as in France, the Western country with the longest payment period (table 3.11). These data are particularly striking because bank credit to nongovernmental sectors relative to GDP fell quite modestly in Czechoslovakia between 1989 and 1992 (from 75 percent to 70 percent) (Svejnar 1993). If we add bank and interenterprise credit and relate the sum to GDP, then the figures we get for 1992 are: Poland 48 percent, Hungary 75 percent and Czechoslovakia 135 percent.

Czechoslovakia certainly seems to be a high-credit economy, which is apparently to be related to the failure of Czechoslovak firms to respond as energetically as Polish and Hungarian firms to the hardening of budget constraints with respect to stocks of inventories (see table 3.12).

How then do we explain the difference between Hungary and Poland, on the one hand, and Czechoslovakia and Russia, on the other?

Table 3.11
Payment Periods East and West (in months)

Czechoslovakia	2.5–3.5
Denmark	1.6
Finland	1.8
France	3.5
Germany	1.6
Hungary	1.5–1.7
Ireland	2.0
Italy	3.0
Netherlands	1.7
Norway	1.6
Poland	1.5–1.8
Sweden	1.6
Switzerland	2.0
UK	2.6

Source: Fan and Schaffer (1993). Central European figures are for payables and receivables for goods and services relative to turnover, except in the case of Czechoslovakia, where they are for total payables and receivables relative to turnover.

Table 3.12
Enterprise Inventories (Outside Agriculture) as a Percentage of Annualized GDP

	1988	1989	1990	1991
Poland	33	19[a]	21	20
Hungary	46	43	37	34
Czechoslovakia	76	76	76	67

Note: [a] Biased downwards as a result of near hyperinflation in late 1989.

Source: Fan and Schaffer (1993).

Also, what is the similarity between a country (Russia) whose policy has been very loose from a macroeconomic point of view and one (Czechoslovakia) which is the exemplar of a tight policy? The contrast between Poland and Russia may have stemmed from the degree of credibility of stabilization policies in the two countries. Firms in Poland seem to have believed that stabilization would happen and were therefore unwilling to grant credit to their customers, fearing they were unlikely to have been repaid as their customers continued to face hard budget constraints. In Russia, with stabilization not credible, firms expected their customers to recover access to soft budgets after the failure of the stabilization attempt and therefore to be able to pay their debts. The only problem facing suppliers, in their own view, was to charge a sufficiently high price to compensate for the expected inflation during the period of the interenterprise loan (Rostowski 1993).

The credibility of the reform program also seems to have been growing in Hungary. Not only do receivables decline as a share of GDP (as we saw in table 3.10), but payment arrears registered by the National Bank of Hungary, which account for only a very small proportion of receivables, show a tendency to increase in the first years of the transition but then exhibit a sharp decline as the automatic bankruptcy trigger and stringent financial discipline via the banks are introduced (see table 3.13).

These results suggest that there is something in Köves's (Szanyi 1995) idea of the Hungarian bankruptcy law as a form of "supply-side shock therapy," having some of the same effects as Poland's "demand-side shock therapy." Not only did output fall as a result of both shocks, but payment discipline also improved significantly.

In Czechoslovakia, on the other hand, payment discipline deteriorated significantly at the beginning of the transition period. This may be

Table 3.13
Intercompany Payment Arrears in Hungary (HUF billion)

Date	Payment arrears	Date	Payment arrears
1990		**1993**	
January	81	January	77
March	–	March	103
June	–	June	81
September	–	September	93
December	90	December	82
1991		**1994**	
January	116	January	77
March	119	March	56
June	138	June	78
September	140	September	50
1992		November	65
January	174		
March	188		
June	136		
September	79		
December	74		

Source: Szanyi (1995), National Bank of Hungary's blacklist for bill of exchange rediscount activity.

because Czechoslovakia implemented a degree of supply-side gradualism: it suspended the operation of its bankruptcy law until mid-1993, two and a half years into transition.[16] Furthermore, softness in the Czech government's approach to firms in the area of IED is confirmed by the fact that a number of multilateral clearings of IED took place, something which occurred neither in Hungary nor in Poland and is typical of such transition and stabilization laggards as Russia, Romania, and Ukraine! Unfortunately, no data are as yet available for receivables in the Czech Republic for the period 1992–94, which would allow us to verify whether—as hypothesized—IED continued to grow as long as the bankruptcy law was suspended.

Accommodation via Relaxation of Enterprise Taxation

Barbone and Marchetti (1994) argue convincingly that subsidy reductions contributed to the fall in enterprise profits and show that tax revenues from enterprise profits either remained unchanged (in Hungary) or actually increased (in Czechoslovakia and Poland). It is useful, however, to proceed in a more straightforward way and examine what happened to the total gross tax burden on enterprises, not just profit taxes, in order to see whether this burden was reduced to accommodate the otherwise deteriorating financial position of enterprises (see table 3.14).

Table 3.14
Gross Tax Burden on Enterprises (Percentage of GDP)

	1989	**1993**
Bulgaria	36.9	19.8
Czech Republic	32.9[a]	26.8
Hungary	27.9	24.9
Poland	22.2	24.9
Romania	20.3	18.6

Notes: [a] Czechoslovakia.

The taxes involved are: profits tax, wage tax, social security payments and excess wage tax (only in Poland).

Source: *IMF World Economic Outlook* 1994.

Thus, taxes on enterprises increased as a percentage of GDP in Poland, while they fell somewhat in Czechoslovakia (the Czech Republic) and Hungary. In the latter two cases, however, if we adjust for the fall in subsidies to producers (*á la* Barbone and Marchetti), we get a net increase in the total tax burden on enterprises of about 8.2 percent of GDP in the Czech Republic and 3.5 percent of GDP in Hungary.[17] The figure for Bulgaria is of quite a different dimension, with the gross tax burden on enterprises falling by 17.1 percent of GDP, while total subsidies fell by 10.7 percent of GDP. Bulgaria thus differs from the Central European countries in being the only one for which the total net tax burden on enterprises probably fell quite sharply.[18]

The tax regime has not generally been used to relax budget constraints on enterprises in Central Europe.[19] However, the accumulation of tax arrears by firms has been a source of accommodation in Central European post-communist Economies. Schaffer's (1995) estimates of the value of tax and social security arrears are shown in table 3.15.

These data suggest that although the stock of tax arrears is highest in Hungary, the flow of arrears in recent years has been highest in the Czech Republic. Survey data from 200 firms each in Hungary and Poland show that tax arrears are strongly negatively correlated with

Table 3.15
Tax and Social Security Arrears as a Percentage of GDP (end of period)

	1991	1992	1993
Czech Republic	–	2[a]	4[a]
Hungary	–	5.8[a]	6.9
Poland	3.7	3.8	4.6
Slovakia	–	–	5.4

Note: [a] approximate figures.

Source: Authors' own calculation.

profits, and with state ownership (but not with size) in Poland. The flow of tax arrears to manufacturing is about 1 percent of GDP in the two countries and as such is greater than the flow of overt subsidies. Schaffer concludes that "in a limited, but still important sense we are seeing the re-emergence of the 'soft-budget constraint' in these transition countries." It is worth noting that, at least until 1993, the extent of this phenomenon was very limited, not exceeding 2 percent of GDP per annum in any country, a number that may have been significantly smaller than the accumulation of bad debts in banks.

The Fiscal Stance of General Government and Accommodation

Czechoslovakia (and subsequently the Czech Republic) shows a continued commitment to fiscal balance throughout the period after the fall of communism, although there was not a totally insignificant deficit in 1991, the year of the CMEA trade and Soviet import shocks. The initial year of transition and stabilization in Poland registered a large swing of 10.5 percent of GDP from deficit to surplus, showing the government's determination to harden budget constraints throughout the economy. The almost equally large swing in the opposite direction in 1991, however, was not the result of a desire to accommodate the CMEA and Soviet import shocks but was rather the result of the revenue effects of these shocks not having been foreseen. Expenditure was cut, although not sufficiently enough to prevent a very large deficit from emerging. However, whatever the intentions of the government, the effect was that the fiscal stance in Poland in 1991 and 1992 was far more accommodative than in 1990 and, possibly more importantly, far more accommodative than in Czechoslovakia (later the Czech Republic), which was hit by exactly the same external shocks and which also undertook a rigorous stabilization program. As table 3.16 shows, improving revenues and continuing expenditure cuts resulted in a significant reduction in the deficit in 1993. A similar situation to that in Poland developed in Hungary from 1991, but on a far more serious scale, as a result of trade shocks and the effects of the new bankruptcy law on profits (company profits and, above all, bank profits). The revealing of bad bank debts not only reduced profits on tax revenues from banks but also required a massive increase in expenditures to finance bank recapitalization (cumulatively all Hungarian recapitalizations amounted to the equivalent of 9 percent of one year's GNP). The difference between Poland and Hungary, however, is that in the latter country, the authorities began to take action only in 1995 to reduce the deficit, whereas in Poland the deficit was reduced to a still excessive 3 percent of GDP from 1993.[20]

Table 3.16
General Government Fiscal Balance (Percentage of GDP)

	1989	1990	1991	1992	1993
Bulgaria	-1.7	-8.8	-8.6	-7.0	-12.8
Romania	7.4	1.1	0.6	-4.6	-0.2
Czech Republic	-2.8[a]	-0.4[a]	-2.1[a]	2.0[a]	1.0
Hungary	-1.4	0.5	-2.2	-5.6	-6.4
Poland	-7.5	3.0	-6.5	-6.8	-2.9

Note: [a] Czechoslovakia.

Source: IMF World Economic Outlook, October 1994, p.p. 80–83.

The story is very much the same in Bulgaria as it is in Hungary, only on a much larger scale. Most of the inflationary financing in Romania came through subsidized credits from the central bank that went directly to business—i.e., the source of accommodation was the quasi-budget deficit of the central bank, rather than the fiscal accounts of the general government.

Accommodation via Exchange Rate Policy

We have already seen earlier in this chapter that, with the possible exception of Czechoslovakia, the countries of Central Europe cannot be considered to have overdepreciated when they began their transition and shifted to internally convertible currencies. In fact, again with the exception of Czechoslovakia, these countries began the transition with significant real appreciations of their currencies (table 3.17).

Table 3.17
Real[a] and Nominal Effective Exchange Rates against the US Dollar

	Czechoslovakia		Hungary		Poland	
	Nominal	Real	Nominal	Real	Nominal	Real
1988	80.0	100.0	79.7	100.0	4.5	100.0
1989	83.8	94.8	93.5	98.5	15.1	93.9
1990	100.0	82.4	100.0	112.4	100.0	103.1
1991	162.2	86.4	118.2	126.1	111.3	137.6
1992[b]	155.5	97.5	124.9	134.0	143.7	136.4
1993[c]	160.5	105.3	145.4	129.0	191.0	135.7
1994[d]	154.8	115.7	167.2	119.8	240.8	142.9

Notes:
Base year for real rates 1988, base year for nominal rates 1990.
[a] Real indices obtained through deflating the effective nominal rates with PPI; an index value below 100 represents real depreciation of domestic currency.
[b] Figures exclude fourth quarter of 1992 for Czechoslovakia (or Czech Republic).
[c] Czech Republic.
[d] Figures for 1994 are based on the third quarter for Czech Republic and Poland and on the second quarter of the same year for Hungary.
Sources: Statistical year books of the three countries; IMF, ***International Financial Statistics***, various issues, and authors' calculations.

The Polish shift to convertibility in 1990 saw a real appreciation of about 10 percent, while in Hungary the more gradual introduction of convertibility during 1989–92 was accompanied by a real appreciation of 36 percent. In fact, these figures understate the true degree of real appreciation in these two countries, as the nominal exchange rates used to calculate the real rates before convertibility was introduced are official rates that overvalue the domestic currency.[21] There was a large real depreciation in Czechoslovakia in 1990 (of 13 percent), but the shift to convertibility in 1991 was also accompanied by a real appreciation, albeit a modest one, of 5 percent.

Czechoslovakia, and the later Czech Republic, with its fixed nominal exchange rate policy and its continuous real appreciation, clearly did not accommodate anti-reformist or anti-restructuring pressures via its exchange rate policy. Indeed, between 1991 and 1994, the currency appreciated in real terms by 34 percent. The situation was quite different in Hungary, where there were two clearly distinguishable phases: (1) 1989–92, when the real exchange rate appreciated sharply; and (2) 1992–4, when it depreciated by 10.6 percent.[22] Policies during the latter phase, however, should not be thought of as intentionally accommodative to cost pressures on enterprises. Rather, it was the inevitable result of the need to obtain an improvement in the balance of payments, which had been badly affected by the period of real appreciation.

The Polish story is again different: sharp real appreciation during 1990, and then a fairly constant real exchange rate, were maintained by a nominal devaluation that closely shadowed PPI inflation.[23] Thus, from 1991 the exchange rate was not used as a nominal anchor in Poland, and to that extent exchange rate policy can be considered to have been accommodative. The Polish experience during the second half of 1994 and early 1995 is particularly striking. Despite rapidly accumulating reserves, the exchange rate crawl was only slightly slowed, consequently consumer price inflation in 1994 was 30 percent, only 5 percent down from 1993, the poorest result to date since the transition in Poland began.[24]

Accommodative Protectionism

As we can see from figures 3.1 and 3.2, protectionism has remained low with a slight upward trend in Czechoslovakia (after 1992 in the Czech Republic) between 1989 and 1993.[25] There was a slight reduction in tariffs in Hungary in 1991. If we look at the average tariff level weighted by the importance of each good in imports, we can see that this level was maintained into 1992.[26]

The clearest case of accommodative protectionism, however, is Poland, where tariffs were slashed by two-thirds (on a weighted basis) at the same time currency convertibility was introduced in 1990. This policy was followed by a return to pre-reform levels in 1992 under Jan Olszewski's government (i.e., there was a tripling of the average weighted tariff level), partly in response to populist political pressure but also as a revenue raising measure, so as to limit the rapidly growing budget deficit.[27] However, it should be noted that the budgetary aims of the policy could have been achieved, at least in the case of some goods, without discriminating against imports. For instance, much higher registration fees for cars, particularly for luxury cars, could have been designed to collect as much revenue as the increased tariffs. The deci-

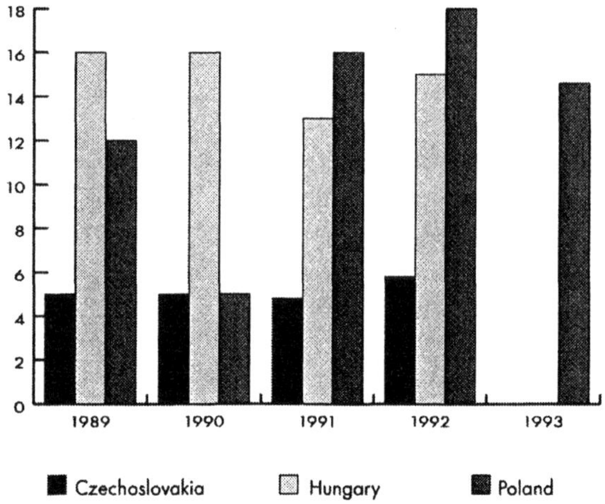

Figure 3.1: Average Tariff Level 1989–93 (unweighted)
Source: EBRD, *Transition Report* 1994, p.114.

sion to use tariffs rather than registration fees thus shows a desire to accommodate the pressures on domestic producers, as well as improving budgetary accounts.[28] It was only under the more mainstream Hanna Suchocka government that tariffs once again declined in 1992, but this time the reduction was far more modest than in 1990. The left-wing government, in power since 1993 in Poland, has once again increased tariffs significantly, particularly for agricultural goods.

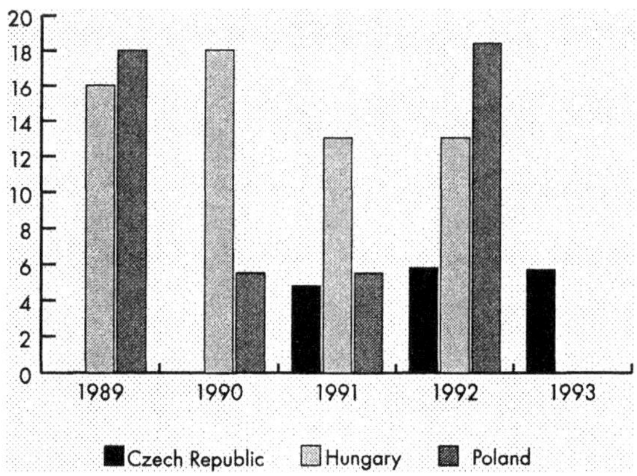

Figure 3.2: Average Tariff Level 1989–93 (weighted)
Source: UN *Economic Bulletin for Europe* 1992, Vol. 44 N.Y., 1993.

Conclusion

With regard to the measurement of shocks, it appears that two of the commonly mentioned macroeconomic shocks have had significant effects, while two others did not. Trade shocks (i.e., a massive fall in CMEA and Soviet imports) had significant effects on all the countries concerned (see table 3.6). In fact, if Rosati is correct, these two shocks account for the bulk of the fall in GDP in most Eastern European transition economies, and little remains to be explained (except in Bulgaria and Czechoslovakia).[29] A second enterprise shock that was clearly significant was the removal of subsidies (table 3.4). Interestingly, this shock was largest in Czechoslovakia, the country for which trade shocks do not seem to account for the fall in output. Very little could be established relating the reduction in real credit that occurred at the beginning of the transition in all the Central European countries to the fall in output, suggesting that there is some doubt regarding the extent to which the reduction of real credit caused a shock that forced producers to adjust. On the other hand, the change in the nature of credit—rather than in its quantity—must have caused a fundamental change in the operating environment of firms.[30] Finally, the introduction of current account convertibility was not generally accompanied by a clear overdevaluation of currencies (table 3.7). Thus, only in Czechoslovakia and Bulgaria could overdevaluation have been a factor contributing to output falls and a negative shock to the average producer. Indeed, in Hungary the move to convertibility was accompanied by real appreciation, both relative to the previous situation and relative to comparable countries!

On the matter of accommodation, the countries of Central Europe have differed considerably regarding the accommodative policies each has taken. All three countries have pursued some degree of accommodation via bank lending to enterprises, with substandard and worse loans accounting for between a fifth and a quarter of bank credit in all three countries by 1993. However, in terms of their impact on firms and costs to the economy, ultimately to the taxpayer or the depositor, these policies were of a very different magnitude in the various countries, cumulatively accounting for over 17 percent of one year's GDP in the Czech Republic, over 12 percent in Hungary, and over 5 percent in Poland.

With regard to interenterprise debt, Czechoslovakia (and the later Czech Republic) pursued a far more permissive policy than either

Hungary or Poland. Whereas it is hard to measure the amount of accommodation that took place in that country as a result of the authorities' toleration of IED build-up (IED is not classified as substandard or otherwise in any statistics), this latitude is reflected both in the fact that Czechoslovakia (and the later Czech Republic) has indulged in multilateral clearings of IED; in fact, IED is much larger in the Czech Republic than elsewhere and grew much faster in Czechoslovakia than elsewhere in Central Europe during the early phases of transition. Again, this latitude is reflected in the persistence of much higher levels of inventories in Czechoslovak non-agricultural firms than in their Polish or Hungarian counterparts and in the failure of these levels to decline, as they did in the other two countries (table 3.12).

Reductions of the gross tax burden on enterprises were not generally used as an accommodation mechanism in Central European countries during 1989–93 (in the sense that they undercompensated the fall in budgetary enterprise subsidies). Czechoslovakia (and the Czech Republic as its heir) had the largest fall in the gross burden as a share of GDP (table 3.14), but this was accompanied by an even larger fall in enterprise subsidies, with a similar situation holding in Hungary (compare table 3.4). The gross tax burden on enterprises in Poland actually increased, despite a reduction in subsidies. Only in Bulgaria does the reduction in the gross tax burden on enterprises seem to have been significantly larger than the reduction in subsidies to them. Tax and social security arrears were also relatively small (table 3.15) and—more importantly—were growing quite slowly in both Hungary and Poland during 1991–93. The fastest rate of growth of tax arrears in 1992 and 1993 seems to have been in the Czech Republic, although even here this accumulation was only the equivalent of approximately 2 percent of GDP in each year, a figure that is significantly less than the accumulation of risky bank debts in the same country (table 3.9).

General government fiscal balance, which provides some overall indication of accomodative economic policy, shows, as expected, very rigorous fiscal measures being pursued in the Czech Republic from 1992 onward (table 3.16). In both Hungary and Poland, on the other hand, there was a marked deterioration from 1991. The critical difference is that to some extent Poland brought this deterioration under control from 1993; this is not the case for Hungary, where very large deficits continued into 1995. Bulgaria shows massive and uncontrolled deficits, while low Romanian deficits are the result of accommodation occurring via the central bank rather than the treasury.

The nominal exchange rate was used rigorously as an anchor in Czechoslovakia, and the later Czech Republic, throughout the post-1991 period. Nominal depreciation in Hungary was kept below the rate of PPI inflation during 1989–92, exerting a strong disciplining effect on the traded goods sector as the real exchange rate appreciated (table 3.17). In the subsequent period, this policy was reversed in order to protect the country's international reserves, which relaxed the pressure on producers to adapt and thus was to some extent accommodative. After the sharp real appreciation of 1990–91 in Poland, the real exchange rate was kept roughly constant—i.e., it was accommodated to domestic inflationary pressures on PPI, although fortunately there was no attempt to really loosen up on the producers of tradeables by pursuing a policy of active real devaluation. As a result, the nominal exchange rate was not used as a tool of anti-inflationary policy, which would have mattered less if the other tools—monetary and fiscal policy—had been wielded more vigorously.

Protectionism was not used as an accommodative policy to any great degree in either Czechoslovakia (later the Czech Republic) or in Hungary. However, it was used quite clearly in Poland, particularly under the Olszewski government (and again since 1994 under the post-communist government).

All of the Central European countries pursued accommodative policies to some degree, but each tended to use a different mix of these policies. Accomodative policies in Poland took the shape of protectionism (from 1992) combined with the failure to use the nominal exchange rate as an anchor after 1991. Poland's fiscal stance was also allowed to deteriorate sharply in 1991 and 1992 and only improved from 1993. On the other hand, the accumulation of bad bank debts and tax arrears and the growth and multilateral clearance of interenterprise debt played a relatively small or indeed nonexistent role in Poland. The main instrument of accommodation in Hungary has been the fiscal deficit, allowing a lower level of corporate taxation, with the accumulation of bad bank debt in second place. Hungary's exchange rate policy became somewhat more accommodative after 1992. Neither protectionism nor the accumulation of IED were important in Hungary. Accommodation in Czechoslovakia occurred mainly in its most invisible forms: bad debt accumulation and the growth and multilateral clearance of IED. The Czech Republic has also been the country with the highest recent growth of tax arrears. The structural effects of these policies can be seen in the failure of inventories to decline from their massive levels as late as the end of 1991. On the other hand, fiscal, exchange rate, and tariff policies were exemplary. Given the sensitivity of the Czech government to foreign criticism, it may not be accidental that the less observable accommodative policies have been adopted there.

Although it has been possible to identify which country has favored which accommodative policies, many of the policies remain incommensurable. Consequently, it has proved impossible to conclude which country in Central Europe has pursued the least and which the most accommodative policy. Accommodation has occurred on a significant and probably similar scale in all three countries. At the same time, it must be stated that in none of the three Central European countries has accommodation been so extensive as to bring a halt to enterprise adjustment and restructuring, let alone to threaten a reversal of the reforms.

References

Barbone, L. and D. Marchetti. 1994. Economic transformation and the fiscal crisis. Policy research working paper no. 1286 (April). Washington, D.C.: World Bank.

Calvo, G. and F. Coricelli. 1993. Output Collapse in Eastern Europe. *IMF staff papers,* 40, no. 1 (March): 32–52.

Calvo, G. and F. Coricelli. 1995. Inter-enterprise arrears in economies in transition. In *Output Decline in Eastern Europe: Unavoidable, External Influence or Homemade*, edited by R. Holzman, J. Gacs, and G. Winckler. London: Kluwer Academic Publishers.

Commander, S., and F. Coricelli. 1992. Output decline in Hungary and Poland in 1990–1: Structural change and aggregate shocks. Policy Research Dept. Working Paper no. 1036. Washington, D.C.: World Bank.

Dittus, P. and S. Prowse. 1994. Corporate control in Central Europe and Russia: Should banks own shares. Paper delivered at conference, Corporate Governance in Central Europe and Russia. Central European University and World Bank, December 12–16, 1994, Washington, D.C.

Edwards, S. 1986. Are devaluations contractionary? *Review of Economics and Statistics* 68, no. 3 (August): 501–508.

European Bank for Reconstruction and Development. 1994. *Transition Report.* London: European Bank for Reconstruction and Development.

Fan, Q., and M. Schaffer. 1994. Government financial transfers and enterprise adjustments in Russia, with comparisons to Central and Eastern Europe. London School of Economics, Centre for Economic Performance. Working Paper, no. 394.

Glowny Urzad Statystyczny. *Statistical Bulletin—Poland, Czech Republic, Hungary and Slovakia* (Quarterly). Various issues. Warsaw: Glowny Urzad Statystyczny.

Gomulka, S. 1995. The financial situation and bad debts of enterprises in Poland. In *Output Decline in Eastern Europe: Unavoidable, External Influence or Homemade,* edited by R. Holzman, J. Gacs, and G. Winckler. London: Kluwer Academic Publishers.

Grosfeld, I. and G. Roland. 1996. Defensive and strategic restructuring in Central European enterprises. *Journal of Transforming Economies and Societies* 3, no. 4: 21–46.

Gylafsson, T. and M. Schmid. 1983. Does devaluation cause stagflation?, *The Canadian Journal of Economics* XVI, no. 4 (November): 641–654.

International Monetary Fund. *International Financial Statistics.* Various issues. Washington, D.C: International Monetary Fund.

International Monetary Fund. 1994. *World Economic Outlook.* Washington, D.C.: International Monetary Fund.

Khan, M. and E. Clifton. 1992. Inter-enterprise arrears in transforming economies: The case of Romania. International Monetary Fund Papers on Policy Analysis and Assessment. Washington, D.C.: International Monetary Fund.

Layard, R. and A. Richter. 1994. Who gains and who loses from Russian credit expansion. *Communist Economies and Economic Transformation* 6, no. 4: 459–470.

Ministry of Industry and Trade of the Czech Republic. 1994. *Analysis of Economic Development in the Czech Republic and in MIT Organizations in 1993.* Prague: Ministry of Industry and Trade.

Pinto, B. and S. van Wijnbergen. 1994. Ownership and corporate control in Poland. Policy Research Depatment Working Paper no. 1308. International Finance Corporation.

Rodrik, D. 1994. Foreign trade in Eastern Europe's transition: Early results. In *The Transition in Eastern Europe,* edited by O. Blanchard, K. Froot, and J. Sachs. National Bureau of Economic Research, University of Chicago Press.

Rosati, D. The impact of the Soviet trade shock on output levels in Central and Eastern European economies. In *Output Decline in Eastern Europe: Unavoidable, External Influence or Homemade,* edited by R. Holzman, J. Gacs, and G. Winckler. London: Kluwer Academic Publishers.

Rostowski, J. 1993. The inter-enterprise debt explosion in the former Soviet Union: Causes, consequences, cures. *Communist Economies and Economic Transformation* 5, no.2: 131–159.

Rostowski, J. 1995. The banking system, credit and the real sector in transition economies. In *Banking Reform in Central Europe and the Former Soviet Union,* edited by J. Rostowski. Budapest: Central European University Press.

Schaffer, M. 1995. Government subsidies to enterprises in Central and Eastern Europe: Budgetary subsidies and tax arrears. In *Tax and Benefit Reform in Central and Eastern Europe,* edited by D.M.G. Newberry. London: Centre for Economic Policy Research.

Svejnar, J. 1993. Czech and Slovak Federal Republic: A solid foundation. In *Economic Transformation in Central Europe: A Progress Report,* edited by R. Portes. London: Centre for Economic Policy Research and European Communities.

Szanyi, M. 1995. Measuring transition in East-Central Europe: The case of budget constraints. San Francisco: International Center for Economic Growth.

United Nations. Department for Economic and Social Information and Policy Analysis. Statistical Division. *National Account Statistics.* 1993. *Trends in International Distribution of Gross World Product, 1993.* Series 10 (special issue), no.18. New York: United Nations.

Notes

1. There need not have been any intention to "overdevalue," but rather to avoid underdevaluation.

2. The results are even worse if quarterly real credit is lagged behind industrial output with the following correlation coefficients: $t - 1 = -0.014$; $t - 2 = 0.0369$; $t - 3 = 0.0538$.

3. See Svejnar (1993). In fact, the tightening of credit to state enterprises in Poland was greater than appears in table 3.2; in the second half of 1990, all nominal increases in credit granted by the nine regional banks in Poland were earmarked for the private sector, and the same policy was pursued throughout 1991 in Czechoslovakia. This policy was considerably loosened in Poland in 1991, with credit to the private sector targeted to grow only twice as fast as that to SOEs.

4. In Czechoslovakia, where inflation was very low before the transition, enterprises continued to obtain part of the seigniorage from money creation by getting credit which they were not expected to repay.

5. Two kinds of links operated: (1) the higher the level of output, the higher the level of credit granted by the state owned banks; (2) the higher the level of credit, the higher the level of output (because enterprise managers wanted to prove their efficiency to superiors and thus obtain a promotion, and higher subsidy levels made it possible to increase production).

6. Given the absence of bad credit under the old regime, banks had to invest in obtaining credit-allocation skills. They were unlikely to do so simply as a result of the government's statement that a given (pre-stabilization) increase in nominal credit was final. (Such a credible one-time increase is how Calvo and Coricelli suggest that real credit can be maintained during stabilization.) Only when the government actually failed to increase nominal credit to compensate for preceding inflation, would the introduction of the new regime become credible and banks actually invest in credit-allocation skills.

7. While it is true that budgetary subsidies are a flow and real bank credit is a stock, the two magnitudes would be additive if both occur in the same period of time (one year). We would be adding a reduction in the flow of subsidies as a percent of GDP in that year to a reduction in the stock of real bank credit as a one-time negative flow in the same year. This approach is problematic because the figures for subsidy reduction cover a number of years, while the reductions in bank credit took place in a single year in Czechoslovakia and Poland.

8. Not all subsidies were paid to enterprises, although the vast majority were in both Poland and Czechoslovakia (table 3.4).

9. The matter is more complex: if credit is effectively nonrepayable, then it is the real value of the flow of new credit that represents the subsidy to borrowers. This is effectively paid for out of an inflation tax by money holders (Layard and Richter 1994). To the extent that credits are repayable, the amount by which the real interest rate on loans is negative would measure the subsidy value of bank credit.

10. These are the effects that correspond to trade creation and trade diversion when a common market is established.

11. Rosati was unable to calculate the pure terms-of-trade effects for either Bulgaria or Czechoslovakia.

12. The PPP numbers quoted here imply GDP per capita levels, which probably underestimate Polish GDP and overestimate Czechoslovak GDP. The three years of monthly average wage rates of about $200 in both Poland and the Czech Republic casts doubt on these numbers, particularly as most consumer goods are significantly cheaper in Poland than in the Czech Republic. This scenario would mean that overdevaluation was somewhat stronger than table 3.7 suggests in Poland in 1990 and somewhat weaker in Czechoslovakia in 1991.

13. Their figure for 1992 for the Czech Republic is 19 percent, which is consistent with that of the Czech Ministry of Industry and Trade. However, the National Bank of Hungary gives figures for the three categories of problem loans in Hungary as: end 1992, 11.5 percent; end 1993, 17.5 percent (Szanyi 1995). Both are far below those given by Dittus and Prowse.

14. Bank credit to non-governmental, non-financial businesses is about 45 percent of GDP in Hungary and 21 percent of GDP in Poland.

15. The nominal value of IED of Rbs. 39 billion and Rbs. 3,000 billion for the end of December 1991 and the end of June 1992, respectively, (Rostowski 1993) was divided by 1991 nominal GDP in the first case and by nominal GDP in the second and third quarters of 1992, multiplied by two in the second case. The same procedure was used for bank credit. The end of June 1992 is the midpoint for the second and third quarters of 1992. This procedure probably gives a good approximation to total 1992 GDP according to prices at the end of June 1992. Since there was significant inflation (of about 100 percent) during 1991, though most of it was in February 1991, nominal GDP in 1991 probably underestimates 1991 nominal GDP at December 1991 prices.

As a result, IED and bank credit as shares of GDP in December 1991 are probably somewhat overestimated.

16. This is not to deny the positive supply-side effects of mass privatization; they do not seem to have found any expression, however, in an improvement in payment discipline.

17. This figure for Poland is about 7.7 percent of GDP.

18. If subsidies to producers in Bulgaria fell by a smaller share of GDP than did total subsidies, as was the case in all the Central European countries, then the fall in the total tax burden on the net of subsidies to producers of enterprises will have been at least 6.4 percent of GDP.

19. Even in Bulgaria, the fall in the tax burden was mainly the result of the government's failure to raise tax revenue.

20. Given the very low ratio of domestic broad money to GDP, the inflationary effects of a given deficit, relative to GDP, will be higher in Poland than in Hungary.

21. With many transactions taking place at black- or free-market (auction) rates, the right preconvertibility rate is some weighted average of the official and freer exchange rates. Such a rate would give a lower weight to the domestic currency before convertibility and therefore show a smaller nominal depreciation upon convertibility. Since the price index used to arrive at the real exchange rate—the PPI—is not affected, the actual real appreciation must be larger or—in the case of Czechoslovakia—smaller.

22. This tendency has continued into 1995 and was reversed only in 1996.

23. Most of this was achieved through a preannounced crawling peg devaluation, although discrete devaluations also occurred.

24. Ultimately, the accumulation of international reserves was so large that the zloty had to be floated in May 1995, which resulted in a 4 percent nominal appreciation.

25. Low tariffs did not prevent the economy from being almost entirely protected by central planners' complete control of foreign-currency allocation.

26. It was almost entirely reversed in 1992, if we take the unweighted average.

27. On an unweighted basis, there was already a sharp increase in 1991. However, the difference between the two measures shows that the Bielecki government in 1991 increased a large number of tariffs on goods that were hardly imported at all. It seems that this was done intentionally, so as to respond to political pressure in favor of protec-

tionism without doing too much economic damage. It was only under Olszewski that "large-ticket" imports, such as cars, were hit by high tariff levels.

28. Eminent Western advisers were closely involved—by their own account—in the decision to raise tariffs under the Olszewski government.

29. This need for explanation goes in opposite directions in the case of Bulgaria, depending on whether the effects on GDP are at PPP or market rates of exchange.

30. The present authors would argue that for this qualitative change to take place, the real quantity of credit had to be allowed to decline if this was the consequence of imposing constraints on its nominal quantity.

4 Downsizing as an Exit Mechanism: Comparing the Czech Republic, Hungary, and Poland

Ewa Balcerowicz, Iraj Hoshi, Jan Mládek, Tamás Novák, Alison Sinclair, and Miklós Szanyi

In the early stages of economic transition, the legal and institutional framework for classical forms of exit, to be discussed in chapters 5 through 8, are usually either nonexistent or in their infancy. But enterprises, subjected to the shocks of transition, will still experience the pressure for exit and will embark on a variety of informal exit processes. One of the most important and commonly utilized of these processes is *downsizing*, defined as a systematic and significant reduction of resources deployed in an enterprise.[1] Here, the term "exit" refers to the exit of resources from enterprises rather than the exit of enterprises from the market.

Even when classical exit mechanisms are in the process of development, downsizing as an informal exit mechanism will remain an option available to enterprises in financial difficulty. In general, before embarking on bankruptcy or liquidation procedures of the type discussed in the next four chapters, owners and managers will attempt to reverse the poor performance of their enterprises by altering their resource deployment. They may decide to reduce their operations in some product markets and redeploy these resources in others or to release these resources altogether, reducing their hoarding of labor and assets. The latter course of action, more common in the early stages of transition, constitutes exit by downsizing and is embarked upon in the interest of owners or under the pressure of creditors.

The purpose of this chapter is to analyze the extent and specific features of the downsizing process in the Czech Republic, Hungary, and Poland and compare the experiences of these three countries in the early years of their transition to a market system. For this purpose, we have chosen to focus on the largest enterprises in the manufacturing sector of these economies and study the changes in their employment, output, and labor productivity resulting from the pressure for exit. Given the difficulties of obtaining accurate information on the value of enterprise assets and the problems associated with their measurement in the immediate post-central planning period, we have not considered changes in these assets. Instead, we have concentrated on the movement of labor among enterprises, branches of manufacturing, and sectors of the economy.

The aggregate data for all three countries clearly indicate that there has been a significant, and at times drastic, reallocation of labor out of the traditional sectors of the economy (agriculture and industry) into new sectors and small entrepreneurial activities. As Appendix 4.1 shows, between 1990 and 1994 employment in agriculture and industry fell sharply in all three countries—by 46 percent and 20 percent, respectively in the Czech Republic, 68 percent and 33 percent in Hungary, and 14 percent and 21 percent in Poland. At the same time, employment in newly developing sectors, such as financial services, increased significantly (though from a much smaller initial level) by some 170 percent in the Czech Republic, 53 percent in Hungary, and 32 percent in Poland.

During the same period, the total number of people employed in existing firms fell by nearly half a million in the Czech Republic, 1.3 million in Hungary, and 2 million in Poland, while the number of private entrepreneurs running their own businesses increased by 1 million in the Czech Republic, half a million in Hungary, and over 1 million in Poland. These changes indicate the extent of reallocation of resources from larger to smaller enterprises as well as among different sectors of the economy, since private entrepreneurs running their own businesses usually operate in trade and services. Downsizing in the traditional sectors has facilitated, indeed forced, the redeployment of resources to new and more efficient uses. What is even more important is that, despite a widely held view, enterprises operating in the traditional sectors in the Czech Republic have indeed undergone significant downsizing and restructuring.[2] We will return to this issue when we look at the extent of downsizing in the three countries.

Although downsizing has taken place in almost all sectors of the economy, this chapter concentrates on the manufacturing sector. Before discussing the samples and empirical results, it may be useful to draw attention to an important methodological issue regarding the interpretation of the downsizing process, i.e., whether or not downsizing should be seen as a positive outcome of the enterprise adjustment process. The observed changes in output and employment are the sum total of adjustments made by firms, with a variety of managerial incentives and motivations, in response to the shocks of transition. While we do not know, and cannot observe, the precise reason for each type of adjustment made by a firm, we do notice the overall results of the interaction of several forces whose strengths vary in different firms and industries depending on the managers' reaction to changes in the prevailing incentive system and in their market environment. In some cases, managers may respond passively to the shocks, accepting a loss of markets and a reduction in sales, followed by a forced reduction in employment.[3] In others, they may take a more proactive attitude to outside pressures by streamlining their production process and reducing overmanning; in short, reducing their costs in order to survive. In a third group of firms, managers may embark on a course of action designed to reverse the effects of transition shocks by changing their production methods, improving the design and quality of their products, embarking on new investment projects, and enhancing their marketing and promotional efforts.[4] The data on changes in the output and employment of enterprises that are grouped together according to their size, ownership, and activity represent the overall outcome of all these processes without identifying the precise reasons for changes in individual firms.

It should be pointed out that in the early transition period, many enterprises reduced their employment of labor and capital for reasons other than those mentioned above. Large enterprises were sometimes divided into several smaller units and privatized separately. There were many cases of demergers, spin-offs, and asset-stripping, with the noncore activities of enterprises often separated and sold off which also resulted in a reduction of employment levels. On the whole, large enterprises that underwent these types of change have been excluded from our sample so that we can focus on the downsizing process alone.[5]

In this chapter, we treat downsizing and the contraction of employment as a welcome development, reflecting the managers' ability and willingness to deal with the inherited hoarding of labor and overmanning as a precondition for a necessary reallocation of resources between enterprises and sectors. Such a release of resources is particularly important in the three samples under consideration, as they consist of the largest manufacturing enterprises, often operating in highly concentrated branches of industry in each country. But it should be kept in mind that proactive and dynamic managers, possibly under the influence of a foreign partner, may be able to counteract contractionary processes by engaging in active strategic restructuring of the type discussed earlier.[6]

Sample of Largest Manufacturing Enterprises

Our sample consists of the largest 200 manufacturing firms in the Czech Republic and Poland and the largest 150 in Hungary.[7] The term "largest" refers to a ranking by sales revenue at the beginning of the transition period, 1989 in Hungary and Poland and 1990 in the Czech Republic. Only those firms that survived as one company from the beginning of the transition period to the end of 1993 were retained in the sample. Large holding companies and trusts that were broken up into smaller units during the period under consideration were excluded from the study. Similarly, enterprises that filed for bankruptcy or liquidation during this period, particularly numerous in Hungary, were also excluded, as these followed other forms of exit that will be discussed in the other chapters. In a small number of cases, firms that had been transformed to privately owned limited liability companies and for which the relevant information had become unavailable were also excluded.

The study of changes in the largest manufacturing enterprises is important for a variety of reasons, not least because these enterprises account for a significant share of industrial activity in each country and exercise a major influence over the direction of change in the economy as a whole. It is generally expected that large enterprises, as the symbol and the main form of economic organization under socialism, will be rather slow in adjusting their behavior to the emerging market-oriented conditions because of the absence of effective ownership interests, the uncertainty surrounding their eventual privatization, their monopolistic market position, and their economic and political significance for their particular regional or local economies. The restructuring of these firms is, therefore, an important indicator of successful transition, and their adjustment may indeed be regarded as a benchmark with which the adjustment patterns of other enterprises in the economy can be compared. Figure 4.1 shows the relative importance of the sample in the manufacturing employment of each country.[8]

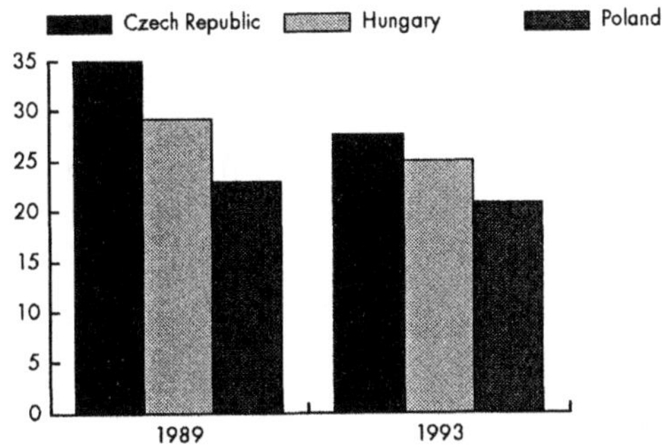

Figure 4.1: Share of the Largest 200 Firms in Manufacturing Employment

Source: Authors' calculations.

The firms in three samples accounted for between 22 percent and 35 percent of manufacturing employment at the beginning of transition and between 20 percent and 28 percent at the end of 1993. In terms of manufacturing output,[9] the samples accounted for one-third to one-half in the three countries (see Appendix 4.2 for details). Both at the beginning of the transition process and in 1993, the Czech sample had the largest share of manufacturing employment, though of the three it also experienced the largest decline in its share. The share of sample enterprises in total manufacturing employment declined by about 7.4 percent in four years, indicating a more rapid change in these firms than in the manufacturing sector as a whole. In the other two countries, however, the relative importance of the large firms changed much less. Over a five-year period, the share of the largest firms declined by only 2 percent in Poland and by 5 percent in Hungary.[10] The slower change in these two samples could reflect a variety of factors, including the slower pace of privatization, particularly of large firms, in Poland and Hungary and the impact of pretransition reforms in both countries.[11]

The share of sample enterprises in total employment in the economy also decreased in all three countries, again by a larger proportion in the Czech Republic than in the other countries (see appendix 4.2). Given the relatively large and overextended manufacturing sector and the prevalent overmanning in planned economies, this decline is not surprising. What we observe is a process of resource reallocation from manufacturing to nonmanufacturing firms and from large to small firms, particularly noticeable in the Czech Republic.

All three samples display a combination of relative stability and a considerable repositioning of their constituent enterprises. Of the top ten firms at the beginning of the transition period in each country, seven had remained on the list in 1993. For the group consisting of the top fifty firms, there was more movement, with the number of firms remaining in the top fifty in 1993 ranging from thirty-six in the Czech sample to twenty-nine in the Polish and twenty-two in the Hungarian sample.

Changes in Output and Employment

The change in the aggregate output, employment, and labor productivity of the samples are illustrated in figure 4.2, with the precise numerical values presented in appendix 4.3. For all three countries, both the output and employment of the largest manufacturing firms declined every year during the period under consideration, with the exception of output in the Polish sample, which began to increase in 1994 (two years later than the upturn in industrial production and GDP).[12] The decline in output and employment, though significant everywhere, w as not uniform across the three samples. Hungarian firms experienced the sharpest decline both in output (by 60 percent) and employment (by 47 percent) between 1989 and 1993. Polish firms, on the other hand, experienced the least decline (38 percent in output and 33 percent in employment) over the same period, with the Czech firms' decline falling somewhere between the two.

After an initial fall in all three countries, labor productivity began to improve slowly—first in Poland, as the country came out of recession, and then in Hungary.[13] It stabilized in the Czech Republic after one year of decline. By 1994 the Polish firms in our sample had regained their pretransition levels of labor productivity.[14] As in the case of output, the fall in labor productivity for the Hungarian sample was by far the sharpest, nearly 40 percent in the first two years of transition.

The decline in labor productivity in the early transition period appears to be a characteristic common to all economies in transition. In the first year of transition, with the freeing of prices, many enterprises, especially larger ones, enjoyed an improvement—albeit temporary—in their financial position, which to some extent enabled them to accommodate the shocks and avoid reducing employment in line with falling sales.[15] The restrictive labor market practices and social values and norms inherited from the past made large-scale layoffs socially and politically undesirable and difficult. Moreover, the uncertainties associated with the early days of transition, particularly regarding ownership transformation and macroeconomic policy changes, discouraged firms from

Output (1989 prices)

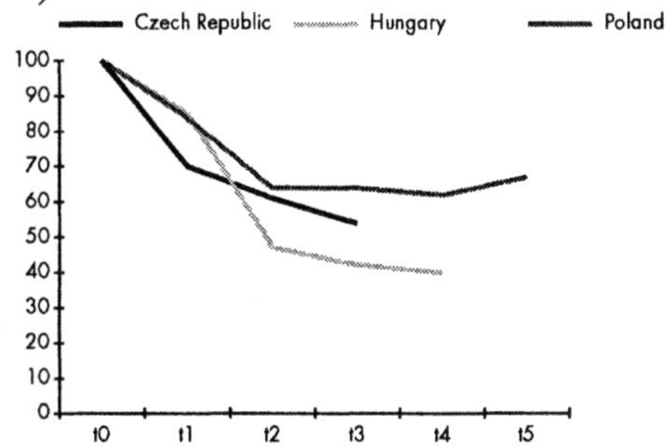

Employment

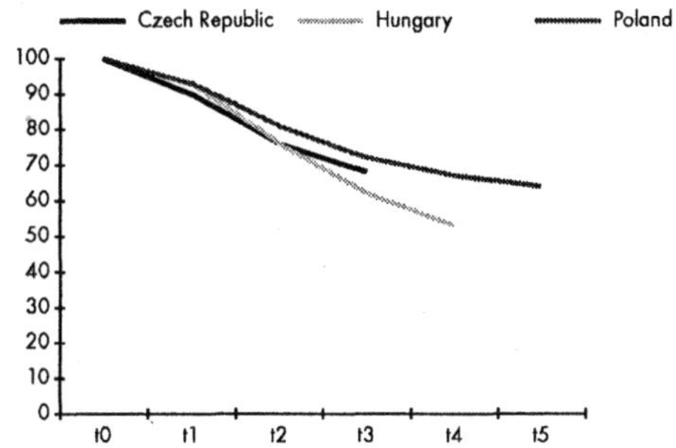

Labour productivity

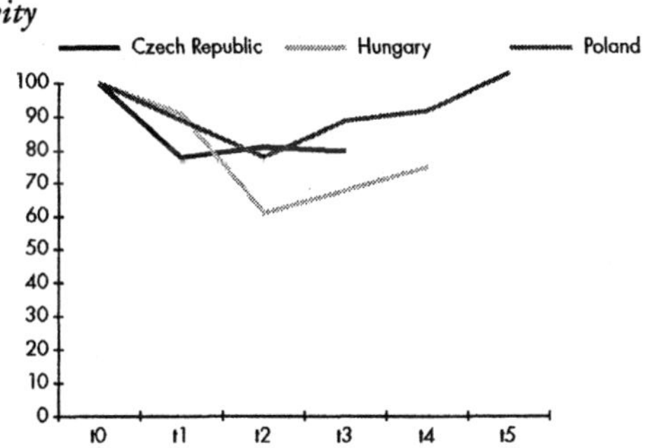

Figure 4.2 Changes in Output, Employment, and Labour Productivity of the Three Samples

Notes: For the Czech Republic t0=1990, t1=1991, t2=1992, t3=1993, t4=1994, while for Hungary and Poland t0=1989, t1=1990, t2=1991, t3=1992, t4=1993, t5=1994.

Source: The figures for manufacturing output and employment are from EBRD, *Transition Report 1996*, p. 118. For the description of the sample in each country, see the text.

reacting quickly to changes in demand. The large decline in output in 1990 and/or 1991, therefore, was not accompanied by a similar reduction in employment. But as competition increased, reforms became credible and privatization proceeded, enterprises began to change their behavior and to respond to market signals. Consequently, in 1991 and 1992 most enterprises embarked on large reductions in employment following further—though somewhat smaller—reductions in output, resulting in a rise in labor productivity. Further reductions in employment continued in most enterprises in 1993 (again, particularly sharp in Hungary), helping to stabilize or even increase labor productivity.

We have already pointed out that, depending on their particular circumstances and managerial incentives, enterprises may undergo a variety of restructuring processes. The output and employment responses of individual enterprises may therefore be very different in firms of different size, ownership, or sector. The aggregate data presented in figure 4.2 (and in Appendix 4.3) hide variations at the enterprise level in each of the three countries. This variation is illustrated in table 4.1, which shows the mean, range, and standard deviation of annual changes in output and employment of enterprises in each sample, together with the decline in the manufacturing sector's output and employment in each country.

All three samples were characterized by a large variance in both the output and employment responses of firms. The large variations across firms reflect differing levels of pressure and differing responses to government reforms. Despite this variation, it is the magnitude of the response of large enterprises, in comparison with the industrial sector as a whole, that is worth noting. In all three countries, the largest enterprises underwent a more severe downsizing than was experienced in each country's industrial sector. In the first three to four years of transition, output levels in these enterprises declined more than industrial production. Aside from the occasional exception (Hungary in 1990 and Poland in 1992), the employment response was also similar—large enterprises reduced their employment level by a larger percentage than manufacturing employment. Even when industrial production had picked up (as in Poland in 1992), the output decline in large enterprises was still coming. Another interesting feature of enterprise response to transitional shocks is the uniformity of their responses: for the period as a whole, the great majority of enterprises in the three samples registered a decline in both output and employment (in about 140 out of 150 enterprises in Hungary and 180 out of 200 in the other two countries).[16] The number

Table 4.1
Annual Changes in Output and Employment of the Sample of Largest Manufacturing Firms[a] in the Czech Republic, Hungary, and Poland, 1991–94 (Percentage)

Output[b]	**1990**	**1991**	**1992**	**1993**	**1994**	**1990–93**
Czech Republic						
Mean	na	-29	-14	-9	na	-45
Range		-71 to 123	-80 to 67	-68 to 115		-90 to 123
Standard deviation	23	22	26		27	
Manufacturing output[c]	-3.5	-26.4	-14.5	-9.9	0.2	-43.3
Hungary						
Mean	-14	-45	-9	-5		-47
Range	-76 to 50	-91 to 1	-96 to 43	-80 to 14		-96 to 71
Standard deviation	11	19	24	30		25
Manufacturing output[c]	-10.3	-21.1	-8.2	3.3	9.3	-25.2
Poland						
Mean	-27	-26	-8	-7	-6	-36
Range	-87 to 131	-96 to 110	-91 to 1,156	-87 to 427	-90 to 239	-95 to 167
Standard deviation	28	28	87	40	33	44
Manufacturing output[c]	-24.1	-12.3	4.8	12.2	13.7	3.1
Employment						
Czech Republic						
Mean	na	-11	-14	-8	na	-30
Range		-48 to 72	-93 to 33	-45 to 51		-88 to 54
Standard deviation	12	16	11		18	
Manufacturing employment[c]	-3.1	-11.8	-7.5	-6.6	-3.7	-23.8
Hungary						
Mean	-7	-18	-18	-14		-24
Range	-35 to 37	-95 to 36	-70 to 15	-48 to 13		-90 to 9
Standard deviation	14	16	18	19		17
Manufacturing employment[c]	-10.6	-3.9	-17.1	-12.9	1.9	-30.6
Poland						
Mean	-5	-10	-8	-4	-2	-23
Range	-92 to 19	-89 to 9	-90 to 42	-93 to 121	-69 to 48	-96 to 60
Standard deviation	10	12	18	13	14	21
Manufacturing employment[c]	-3.7	-0.4	-10.5	-2	-4.7	-12.6

[a] Largest firms refers to 200 largest manufacturing firms in the Czech Republic and Poland, and 150 in Hungary.
[b] All output figures are at constant 1989 prices.
[c] These figures refer to the decline in output and employment of the manufacturing sector as a whole.

Source: The figures for manufacturing production and employment are from EBRD, *Transition Report 1996*, p. 118. For the description of the sample in each country, see the text.

Table 4.2
Number of Contracting and Expanding Enterprises in the three samples, 1989–94

	Output[a]		Employment	
	No. of firms	Total contraction or expansion[b] (%)	No. of firms	Total contraction or expansion[b] (%)
Czech Republic[c]				
1990–93				
Contracting	187	-45%	180	-32%
Expanding	10	35%	5	19%
1991				
Contracting	180	-33%	177	-12%
Expanding	16	33%	8	19%
1992				
Contracting	153	-19%	172	-17%
Expanding	39	19%	11	8%
1993				
Contracting	142	-20%	157	-13%
Expanding	51	13%	28	5%
Hungary				
1990–93				
Contracting	141	-55%	146	-43%
Expanding	9	22%	4	5%
1991				
Contracting	144	-45%	133	-20%
Expanding	6	2%	14	13%
1992				
Contracting	100	-24%	133	-20%
Expanding	50	15%	14	16%
1993				
Contracting	97	-21%	131	-15%
Expanding	53	19%	18	4%
Poland				
1989–94				
Contracting	175	-49%	183	-37%
Expanding	25	40%	17	12%
1990				
Contracting	163	-30%	161	-8%
Expanding	37	15%	38	6%
1991				
Contracting	166	-30%	177	-13%
Expanding	34	22%	23	4%

	Output[a]		Employment	
	No. of firms	Total contraction or expansion[b] (%)	No. of firms	Total contraction or expansion[b] (%)
1992				
Contracting	133	-17%	170	-13%
Expanding	67	10%	29	4%
1993				
Contracting	141	-13%	142	-12%
Expanding	59	27%	58	9%
1994				
Contracting	78	-16%	132	-10%
Expanding	122	25%	68	9%

Notes:
[a] At constant 1989 prices.
[b] Total contraction (expansion) shown for a group of firms can be thought of as the weighted average contraction per enterprise, where the weights are equal to the relative size of each firm.
[c] The number of contracting and expanding firms may not add up to 200 because of missing observations in individual years.

Source: The figures for manufacturing production and employment are from EBRD, Transition Report 1996, p. 118. For the description of the sample in each country, see the text.

of contracting firms and the extent of their contractions are illustrated in table 4.2, which also shows the very small number of enterprises experiencing expansions.

The pattern of change in both output and employment is similar to that seen in figure 4.2 (and Appendix 4.3). The rate of decline of output always exceeded that of employment in contracting firms. The contraction in output was greatest in 1990 or 1991 (depending on the country), whereas the largest contraction in employment occurred one year later, in 1991 or 1992.

The number of expanding firms (in terms of both output and employment) gradually increased year after year, though the number of those expanding during the period as a whole remained very small—ten firms in the Czech sample, nine in the Hungarian sample, and twenty-five in the Polish sample, if measured by output. If measured by employment, the number of expanding firms was five in the Czech sample, four in the Hungarian sample, and seventeen in the Polish sample. In the Polish sample, which extends to 1994, the majority of firms experienced a rise in their real output (and about one-third of them in their employment) by 1994, reflecting the general growth of the economy and a relative success in the transition to a market system. Output consistently increased faster than employment in expanding firms, indicating an increase in labor productivity.

Table 4.2 also reflects a certain degree of reallocation of resources among firms during the period under consideration. Firms with insufficient market demand or insufficient resource utilization were releasing resources through informal exit. Some of these resources were being absorbed by firms that were successful in improving their resource deployment or expanding their markets. A process of new and better firms replacing old and inefficient ones, rather than patterns of change within firms themselves, accounts for the rise in labor productivity over the period; again, evidence of the importance of exit to economic restructuring.

Effect of Enterprise Size on the Downsizing Process

Does size matter? Are large firms more or less predisposed toward downsizing? To answer this question, we have divided each sample into four subgroups according to their initial size (in 1990 for the Czech sample and in 1989 for the Polish and Hungarian samples) and analyzed the trends of output and employment for each size-group. The results are shown by country in figure 4.3 for output and figure 4.4 for employment. (The precise figures for each group and each sample are shown in Appendix 4.4)[17] Figures 4.3 and 4.4 show a number of interesting similarities and differences both within each sample and among the three samples. In the Czech sample, all four size-groups have undergone approximately the same degree of contraction of output and employment.[18] Irrespective of the degree of accommodation, all size-groups reacted to shocks in a similar manner. Macroeconomic policy reforms and the relatively speedy privatization program brought enterprises of different size-groups under some degree of market discipline sooner and contributed to their somewhat uniform behavior.

In the Hungarian sample, however, we note that the largest firms show the greatest fall in output. (Appendix 4.4 shows that the largest ten firms experienced an even greater fall in output than the largest fifty firms.) One explanation is that the Hungarian sample contains some fifteen to twenty large firms that faced severe financial difficulty and were heavily dependent on the state. These firms reduced their output and employment disproportionately in the period under consideration, resulting in a sharp decline in output and employment of the size-group containing the fifty largest firms.[19] If these firms were deleted from the

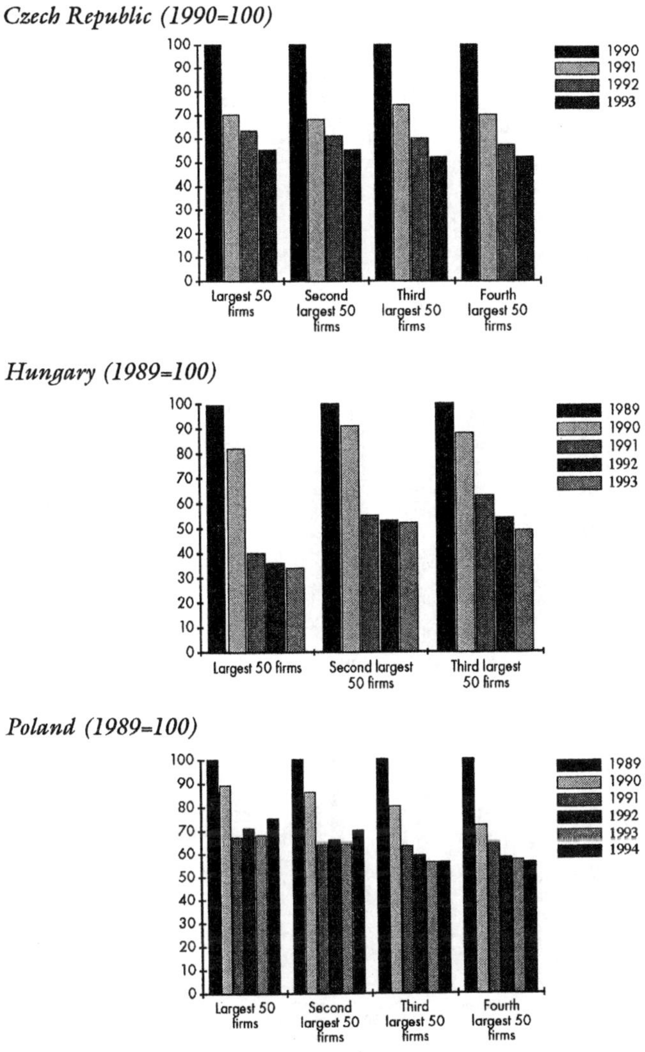

Figure 4.3: Changes in Output of Different Size-Groups in the Three Samples, 1989–94)

Source: The figures for manufacturing production and employment are from EBRD, *Transition Report 1996*, p. 118. For the description of the sample in each country, see the text.

list of the largest fifty enterprises, the behavior of the remaining enterprises would be very similar in different size-groups—a situation like that of the Czech sample.[20]

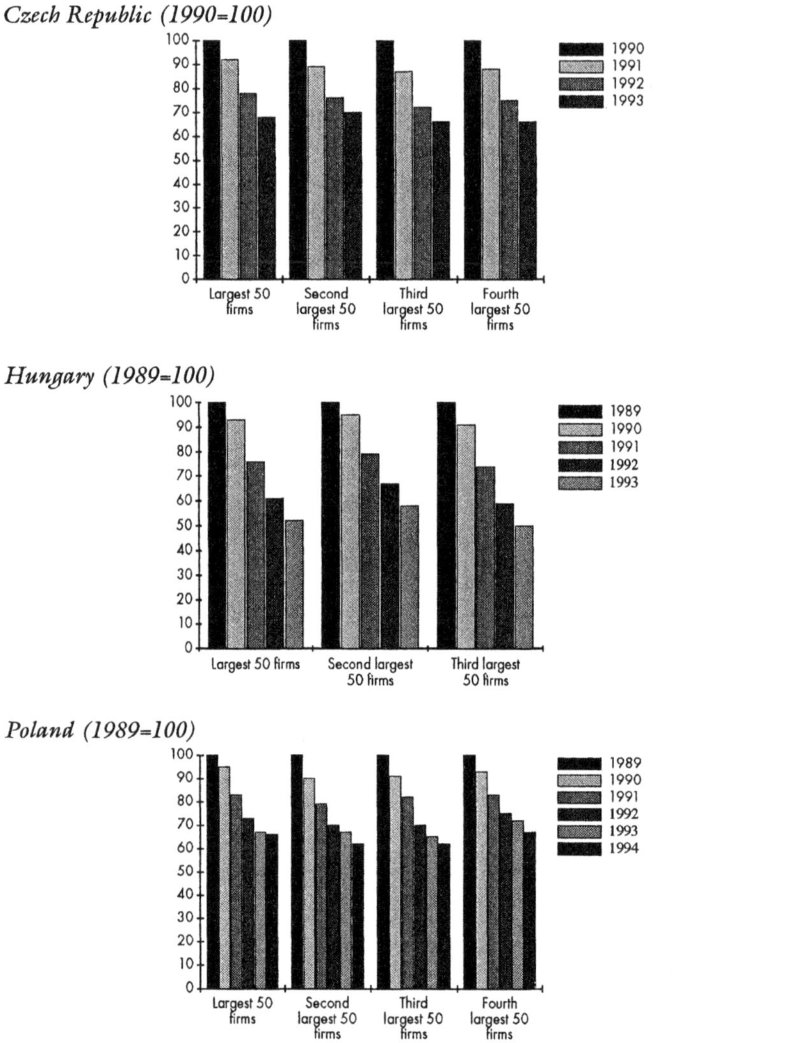

Figure 4.4: Changes in the Level of Employment of Different Size-Groups in the Three Samples, 1989–94

Source: The figures for manufacturing production and employment are from EBRD, ***Transition Report 1996***, p. 118. For the description of the sample in each country, see the text.

In the Polish sample, the largest size-group shows the smallest fall in output in comparison with other size-groups.[21] Firms in this size-group were able to postpone or slow down the downsizing and restructuring process because they enjoyed a high degree of market power in concentrated industries and were, in this period, still largely state owned. The competitive pressure for downsizing was weak and so was their own incentive for this course of action. But, at the same time, the decline of the largest firms was reversed before that of other size-groups, and the largest firms began to expand their output in 1992.

The difference in the employment response of different size-groups in each sample is much less pronounced, almost disappearing in the Czech and Polish samples.[22] Employment, as we have already pointed out, does not change as soon as there is a fall in demand, which is reflected very quickly in a fall in sales and output. Moreover, the tendencies influencing and determining the rate of labor shedding are very similar in all large enterprises irrespective of their exact size. Thus, overall, we conclude that there is no discernible and unambiguous link between the degree of downsizing and the size of enterprises, at least within our samples of the largest manufacturing enterprises.[23]

Effect of Enterprise Ownership on Downsizing

We now turn to the possibility of a link between enterprise ownership and the extent of downsizing. For this purpose, we divided the enterprises in each sample into three subgroups—state-owned, private (domestic), and foreign-owned firms—depending on who owned the majority (over 50 percent) of their shares in 1994. Table 4.3 shows the distribution of firms in each sample by ownership. The privatization of large firms in Poland has been much slower than in the other two countries, and the large majority of big firms in our Polish sample (87.5 percent) were still state owned in 1994. Because the number of foreign-owned firms in the Polish

Table 4.3
Number of State-Owned, Private and Foreign-Owned Firms in the Czech and Hungarian Samples in 1994

	State Owned	Private domestic	Foreign Owned
Czech sample (200 firms)	94	92	14
Hungarian sample (150 firms)	65	45	40
Polish sample (200 firms)	175	21	4

Source: The figures for manufacturing production and employment are from EBRD, *Transition Report 1996*, p. 118. For the description of the sample in each country, see the text.

sample is very small (only four firms), it is difficult to draw any meaningful conclusion about the behavior of this group.

The ownership status of firms in each sample has been changing since 1990, with the number of private (domestic) and foreign-owned firms gradually increasing as privatization and new entry proceed. The position defined in table 4.3 is one that has been arrived at over the four-year period. We assume that managerial incentives and behavior are influenced not only by an actual change in ownership but also by expectations and by the process of privatization itself, with domestic or foreign owners involved in negotiations with the firm prior to its privatization. The expectation of a change in ownership and the desire to protect their own positions can motivate the managers to behave in a manner consistent with the interests of future owners.[24]

It is generally expected that different owners create different incentives for managers. Foreign-owned firms, for example, are expected to be more dynamic and innovative, to engage in strategic restructuring (involving changes in technology, product mix, marketing activities, and new investments), and to return to growth quicker than other firms. At the same time, foreign investors will be more attracted to firms with brighter prospects and fewer restructuring needs in the first place. Here we face a typical "sample selection" problem that makes it difficult to infer a causality between the degree of downsizing and the type of ownership. In either case, although there may be downsizing in these enterprises too, the process should be less drastic than in state-owned or private firms without the same access to foreign technology, capital, and expertise.

Figures 4.5 through 4.7 present the changes in output, employment, and labor productivity for each of the three subgroups in each sample—except for Poland where, because of the very small number of foreign-owned firms, we have only shown the changes in output, employment, and labor productivity of state-owned and private firms. The data underlying these tables are presented as Appendix 4.5. Figures 4.5 through 4.7 show that, on the whole, foreign firms performed better than state-owned and private firms. While all three subgroups experienced a decline in output, the extent of the decline was smaller for foreign-owned firms than for the other two subgroups in the Czech Republic and Hungary. The extent of contraction in employment, however, was only slightly less in foreign-owned firms than in domestic firms in the Czech Republic and was almost identical in the two groups in Hungary. Consequently, labor productivity increased much faster in

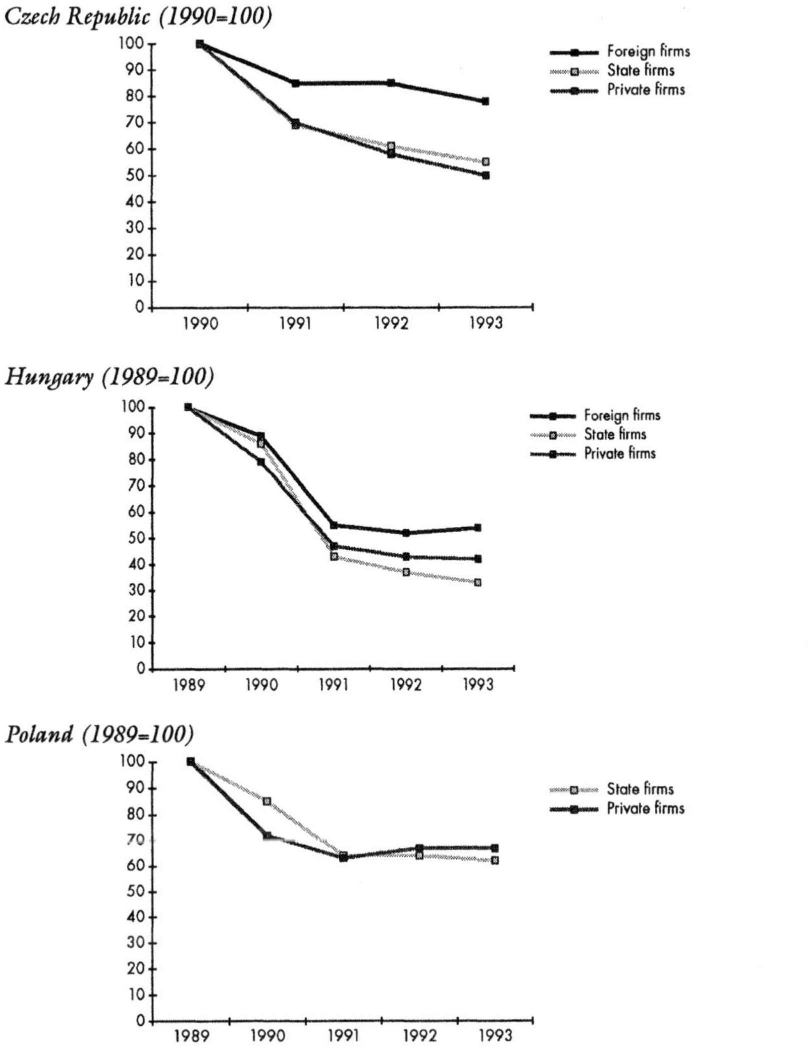

Figure 4.5: Changes in the Output of Sample Firms According to Type of Ownership, 1989–93

Source: The figures for manufacturing production and employment are from EBRD, *Transition Report 1996*, p. 118. For the description of the sample in each country, see the text.

foreign firms than in domestic firms. Thus, our expectation that foreign firms performed better than state-owned and private firms was confirmed. Enterprises bought by foreign firms not only enjoyed the benefits associated with better technology and management but, often, were

Czech Republic (1990=100)

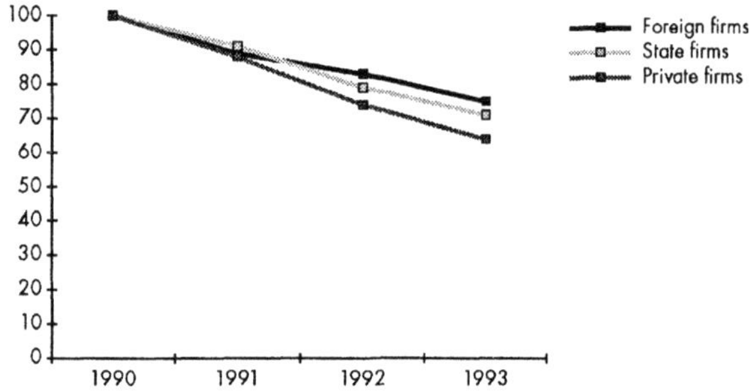

Hungary (1989=100)

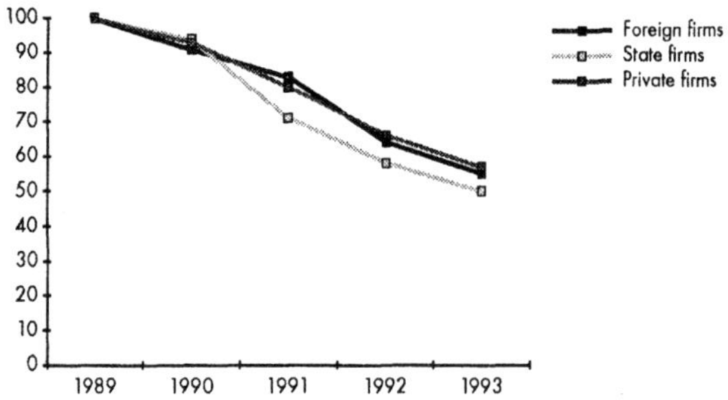

Poland (1989=100)

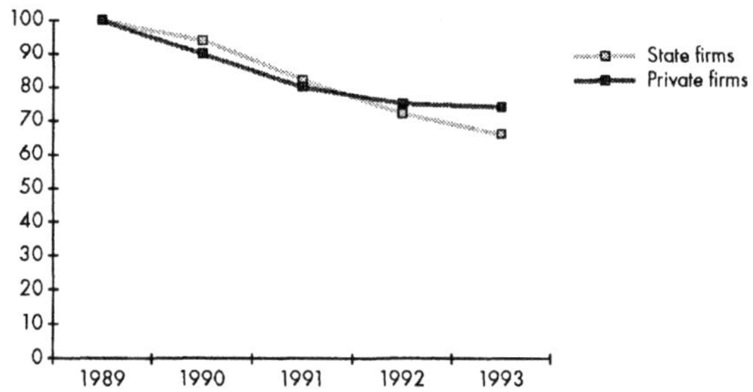

Figure 4.6: Changes in the Employment of Sample Firms According to Type of Ownership, 1989–93

Source: The figures for manufacturing production and employment are from EBRD, *Transition Report 1996*, p. 118. For the description of the sample in each country, see the text.

performing better and faced better market conditions in the first place. Foreign firms may have been good at picking winners.

What are the differences between private (domestic) and state-owned firms? Figures 4.5 through 4.7 generally indicate the absence of a uni-

Czech Republic (1990=100)

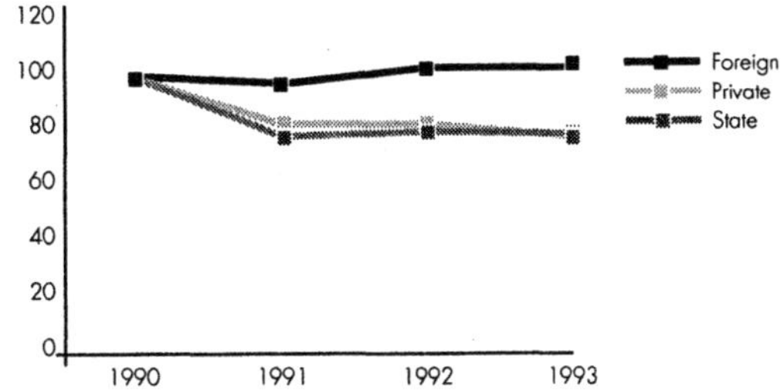

Hungary (1989=100)

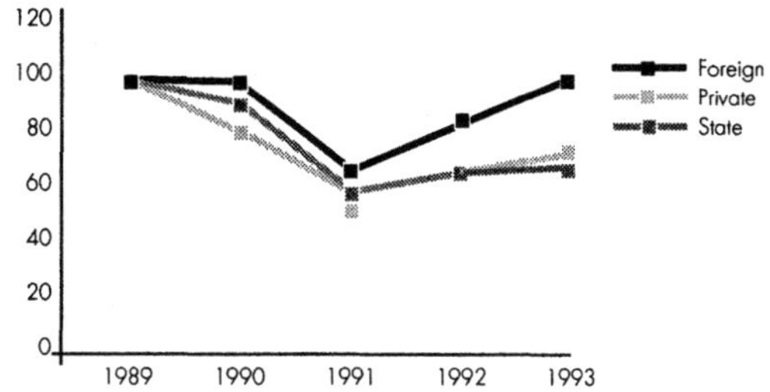

Poland (1989=100)

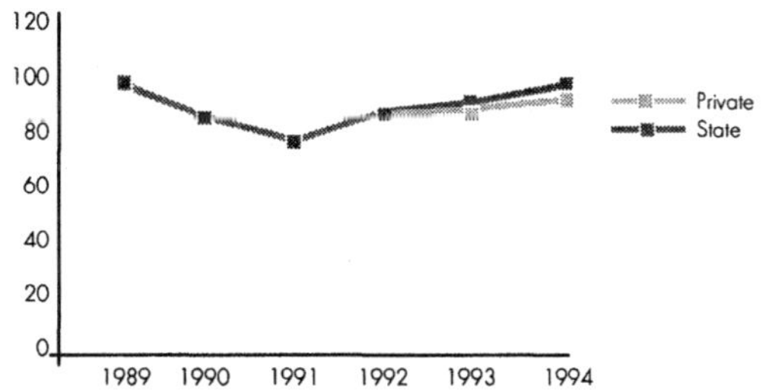

Figure 4.7: Changes in the Labour Productivity of Sample Firms According to Type of Ownership, 1989–93

Source: The figures for manufacturing production and employment are from EBRD, *Transition Report 1996*, p. 118. For the description of the sample in each country, see the text.

form and significant difference between the two groups. Many reasons may account for the similar behavioral pattern. In the Czech Republic, for example, most of the state-owned firms in the sample in 1994 were already in the process of voucher privatization and, for reasons explained

Table 4.4
Changes in Output and Employment of Sample Enterprises in Different Branches of Manufacturing (Percentage)

Branch	No. of firms	No. of contracting firms[a]	Change in output[b] (all sample firms)	Change in employment (all sample firms)
Czech Republic, 1990–93				
Food	26	19	-18	-17
Textiles and clothing	23	23	-51	-37
Leather	4	3	-51	-54
Wood	10	10	-56	-27
Pulp, paper, printing and publishing	7	7	-40	-30
Coking and oil	2	2	-48	-12
Chemicals	20	20	-37	-26
Rubber and plastic	5	4	-30	-12
Ceramics and glass	11	9	-49	-26
Metals	16	13	-41	-18
Machinery	55	54	-47	-37
Electrical and electronics	13	10	-56	-36
Transport	6	4	-42	-46
Other	2	2	-21	-19
Hungary, 1990–93				
Food	59	58	-43	-37
Textiles and clothing	7	7	-64	-49
Leather	3	3	-68	-46
Wood	3	2	-67	-42
Pulp, paper, printing and publishing	9	6	-73	-64
Coking and oil	1	1	-50	-38
Chemicals	18	18	-44	-25
Rubber and plastic	5	5	-55	-35
Ceramics and glass	11	11	-59	-48
Metals	9	9	-82	-70
Machinery	16	16	-55	-46
Electrical and electronics	9	9	-60	-59
Transport	3	3	-38	-36
Poland, 1989–94				
Food	29	20	-29	-27
Textiles and clothing	19	19	-65	-37
Leather	5	5	-94	-81
Wood	3	3	-71	-48
Pulp, paper, printing. and publishing	4	4	-5	-26
Coking and oil	10	6	+31	-4

Branch	No. of firms	No. of contracting firms[a]	Change in output[b] (all sample firms)	Change in employment (all sample firms)
Chemicals, rubber and plastics	43	41	-31	-31
Ceramics and glass	3	3	-30	-27
Metals	11	11	-55	-34
Machinery	10	10	-69	-49
Electrical and electronics	15	15	-58	-41
Transport	19	18	-40	-38
Building materials	3	3	-20	-45
Metallurgy	26	25	-39	-32

[a] Contraction refers to changes in employment; [b] At constant 1989 prices.

Source: The figures for manufacturing production and employment are from EBRD, *Transition Report 1996*, p. 118.

earlier, their behavior may well have been influenced by the expectation of being privatized. This, expectation can explain why the output, employment, and productivity responses of the two groups were so similar. The Polish scenario is rather mixed and, given the very large difference between the size of the two subgroups (175 and 21), it is difficult to make a meaningful comparison. Private firms in Hungary did have a smaller decline in output and employment and a slightly improved labor productivity than state-owned firms, but the difference was slight.[25] In order to discern differences in behavior among firms of different ownership types, one would need to examine patterns of change in far more detail than is allowed by our dataset.

Downsizing in Different Branches of Manufacturing

Should the extent of downsizing be different in different branches of manufacturing? It has been suggested that traditional industries, such as textile and heavy industry, would not be able to cope with the new competitive environment as well as the technologically based modern sectors like electronics and electrical machinery industries. This would imply that the development of competitive markets would lead to more exits from the traditional branches of industry than from modern branches. Table 4.4 shows the changes in the output and employment of firms in different branches of manufacturing in the three samples as well as the number of declining firms in each branch. The overwhelming impression conveyed by table 4.4 is that for all three samples, almost all firms in all branches of manufacturing underwent a significant downsizing (exit of resources), with no activity, traditional or modern, light or heavy, escaping contraction. The reduction in employment in each branch was generally smaller than the reduction in output, resulting in falling labor productivity over the entire period under consideration, although not necessarily in every year. The most notable case of decline was the Polish leather industry, with a 94 percent decline in output and an 81 percent decline in employment, largely caused by the liberalization of foreign trade and the removal of subsidies. The one exception to the general decline was the coking and oil sector in Poland, in which four out of ten firms experienced an expansion of output, and where the total output of the industry increased by 31 percent.[26]

An interesting feature of table 4.4 is the position of the food industry, which, despite its overall contraction, contained most of the expanding firms in Poland and the Czech Republic (though not in Hungary). In the Polish sample, there were seventeen expanding firms in the 1989–94 period, nine in the food industry. In the Czech sample, there were five known cases of expansion between 1990 and 1993, four in the food industry. In other words, large firms in the food industry dominated the expanding sectors of both economies.

Table 4.4 clearly indicates that, in all three samples, firms have been subject to downsizing irrespective of their technological level or ability to cope with competition. Downsizing in all branches of the manufacturing sector suggests that the redeployment of resources among branches may have been less than that among firms in individual branches. The extent of the reallocation of resources within industries can be demonstrated by analyzing the change in the share of employment in each branch accounted for by the sample firms in that branch. A decline in this share implies that enterprises in the sample have been subject to heavier downsizing than the branch as a whole, while an increase in this ratio means that sample enterprises have experienced a milder downsizing than the branch as a whole.

The sample's share of employment in each branch over the period under consideration is shown in table 4.5. For most branches, the share of branch employment accounted for by firms in the sample has been declining over time, indicating that the downsizing process has been more thorough for the sample firms (i.e., the larger firms in each branch) than for the branch as a whole. This also means that the majority of industries have experienced a process of deconcentration, with shares of the largest enterprises declining in most branches. Thus in the Czech sample, the share of sample firms in their branch employment showed a reduction in nine out of fourteen branches and no significant change in the remaining five. In the Hungarian and Polish samples, a decline was recorded in seven out of thirteen branches and in thirteen out of fourteen branches, respectively. Sample firms in three branches in Hungary (none in Poland), showed a significant increase in their employment

Table 4.5
Changes in the Samples' Share of Branch Employment (Percentage)

Czech Republic	**Share in Branch Employment**		
	1991	**1992**	**1993**
Food	17	18	17
Textiles and clothing	43	42	39
Leather	54	42	33
Wood	55	55	47
Pulp, paper, printing and publishing	39	40	36
Coking and oil	80	79	71
Chemicals	83	83	84
Rubber and plastic	48	48	45
Ceramics and glass	30	31	27
Metals	44	46	44
Machinery	70	65	63
Electrical and electronics	16	17	18
Transport	21	18	18
Other	4	4	4

Hungary	**Share in Branch Employment**		
	1991	**1992**	**1993**
Food	43	38	37
Textiles and clothing	19	19	20
Leather	19	18	16
Wood	18	17	18
Pulp, paper, printing and publishing	12	14	15
Coking and oil	90	88	85
Chemicals	76	73	70
Rubber and plastic	64	64	64
Ceramics and glass	36	27	26
Metals	29	24	26
Machinery	28	32	34
Electrical and electronics	46	49	51
Transport	59	58	54

Poland	Share in Branch Employment				
	1989	1990	1991	1992	1993
Food	14	12	12	11	10
Textiles and clothing	13	9	11	11	11
Leather	20	12	11	10	7
Wood	5	3	3	2	2
Pulp, paper, printing and publishing	14	13	13	13	13
Coking and oil	14	14	13	13	11
Chemicals, rubber and plastic	56	47	49	48	46
Ceramics and glass	16	13	14	15	15
Metals	22	14	16	16	17
Machinery	14	14	14	13	13
Electrical and electronics	21	17	19	20	22
Transport	49	42	42	39	42
Building materials	5	3	4	3	3
Metallurgy	91	90	91	81	77

Source: Source: The figures for manufacturing production and employment are from EBRD, *Transition Report 1996*, p. 118. For the description of the sample in each country, see the text. Branch employment has been calculated from the Statistical Yearbooks of the three countries, various years.

share. This deconcentration process indicates that a reallocation of resources between large and small firms has been occurring within each branch. The exit of resources from larger firms has been accompanied by the flow of at least some of these resources into smaller firms.

Concluding Remarks

Downsizing is clearly an important exit process in the early stages of transition when classical exit processes have not yet been fully developed. It has occurred extensively in all three countries under consideration despite differences in their transformation strategies. Downsizing has led to a large reduction in the volume of resources used by big manufacturing enterprises in all branches of industry.

It was clear from our data that almost all enterprises in the three samples were subject to downsizing in the early period of transition. Although the precise extent of downsizing varied greatly across enterprises and countries, there is no doubt that a significant and major reallocation of resources took place everywhere. Labor productivity generally fell in the first two or three years of transition because of the delayed employment response to shocks (in comparison with output response). In general, the decline in labor productivity was halted everywhere and in many cases reversed, with enterprises in Poland achieving pretransition levels of labor productivity. We also showed that the downsizing process, within the sample of large firms, was largely independent of size. Different-sized groups within our samples generally behaved in a similar fashion—with the exception of very large firms in the Hungarian sample, which was dominated by a small number of financially troubled firms. In terms of enterprise ownership, the Czech and Hungarian samples indicate that a firm under foreign ownership generally went through a milder form of downsizing, perhaps the result of the firm's better initial conditions and the management's ability to turn the company around quickly. The difference between private (domestic) and state-owned firms was less significant.

In all countries, larger firms in the great majority of manufacturing branches downsized more heavily than their branch as a whole, resulting in a drop in their share of branch output and employment—and also in industrial deconcentration. Downsizing occurred irrespective of the technological level of the particular branch or whether the branch has been modern or traditional.

In this chapter, we have concentrated on changes in employment and output levels as indicators of downsizing because of the reasonably reliable data on these variables. We know, from our own study of individual enterprises and from many other case studies of enterprises in transition, that downsizing has also been accompanied by a reduction in enterprise assets. Many enterprises separated individual plants from their main activities and sold them off either during the process of privatization or later on. Others sold parts of their assets in order to raise funds for a variety of purposes—to reduce their geographic dispersion or simply leave certain markets.[27] The absence of accurate data on assets, however, has prevented us from investigating the downsizing process in terms of the capital assets of enterprises.

The uniformity and the all-pervasive nature of the response of enterprises to the shocks of transition (downsizing) in all branches of industry and in all three countries is a striking feature of the exit process. This uniform behavior reflects the perception held by enterprises that transition is a one-way street and that there is little chance of returning to a soft-budget constraint regime. In short, the transition programs in the three countries were regarded as credible by enterprise managers—a lesson for other transition economies at earlier stages of transition.

Appendix 4.1
Changes in the Level of Employment in Different Sectors and the Growth of Self-Employment, 1990–94 (in thousands)

	1990	1991	1992	1993	1994
Czech Republic					
Agriculture	631	508	425	331	338
Industry[a]	2025	1948	1798	1710	1619
Construction	403	404	408	453	444
Trade and repairs	524	484	544	609	702
Hotel and catering	90	88	101	112	137
Transport. and communications	371	368	366	385	353
Financial intermediaries	28	37	51	65	76
Real estate, renting and business services	382	351	339	303	340
Public sector[b]	693	691	717	724	726
Others	204	178	176	199	147
Total employed	5351	5059	4927	4853	4885
Private entrepreneurs running their own business[c]	0	124	892	1045	1014
Hungary					
Agriculture	547	425	283	207	175
Industry[a]	1282	1147	997	871	856
Construction	250	209	147	125	131
Trade and repairs	422	384	277	227	257
Hotel and catering	71	70	64	57	62
Transport and communications	342	311	346	340	332
Financial intermediaries	43	51	57	61	66
Real estate, renting and business services	106	110	105	90	104
Public sector[b]	852	838	798	826	820
Others	253	187	84	78	79
Total employed	4168	3732	3118	2835	2831
Private entrepreneurs running their own business[c]	393	510	606	688	778
Poland[d]					
Agriculture	4559	4383	3782	3704	3902
Industry[a]	4620	4250	3784	3671	3641
Construction	1243	1116	1024	853	820
Trade and repairs	1389	1561	1806	1872	1863
Hotel and catering			154	168	188
Transport and communications	932	843	905	871	854
Financial intermediaries	181	179	193	218	239
Real estate, renting and business services			523	498	470

	1990	1991	1992	1993	1994
Public Sector[b]					
Others					
Total Employed	16511	15601	14677	14330	14475
Private entrepreneurs running their own business[c]	na	na	na	1626	1718

[a] Mining and quarrying, manufacturing, and electricity, gas and water.
[b] Public administration, defence, education, health and social work.
[c] Beginning of each year. Some of these businesses may have become inactive or stopped operation altogether.
[d] New sectoral classification since 1992, so figures are not strictly comparable.

Sources: ***Statisticka Rocneka Ceske Republiky***, Praha, various issues 1993-1996; ***Rocznik Statystyczny***, Warsaw, various issues 1992–95; ***Statistical Yearbook of Hungary***, Budapest, various issues; the Czech Ministry of Industry and Trade, and EBRD, ***Transition Report, 1996***.

Appendix 4.2
Share of the Largest 200 Firms in Employment and Output (Percentage)[a]

Sample's share in:	1989	1990	1991	1992	1993
Economy's total employment					
Czech Republic	na	11.5	10.9	9.4	8.6
Hungary	na	8.8	8.0	7.8	7.4
Poland	5.2	5.1	4.7	4.4	4.1
Manufacturing employment					
Czech Republic	na	34.9	32.3	29.4	27.5
Hungary	29.1	33.2	29.2	28.0	24.9
Poland	22.8	22.5	21.6	21.3	20.7
Manufacturing output[b]					
Czech Republic[c]	na	na	55.7	55.0	55.4
Hungary	49.2	52.0	41.3	42.0	38.7
Poland	32.5	34.5	31.5	30.4	27.1

[a] The Hungarian figures refer to the 150 largest manufacturing enterprises. The transformàtion programe was implemented from January 1991 in the Czech Republic, a year later than in Hungary and Poland. Therefore we have focused on the adjustment process from 1990 in the Czech Republic and from 1989 in Poland and Hungary.

[b] Value of output sold at current prices.

[c] The total manufacturing output figure used to calculate the 1991 share of the Czech sample is an approximation.

Sources: Own calculations using sample dates *Statisticka Rocneka Ceske Republiky*, Praha, various issues 1993–96; *Rocznik Statystyczny*, Warsaw, various issues 1992–95; *Statistical Yearbook of Hungary*, Budapest, various issues.

Appendix 4.3
Total Output, Employment, and Labor Productivity of the Three Samples, 1989–94

	1989	1990	1991	1992	1993	1994
Czech Republic						
Output (in bn KC)		279	196	171	151	
Employment (1000's)		610	546	464	414	
Labor productivity (in 1000 KC/worker)		457	359	369	366	
With 1990=100						
Output (%)		100	70	61	54	
Employment (%)		100	90	76	68	
Labor productivity (%)		100	78	81	80	
Hungary						
Output (in bn HUF)	800	677	373	337	320	
Employment (1000's)	395	367	302	245	211	
Labor productivity (in 1000 KC/worker)	202	184	124	138	152	
With 1989=100						
Output (%)	100	85	47	42	40	
Employment (%)	100	93	76	62	53	
Labor productivity (%)	100	91	61	68	75	
Poland						
Output (in mml PLN)	3,174	2,666	2,026	2,043	1,982	2,132
Employment (in 1000)	884	823	721	638	593	569
Labor productivity (in 1000 KC/worker)	3.6	3.2	2.8	3.2	3.3	3.7
With 1989=100						
Output (%)	100	84	64	64	62	67
Employment (%)	100	93	81	72	67	64
Labor productivity (%)	100	89	78	89	92	103

Notes: All output figures are valued at 1989 prices. Labor productivity is defined as total value of output sold divided by total employment of each sample.

Source: The figures for manufacturing production and employment are from EBRD, *Transition Report, 1996*, p. 118. For the description of the sample in each country, see the text.

Appendix 4.4
Changes in Output, Employment and Labor Productivity of Different Size-Groups in the Three Samples, 1989–94[a]

	1989	1990	1991	1992	1993	1994
CZECH REPUBLIC						
Output						
Largest 10 firms		100	71	62	55	
Largest 50 firms		100	70	63	55	
Second-largest 50 firms		100	68	61	55	
Third-largest 50 firms		100	74	60	52	
Fourth-largest 50 firms		100	70	57	52	
Employment						
Largest 10 firms		100	96	81	73	
Largest 50 firms		100	92	78	68	
Second-largest 50 firms		100	89	76	70	
Third-largest 50 firms		100	87	72	66	
Fourth-largest 50 firms		100	88	75	66	
Labor productivity						
Largest 10 firms		100	74	77	76	
Largest 50 firms		100	76	80	80	
Second-largest 50 firms		100	77	80	79	
Third-largest 50 firms		100	85	83	79	
Fourth-largest 50 firms		100	80	76	79	
HUNGARY						
Output						
Largest 10 firms	100	76	32	26	28	
Largest 50 firms	100	82	40	36	34	
Second-largest 50 firms	100	91	55	53	52	
Third-largest 50 firms	100	88	63	54	49	
Employment						
Largest 10 firms	100	91	67	53	47	
Largest 50 firms	100	93	76	61	52	
Second-largest 50 firms	100	95	79	67	58	
Third-largest 50 firms	100	91	74	59	50	
Labor productivity						
Largest 10 firms	100	83	48	50	60	
Largest 50 firms	100	88	53	59	65	
Second-largest 50 firms	100	96	70	79	89	
Third-largest 50 firms	100	96	85	91	98	

	1989	1990	1991	1992	1993	1994
POLAND						
Output						
Largest 10 firms	100	100	75	84	79	84
Largest 50 firms	100	89	67	71	68	75
Second-largest 50 firms	100	86	64	66	64	70
Third-largest 50 firms	100	80	63	59	56	56
Fourth-largest 50 firms	100	72	64	58	57	56
Employment						
Largest 10 firms	100	96	89	80	67	69
Largest 50 firms	100	95	83	73	67	66
Second-largest 50 firms	100	90	79	70	67	62
Third-largest 50 firms	100	91	82	70	65	62
Fourth-largest 50 firms	100	93	83	75	72	67
Labor productivity						
Largest 10 firms	100	104	85	104	118	121
Largest 50 firms	100	94	80	96	102	113
Second-largest 50 firms	100	96	81	94	96	113
Third-largest 50 firms	100	87	77	85	86	90
Fourth-largest 50 firms	100	77	77	77	80	84

[a] The division of enterprises into different size groups is based on sales revenue in 1990 for the Czech and Hungarian samples and in 1989 for the Polish sample. Labor productivity is defined as total value of output sold for each subgroup divided by total employment of that subgroup.

Source: *Statisticka Rocneka Ceske Republiky*, Praha, various issues 1993–96; *Rocznik Statystyczny*, Warsaw, various issues 1992–95; *Statistical Yearbook of Hungary*, Budapest, various issues.

Appendix 4.5
Change in Output, Employment, and Labor Productivity of the Sample According to Type of Ownership, 1989–93[a]

	1989	1990	1991	1992	1993
CZECH REPUBLIC					
Output					
Foreign firms (n=14)		100	85	85	78
State firms (n=94)		100	69	61	55
Private firms (n=92)		100	70	58	50
Employment					
Foreign firms		100	89	83	75
State firms		100	91	79	71
Private firms		100	88	74	64
Labor productivity					
Foreign firms		100	95	102	104
State firms		100	76	78	78
Private firms		100	80	80	78
HUNGARY					
Output					
Foreign firms (n=40)	100	89	55	52	54
State firms (n=65)	100	86	43	37	33
Private firms (n=45)	100	79	47	43	42
Employment					
Foreign firms	100	91	83	64	55
State firms	100	94	71	58	50
Private firms	100	93	80	66	57
Labor productivity					
Foreign firms	100	98	66	81	97
State firms	100	92	60	64	66
Private firms	100	85	59	65	73
POLAND					
Output					
Foreign firms (n=4)	100	73	45	53	65
State firms (n=175)	100	85	64	64	62
Private firms (n=21)	100	72	63	67	67
Employment					
Foreign firms	100	83	70	64	62
State firms	100	94	82	72	66
Private firms	100	90	80	75	74

	1989	1990	1991	1992	1993
Labor productivity					
Foreign firms	100	88	65	82	95
State firms	100	91	78	89	93
Private firms	100	80	79	89	91

[a] The ownership status of enterprises refers to 1994. Labor productivity is defined as total sale of output of enterprises in each subgroup divided by total employment of enterprises in that sub-group. "Private firms" category refers to domestic private firms.

Source: The figures for manufacturing production and employment are from EBRD, *Transition Report 1996*, p. 118. For the description of the sample in each country, see the text.

References

Bouin, O. 1996. Enterprise restructuring at different stages of ownership transformation: Poland and the Czech Republic. Paper prepared for Conference, Ownership Transformation and Restructuring Processes in Central and Eastern Europe, Warsaw, April 11–12, 1996.

Capek, A. and P. Mertlik. 1996. Organizational change and financial restructuring in Czech manufacturing enterprises 1990–1995. Prague: Czech National Bank, Institute of Economics. Mimeographed.

Carlin, W., J. Van Reenen, and T. Wolfe. 1994. Enterprise restructuring in the transition: An analytical survey of the case study evidence from Central and Eastern Europe. Working Paper no. 14. London: European Bank for Reconstruction and Development.

Dabrowski, J. M., M. Federowicz, and A. Levitas. 1992. Przedsiebiorstwa panstwowe w drugim roku transformacji gospodarczej-wyniki badan (State-owned enterprises in the second year of transformation. Research Results). Report no. 27. Gdansk: Instytut Badan nad Gospodarka Rynkowa.

European Bank for Reconstruction and Development. 1996. *Transition Report*. London: European Bank for Reconstruction and Development.

Grosfeld, I. and G. Roland 1995. Defensive and strategic restructuring in Central European enterprises. Discussion Paper no. 1135 (March). London: Centre for Economic Policy Research.

Hoppenstedt Bonnier.1995. *Vyznamne podniky Ceske republiky 1995* (The largest firms in the Czech Republic, 1995). Prague: Hoppenstedt Bonnier

Kollo, J. 1995. Short-term response of employment to sales in state-owned and private firms in Hungary 1990–1994. Paper presented at meeting of the World Bank/EDI Project: Employment, Unemployment and Restructuring in Eastern Europe and Russia, Washington, D.C., September 29, 1995.

Novák, T. and M. Szanyi. 1995. Downsizing in Hungarian manufacturing. Budapest. Mimeographed.

Notes

We are grateful to the Central European University Privatization Project, directed by Professors R. Frydman and A. Rapaczynski, for allowing us access to their database of Czech companies and to Katarzyna Pietka and Ryszard Petru for the valuable research assistance they provided in collecting and preparing the Polish data.

1. Downsizing as an exit mechanism is not unique to transition economies. Firms in established market economies also embark on downsizing in response to changes in their market environment or to technological opportunities.

2. This view is based on the theory that the very low rate of unemployment in the Czech Republic is because enterprises have not undergone serious restructuring and have retained much of their excess labor. The diffused share ownership and the absence of strategic owners resulting from the voucher privatization scheme is often blamed for the lack of pressure on enterprises.

3. This type of forced restructuring, involving some large enterprises, especially those located in small towns and regions, is highlighted in Dabrowski et al. (1992).

4. The last two types of responses have been referred to as "defensive restructuring" and "strategic restructuring." See Grosfeld and Roland (1995).

5. However, no adjustment has been made for smaller spin-offs that were not reported publicly and of which we were unaware.

6. While the contraction of employment is seen as a positive response to the shocks of transition, the consequences of a large-scale decrease in employment should not be disregarded. Although the Czech Republic does not suffer from this problem, Hungary, Poland, and other transition economies undergoing downsizing have faced large increases in unemployment that have imposed a severe burden on the state.

7. The Czech sample was extracted from the database of firms participating in the two waves of voucher privatization and supplemented by the list compiled by the CEU Privatization Project and Hoppenstedt Bonnier's *Vyznamne podniky Ceske republiky 1995* (The largest firms in the Czech Republic 1995). The complete set of data could only be constructed up to 1993. The Hungarian sample was based on the list of the 100 largest industrial firms and the list of the 200 largest companies compiled by the popular Hungarian economic weekly magazine *Figyelö* in 1989 and 1990. Using these sources, it was only possible to construct

a full set of data for 150 of the largest 200 companies. The Polish sample was extracted from "Lista 500," a list of the largest 500 manufacturing firms in Poland prepared regularly by the Institute of Economics and initially published by the economic monthly *Zarzadzanie,* since 1993 by the economic weekly *Zycie Gospodarcze* and *Nowe Zycie Gospodarcze*. For all samples, additional sources, including contacts with firms, were used to complete the dataset.

8. Figure 4.1 is based on Appendix 4.2. In the remainder of this chapter, wherever possible, we shall present the data in graphic form in the text with the relevant, and more complete, underlying tables appearing in the appendix.

9. Throughout this chapter we shall use the "value of output sold" as a proxy for output. The figures for sales revenue are deflated by the general producer price index for the Hungarian and Polish samples and by the sector-specific producer price index for the Czech sample in order to identify changes in real output.

10. This difference also contradicts the widely held view about the slow pace of restructuring in the Czech Republic referred to earlier.

11. The pre-1989 reform efforts in Hungary and Poland had already resulted in the creation of many small private firms across the economy, with the consequent reduction in the role of large state-owned manufacturing firms.

12. This reflects the fact that smaller manufacturing firms, as well as the nonmanufacturing sectors, came out of the recession earlier than the largest manufacturing firms.

13. Throughout this chapter, we use the "value of output sold per worker," deflated by the producer price index, as a proxy for labor productivity.

14. It should be pointed out that the rise in labor productivity in 1994 is, to a large measure, due to the massive increase in the sales (and output) of firms in the energy sector. If these firms (ten in all) are deleted from the sample, the decline in output will reach 41 percent in 1994 (rather than 34 percent), and labor productivity will not regain its 1989 level. For more on the situation in this sector, see the last section of the chapter.

15. In the first year of transition, there was also an increase in profits, partly due to the then prevalent cost accounting methods. Even though this was somewhat fictitious, it nevertheless contributed to the delayed adjustment in employment.

16. Moreover, the decline in the output and employment of the sample in each country was, in all years, always greater than that in the manufacturing sector as a whole.

17. Appendix 4.4 also shows the changes in output and employment for the largest ten firms in each sample. Although this is not represented in figures 4.4 and 4.5, the conclusions drawn in this section also apply to the top ten firms of each sample.

18. We used regression analysis to see if there was a statistically significant difference between the output and employment decline of different size-groups. For all three years (1991–93), we were unable to reject the hypothesis that there was no significant difference between different size-groups. The only exception was the output change in 1992 for the smallest two size-groups, which were significantly different from those of other size-groups (at the 5 percent level).

19. This is not to say that other countries did not have their own share of troubled large firms. It seems that the impact of these enterprises on the performance of the largest size-group has been more pronounced in Hungary than in Poland or the Czech Republic. In fact, a glance at the performance of the largest ten firms shows this difference more clearly. As Appendix 4.4 shows, the output of the largest ten firms in the Hungarian sample declined by 74 percent, while those in the Czech Republic and Poland declined by only 38 percent and 25 percent. Interestingly, the same table shows that the smallest size-group in the Hungarian sample suffered a much less severe decline than other groups, and its decline was very similar to that of the similar-sized group in the Czech and Polish samples.

20. Novák and Szányi (1995).

21. Though, as in the case of the Czech Republic, the difference across size-groups is statistically insignificant for all years except 1990.

22. Statistically, changes in employment in different size-groups are not significantly different from zero for any of the years under consideration in either the Czech or the Polish samples.

23. A point of caution: even with the smallest size-group considered in Appendix 4.4, we are still looking at large firms in the manufacturing sector—a sample that may not be the most suitable for showing the impact of size on the extent of downsizing.

24. In the Czech Republic, for example, enterprises participating in voucher privatization knew of their expected status two or three years before the date on which their shares were finally distributed to the new private owners (autumn 1993). Given the lengthy process of attracting

foreign investors, the same is true of firms in which foreign partners have a stake.

25. See Kollo (1995) for more recent results showing that the difference in responses of private and state-owned firms have become more pronounced after 1993.

26. We have already referred to this sector in the context of its disproportionate effect on output and labor productivity of the Polish sample as a whole (note 14). But the expansion observed in table 4.4 is due more to the use of the general producers' price index for deflating the sales revenues of firms in this sector than to a genuine massive expansion in their output. The price of energy rose faster than the average producers' price index, but in the absence of detailed price indices for all product groups and sectors, it was not possible to use sector-specific deflators.

27. See, for example, Carlin et al. (1994); Capek and Mertlik (1996); Bouin (1996).

5 Bankruptcy and Owner-Led Liquidation in the Czech Republic

Iraj Hoshi, Jan Mládek, and Alison Sinclair

The financial position of most Czech enterprises deteriorated rapidly following the implementation of the government's transformation program on January 1, 1991.[1] The initial steps in the creation of a competitive market economy, i.e., the liberalization of prices and foreign trade, the removal of subsidies, and the introduction of positive real interest rates, had a serious impact on the operation and performance of most enterprises. The collapse of the CMEA trade regime followed by the break-up of Czechoslovakia, resulting in the loss of a significant part of export and domestic markets, subjected these enterprises to more shocks and resulted in a further deterioration of their financial position. One of the most immediate and observable manifestations of financial distress was the rising volume of interenterprise debt and the cost of servicing these debts under market conditions, particularly the very high interest rates (see the discussion of interenterprise debt in chapter 3).

When the distorted economic structure inherited from the past—the overextended industrial sectors and undeveloped business and personal service sectors—was subjected to the shocks of a transition resulting from the emergence of competitive conditions and the loss of markets, the pressure for exit began to build in the great majority of enterprises. Authorities in the former Czechoslovakia (and later in the Czech Republic) were aware that the financial difficulties of many enterprises were, largely, the result of production and investment decisions made under the previous regime. Believing that these difficulties should not result in a large-scale exit of enterprises, they embarked on a series of measures to accommodate the pressure for exit. These measures were aimed at reducing the burden of past debts, facilitating the privatization of heavily indebted enterprises, and improving the liquidity of commercial banks holding large volumes of poorly performing debts. The most important of these accommodating measures were: (1) a limited debt write-off in 1991 (Kč 50 billion),[2] (2) the formation of Konsolidacni banka in March 1991 to take over the revolving working capital loans of enterprises from other banks (Kč 110 billion), (3) the postponement of the implementation of the new bankruptcy law until April 1993, (4) the computerized clearing of interenterprise debt in May and September 1993 (costing about Kč 980 million), and (5) the implicit debt write-off for some of the enterprises in the process of privatization.[3]

While the purpose of these measures was not to weaken or reduce the impact of the market-based reforms, they did provide enterprises with a buffer to soften the effect of transitional shocks and indeed prevented the large-scale closure of enterprises in the early phase of transition. The exit process, nevertheless, continued in a variety of forms: almost all enterprises embarked on informal processes such as ***downsizing*** (see chapter 4), many state enterprises (or parts of them) were liquidated by their founding bodies (owner-led exit), and many entered into informal work-out arrangements with their creditors.[4] More importantly, with the implementation of the bankruptcy law in 1993, creditors were enabled to increase the pressure for exit through more formal, creditor-led proceedings. Since then the bankruptcy procedure has become the main form of exit of insolvent or defaulting firms.

Bankruptcy Legislation

The legislation on bankruptcy in the Czech Republic goes back to the Bankruptcy Act of 1914 (under the Austro-Hungarian empire) and its later amended version, the Bankruptcy Act of 1931 (under the first Czechoslovak Republic). Under socialism, the concept and practice of bankruptcy lost its meaning and usefulness and the 1931 act fell into oblivion. After an abeyance of forty years, the vital role of a modern bankruptcy code was again recognized, and the Law on Bankruptcy and Settlements of July 1991 (No. 328/1991) and its major amendments in 1993 and 1996 were adopted to meet the needs of the emerging market economy.[5] Unlike its predecessors, which closely resembled the Austrian bankruptcy code, the 1991 law was based on the German model.[6]

The bankruptcy proceedings are triggered when the firm in financial difficulty (the debtor) is either unable to meet its obligations (default on debt repayment) or is "overburdened by debt" (insolvent). The 1996 amendments introduced a clearer definition of being overburdened by debt: when the firm in debt has at least two creditors and its obligations exceed the value of its assets. (The value of a firm's assets also includes the expected profits from current operations.) The proceeding begins with an application to the regional or municipal court (in whose jurisdiction the debtor is located) by the debtor itself, its liquidator, or its *bona fide* creditors.[7] Until 1996, as with the German code, the court would initiate the bankruptcy proceedings only if the debtor had sufficient assets to cover the cost of the court proceedings. But the recent (1996) amendments require the parties initiating the bankruptcy process to deposit a flat sum of Kč 10,000 with the court to cover the initial cost of the proceedings.[8] Given the extensive liquidity problems faced by many Czech firms in the early 1990s and the fact that many defaulting enterprises had outstanding claims against other enterprises (i.e., they may not have been genuinely insolvent), the government introduced additional conditions for the implementation of the bankruptcy proceedings. First, for a state-owned company to enter the bankruptcy proceedings, the consent of the relevant ministry (as its founding body) was necessary. Second, state-owned enterprises participating in the voucher privatization scheme, with at least 50 percent of their shares in the scheme, were temporarily exempted from the application of the bankruptcy law until after the distribution of their shares to the new owners.

Once an application for bankruptcy is filed, the court will first ascertain that the conditions for the declaration of bankruptcy (default on debt, insolvency, and the existence of at least two creditors) have been satisfied. The court will then offer the debtor a three-month protection period during which the firm may make its last attempt to resolve its financial difficulties.[9] During the protection period, there is a stay of claims against the firm, except for employees' claims and state claims arising from current operations. The protection period is particularly meant to give the newly privatized firms an opportunity to negotiate with their creditors directly and reach a settlement with them before a formal declaration of bankruptcy and before additional costs are incurred.

Upon the expiry of the protection period, the court makes a ruling in the form of a resolution, which includes the appointment of an administrator, declaring the bankruptcy of the firm and setting in motion the bankruptcy process.[10] Once the bankruptcy resolution has been declared by the court, the authority to manage the assets of the bankrupt firm is transferred to the administrator; any disposal of assets in the six-month period before bankruptcy, under specified circumstances, is declared void; all proceedings against the debtor are discontinued; claims for a separate settlement or attempts at withdrawing items from the bankrupt firm's assets may only be initiated against the administrator; and all privatization proceedings (if underway) are suspended. The administrator is required to fulfill his role with due care and is personally liable for any damages resulting from a breach of his duties. He is empowered to annul fraudulent transactions arranged by former managers up to one year before his appointment and is entitled to the reimbursement of his expenses and remuneration according to a set tariff (a percentage of the realized value of assets), which, until recently as we shall see later, has been rather poor and ungenerous.

The administrator compiles a list of the assets and liabilities of the debtor as well as a list of creditors for the court. The list is then presented to review hearings attended by the administrator, representatives of the firm, and creditors. The firm as well as its creditors can oppose the validity or the details of the applications, and any dispute is resolved by the court. The creditors are required (by the 1993 amendments) to form a Creditors' Committee if their number exceeds fifteen. The committee supervises the administrator's activities and is entitled and, if requested by the court, obliged to examine his activities.[11] The bankruptcy resolution is delivered to all participants in the proceedings, to the respective tax authorities, and to the authorities responsible for keeping real estate records. Creditors are invited to file their claims within thirty days from the day on which the bankruptcy resolution was declared. The company may, with its creditors' agreement, continue its operations after the declaration of bankruptcy under the administrator's supervision, if the company's value may be increased. The court-based proceedings against a debtor enterprise may result in any of the following three outcomes: (1) an ordinary settlement, (2) a liquidation, or (3) a compulsory settlement.

Ordinary settlement

At any time before the expiry of the three-month protection period and the declaration of bankruptcy, the debtor may seek the court's permission for an "ordinary settlement," which is essentially a reorganization. If the debtor complies with all the requirements of bankruptcy, it can lodge a settlement plan with the court containing the details of its agreements with creditors. In particular, the plan must include the details of any settlement offered to priority creditors, measures to be taken for the reorganization and refinancing of the enterprise, arrangements for the satisfaction of 45 percent of nonpriority claims within two years, and the details (and the notarized signatures) of anyone guaranteeing the implementation of the plan.[12] In addition to the conditions mentioned above, a debtor applying for a settlement should not have been the subject of a bankruptcy declaration or a settlement proposal in the past five years. The court has the final authority to approve or reject the proposal.

If the court resolves to permit the settlement, it appoints a settlement administrator and will order settlement hearings to take place in order to ascertain the details of the settlement agreed upon by the debtor and the creditors no later then six weeks from the date of the resolution. Once a resolution confirming the settlement has become effective and the debtor promptly fulfills all obligations, the court may issue a further resolution declaring the settlement complete.

Liquidation

Should there be no application for settlement during the protection period, the administrator embarks on the process of asset disposal through auctions or other methods, which must be approved by the court, in order to liquidate the bankrupt firm and satisfy the claims of its creditors. Subsequent to hearings involving the bankrupt firm and the Creditors' Committee, the court may (and often does) impose conditions like a minimum price for assets in order to prevent fraudulent practices. Sometimes these conditions prove too strict and impossible to meet, thus requiring the court to revise them and, ultimately, delaying the resolution of the case.[13] The process of asset disposal will cease if, at any time during this process, the debtor obtains the court's approval for a settlement procedure.

Where creditors' claims have been secured on property or a right of retention (the so-called separate settlement), they are entitled to have their claims settled out of the proceeds from the sale of such property. If a claim is not fully covered by the proceeds, the remainder is considered a separate claim on the assets of the bankrupt firm.

Once the process of disposing assets is complete, the administrator will submit a report to the court that includes the details of the realized value of assets, an account of his own remuneration and costs, and a distribution schedule. In preparing the distribution schedule, the post-bankruptcy claims against the debtor's estate are separated from claims prior to the bankruptcy declaration and are given priority. These include the administrator's remuneration and costs and the claims of creditors and employees of the bankrupt estate who concluded agreements with the administrator (including interest on postbankruptcy credits). The prebankruptcy claims are divided into the following three classes, with no distinction made between the creditors of each class: first-class claims include the claims of employees for wages and subsistence in the three years prior to bankruptcy; second-class claims include the claims of the state, i.e., taxes, fees, duties, and social security contributions arising in the three years prior to the declaration of bankruptcy; all other claims are regarded as third-class claims. Claims in each class are satisfied only if those in the previous class(es) are satisfied in full. Should it prove impossible to satisfy all claims listed in the same class, they are satisfied proportionately.

Compulsory Settlement

From the time of the declaration of bankruptcy up to the preparation of a distribution list, the debtor can propose to conclude the bankruptcy proceeding by means of a compulsory settlement. The application for a compulsory settlement, which can be made only by the debtor, must contain a settlement plan with details of the arrangements for the satisfaction of priority claims, information on the feasibility of the plan, and the notarized signatures of the persons who have agreed to guarantee the implementation of the settlement plan. The plan should also contain provisions for the repayment of at least one-third of the firm's nonpriority debts within one year. The settlement plan must be approved by the majority of creditors accounting for three-quarters of all filed claims (in value terms) and by the court, which has the discretion to reject a proposal for compulsory settlement in certain circumstances even if the creditors approve it.[14]

The bankruptcy law also requires the court to ascertain the *honest intention* of the bankrupt firm applying for the compulsory settlement procedure. This is an important measure designed to dissuade irresponsible managers from using the settlement procedure to buy time and postpone the inevitable—even though it injects an element of subjective judgment into the procedure and makes it more cumbersome. There have been cases in which noncompliance with this provision has resulted in creditors mounting successful appeals and nullifying the compulsory settlement decision.[15]

If the court confirms the compulsory settlement, the debtor is able to manage his property again, and the rights curtailed by the declaration of bankruptcy proceedings are restored. Although the initiation of bankruptcy procedures and the intervention of the administrator will have disrupted the normal business of the firm, the debtor will still have a chance to concentrate on the fulfillment of the settlement plan and avoid liquidation.

The Implementation of Bankruptcy Legislation

Although the bankruptcy law came into effect in full force in April 1993, a number of bankruptcies had been filed and a small number of bankruptcy declarations issued by the courts, with the agreement of the founding ministries, before that date. Table 5.1 shows the total number of firms in various stages of the bankruptcy proceedings in the Czech Republic from 1992 to 1996.

Table 5.1
Number of Firms in Bankruptcy Proceedings, 1992–96

Period	1992	1993	1994	1995	1996	Total 1992–96
No. of filings for bankruptcy	350	1098	1816	2393	2990	8647
No. of bankruptcy declarations (by courts)	5	60	288	480	719	1552
No. of settlements	–	1	2	2	6	11
No. still in protection period	–	–	–	–	3	3
No. still in process	234	688	937	1312	1404	4575
Other solutions[a]	111	349	589	599	858	2506

[a] These include referrals to other legal bodies and rejections (mainly on the ground of insufficient funds to cover the cost of proceedings).

Source: Ministry of Economy of The Czech Republic, 1996.

A number of observations should be made in connection with this table. First, unlike the situation in Hungary, there was no great rush of bankruptcy filings when the bankruptcy law came into effect. The main reason for this is that the Czech law, unlike its Hungarian equivalent, does not require managers to file for bankruptcy following a default on payments. Second, despite the previous observation, the number of bankruptcy applications (filings) rose gradually but significantly after 1993. Third, there is a massive gap between the number of filings and the number of court declarations, indicating the slowness of the legal procedures as well as the limited processing capacity of the legal system (more on this later). The number of cases pending in the early legal process has remained very high. Fourth, because of the restrictive nature of the settlement procedure, the number of settlements remained very

Table 5.2
The Legal Form of Firms in Bankruptcy Declarations

Legal form	1993	1994	1995	1996	Growth (%)		
					1994	1995	1996
Limited companies	22	139	245	415	532	76	41
Individual proprietorships	11	82	140	147	645	71	5
State-owned enterprises	11	26	25[a]	33	136	-4	32
Joint-stock companies	8	20	29	72	150	45	148
Agricultural coops	4	11	24	29	175	118	20
Other coops	4	7	14	11	75	100	0
Partnerships	0	3	3	12	–	0	300
Total	60	288	480	719	380	69	50

[a] The status of one of the state-owned companies had changed in this year.

Source: Ministry of Economy of The Czech Republic, 1996.

low. In fact, because of the complications of this option, some of the settlement cases were subsequently converted to liquidation.[16]

As one would expect, small private companies (limited companies and individual proprietorships) formed since the beginning of transition constitute the bulk of bankruptcy filings. The break-down of bankruptcy declarations according to the legal status of bankrupt firms in the 1993–95 period is shown in table 5.2. This is the sector of the economy characterized by high levels of entry and exit. On the other hand, the number of larger companies (state-owned enterprises and joint-stock companies, some of which were privatized firms) embarking on this process has been relatively small. Unlike Hungary, the number of bigger units going into bankruptcy has remained relatively small, though increasing rapidly in 1996, accounting for 32 percent of bankruptcy declarations in 1993, 16 percent in 1994, 11 percent in 1995, and 15 percent in 1996. These figures reflect the economic and political strength of larger companies, the accommodating policies employed by the government in early 1990s to protect large state-owned firms from bankruptcy during the privatization process, and the high-risk nature of small private firms. Companies privatized in the second wave of voucher privatization were excluded from bankruptcy proceedings until after the distribution of their shares in early 1995. Only then was it possible for their creditors or managers to embark on the bankruptcy process, their numbers appearing in the 1995 and 1996 columns of table 5.2. The sharp increase in the bankruptcy of joint-stock companies in 1996 should be largely attributed to this group of companies. Most of the bankruptcy declarations of state-owned enterprises relate to those in the process of liquidation, initiated by their liquidators (more on this later). Agricultural and other types of cooperatives (producer and consumer) and partnerships constituted a less important component of bankruptcies. Their share of the total has fallen from 13 percent in 1993 to 7 percent in 1996.

Shortcomings of the Bankruptcy Law

With the progress of large-scale privatization, the creditor-led bankruptcy process will gradually become the main form of exit in the Czech Republic and will be increasingly relied on to regulate the affairs of financially distressed firms. Given this fact and despite much downsizing, the restructuring process is still not complete in most Czech enterprises, and financial distress will continue to be a major problem for some time to come; it is crucial that the exit mechanism operates speedily and effectively. This mechanism must be able to simplify the exit of nonviable enterprises and, at the same time, facilitate the reorganization of financially distressed enterprises that may have a viable future under different organizational or managerial regimes. Exit, however, is hampered by a number of serious shortcomings related to the design of the bankruptcy law and the transitional environment within which enterprises operate.

Obligation to File for Bankruptcy

Given the underdeveloped nature of financial markets and the lack of accurate information on the financial status of firms, it is unlikely that all stakeholders become quickly aware of a firm's financial distress. It is therefore important that the bankruptcy procedures should ensure the speedy production and dissemination of information for the benefit of creditors and financial markets.[17] In general, the Czech bankruptcy code does not encourage the production and dissemination of information; for example, until June 1996, when the new amendments came into force, the Czech code did not include an obligation on the part of managers to declare overindebtedness and to file for bankruptcy. The managers' obligation to file for bankruptcy at the appropriate moment is a major step in providing creditors and markets with the most crucial piece of information and in counterbalancing the prevailing information asymmetry.[18] Managers, motivated by the opportunity to earn higher incomes, to lead their company in the postprivatization period, and to establish their own position in the managerial labor market have little incentive to initiate the bankruptcy process on their own volition.[19] Such a step would bring their reign to an end and undermine their objectives. What is potentially even more costly is that, in the face of financial difficulties, managers may embark on less prudent policies and undertake highly risky investment projects in order to save their own jobs. This is why in most market economies, in addition to well-functioning financial markets, the managers are under a legal obligation to declare insolvency and enter the bankruptcy process within a two- or three-week period (see chapter 2).

Bias Against Reorganization

The conditions for reorganization as specified by the bankruptcy law—the satisfaction of 45 percent of nonpriority claims in two years under the ordinary settlement and 33 percent in one year under the compulsory settlement procedures—are very strict, making this option an unlikely outcome of the bankruptcy process.[20] With many Czech firms suffering from high levels of interenterprise debt in their early stages of transition, the prohibitive conditions for settlement make the rehabilitation of financially troubled enterprises rather difficult and may result in the closure of many firms that otherwise might have been able to survive under less restrictive conditions.

The bias against reorganization has its origin in the German bankruptcy code (on which the Czech law is largely based) and its consequences have been widely acknowledged—so that the new German insolvency code coming into effect in 1999 will include measures aimed at improving the possibility of reorganization. The aggregate data on bankruptcy filings (table 5.1) and the result of our own sample survey show that very few bankruptcy filings have resulted in a settlement. In fact, in a number of cases where debtors and creditors had initially reached settlement agreements backed by the courts, they failed to complete the settlement process and had to revert back to the liquidation option of the bankruptcy law.

The tendency against reorganization is compounded by the fact that the Czech bankruptcy code does not allow the possibility of creditors proposing a settlement plan. It has been pointed out that, in some cases, creditors may be willing and able to inject new capital in the firm in return for equity or other guarantees, thus preventing liquidation. Creditors are more likely to be willing to propose a settlement plan in the context of a formal process when all (or most) creditors are involved and an administrator acts as an arbitrator. In addition to the bankruptcy law's bias against reorganization, until recently tax laws also tended to discourage settlements by not allowing the losses arising from a settlement to be written off against profits, thus reducing the tax liabilities of creditors.[21]

Excessive Court Involvement

The bankruptcy process as a whole is excessively court based, and the administrator is required to report to and get the approval of the court on too many occasions. Given the shortage of trained judges and other court personnel who could appreciate and handle complex financial issues, a high degree of court involvement will seriously limit the processing capacity of the system. In a country with an underdeveloped legal system, as Franks, Nyborg, and Torous point out, the bankruptcy code "should attempt to avoid or minimize court procedures."[22] Once the court passes the bankruptcy resolution and appoints an agent to oversee the process, the responsibility for pursuing the case should be transferred to the agent. Being made personally liable for actions that affect the interest of creditors, the agent will be subject to serious legal sanctions. The Czech Republic may draw appropriate lessons from the Hungarian bankruptcy proceedings where the bulk (over 90 percent) of reorganizations were speedily completed without the substantive involvement of the court or the presiding judge (see chapter 6).

The Remuneration of Administrators

The administrators appointed by the court to complete the bankruptcy process have extensive discretion over the assets of an enterprise and play a major role in facilitating or hindering the exit process. The prevailing uncertainty, asymmetric information, and difficulties of monitoring the agents, which can only be expected of real owners with sufficient information, give rise to a classic "principal–agent" problem and all its welfare implications. Until June 1996, the administrator's remuneration was based on a fixed schedule, subject to a not-too-generous maximum limit and was paid only at the end of the bankruptcy process.[23] Consequently, the administrator's incentive to maximize the realized value of assets and bring the case to a speedy and satisfactory conclusion was very weak. Furthermore, as the first group of administrators went through the procedures and their experience became known, few new lawyers showed any interest in taking on administratorships.[24] Also, those who had already accepted the post did not treat bankruptcy work as their priority and did not afford it their full and proper attention. The unsatisfactory reward system created conditions for and encourages self-interested and opportunistic behavior by the agents—the disposal of assets and diversion of value for personal gain.

The principal–agent literature makes it clear that the interests of agents may be closely aligned with those of their principals (creditors or owners) by the use of an appropriate remuneration formula and the strengthening of the rules governing their duties. An improved formula linking the administrator's remuneration to the realized value of assets as well as the speed of completion is essential for creating the right incentive mechanism. An efficient administrator would then aim at maximizing the discounted present value of the firm's assets. Naturally, there is a trade-off between the duration of the bankruptcy or liquidation process and the value of assets realized. The administrator, by virtue of his position and the information at his disposal, is in a position to make the appropriate judgment about this trade-off. However, the optimum decision on the realized value of assets over time would be made only if the administrator has a clearly defined interest in maximizing the discounted value of the firm's assets over a short period of time.

This shortcoming was recognized by the government, and the law was eventually amended in 1996. According to the amendments, which came into effect in June 1996, the administrator's remuneration has changed to a more generous system composed of a fixed remuneration supplemented by a variable component depending on the value of realized assets.

Creditor Passivity

Creditors are the most influential agents of the exit process, with the effectiveness of this process closely related to their willingness to press the debtors for the satisfaction of their claims. The unwillingness of creditors to pursue the debtors undermines the operation of the bankruptcy constraint, weakens the discipline of market forces, and slows down the process of exit and resource reallocation. Transition economies suffer from the "creditor passivity" phenomenon, which has been discussed at length in the literature on transition.[25] In the period under consideration, the creditors, which are other enterprises and banks, have often been state-owned entities with weak incentives to push the debtor into bankruptcy. The weak incentives are due to the persistence of soft budget constraints for creditors themselves, especially state-owned banks, and the long established commercial and personal relationships between the managerial personnel of creditors and debtors.[26] Many creditors and debtors have been heavily dependent on each other because of the socialist system of tying supplier and customer enterprises together. This interdependence was particularly strong in the early stages of transition as firms did not have sufficient time to establish links with new suppliers and customers.

The creditor passivity phenomenon also exists among private creditors where the incentive to pursue debt collection is much stronger than among publicly owned creditors. For them, trying to reach an informal work-out, even using "specialized" firms to put physical and moral pressure on the debtor, is preferable to resorting to courts and filing bankruptcy, given the prospect of a long delay and potentially little return.

The oligopolistic structure of the banking system also contributed to the absence of a strong desire by banks to pursue their debtors. The few large banks dominating the financial markets, which still remain fully or partially state owned and thus sheltered, have been able to maintain high margins despite the poor performance of a considerable proportion of their loans to enterprises. In some cases, banks did not wish to bankrupt their debtors as this would have had a direct impact on their own net worth.[27] In other cases, banks preferred to obtain collateral on new loans rather than embarking on the bankruptcy process, thus enabling themselves to operate outside the bankruptcy law and to seize the assets of a debtor if its condition deteriorated. Furthermore, for many enterprises, banks are not just their creditors but also, through the privatization investment funds, their indirect shareholders. This dual interest weakens the banks' incentive to push the debtor firms into bankruptcy.[28]

The expectation of a bailout by the government was another reason for creditor passivity. Despite the government's repeated declarations to the contrary, many creditors (especially banks) expected some form of intervention in favor of creditors holding bad debts. The Czech Government had indeed embarked on this type of rescue operation in 1991, and governments in other transition economies have done so as well. Many banks believed that the political fallout of large-scale bankruptcies would be too serious for the government to contemplate and continued to behave passively in relation to their debtor enterprises.

The great uncertainty associated with the transition period has been another contributing factor. Sometimes, creditors genuinely expect that the position of the debtor will change in the near future and believe that it is in their interest to wait rather than embark on the bankruptcy process. In other cases, the creditors believe that, in their particular circumstances, they would receive very little if their debtor enters the bankruptcy process—especially as a third-class creditor—and therefore prefer to behave passively.

Creditor passivity, of course, is a phenomenon particular to the period of early transition and will gradually diminish as the privatization of banks gets underway and the restrictions on the entry of foreign banks are relaxed. In fact, we can already observe a gradual change in the more recent period, following the (partial) privatization of banks and the opening of the banking markets to foreign competition.[29] In the more recent period, foreign banks, particularly German and Austrian, have been willing to extend credit to Czech firms from across the border. This has increased the competitive pressure on banks and has contributed to their increased willingness to take action against defaulting enterprises. Unlike the earlier period, banks are now becoming much more active in pursing their claims against defaulting enterprises in bankruptcy courts. At the same time, they are demanding a high degree of collaterialization, of the order of 125 percent to 200 percent, often in the form of real estate, before extending credit to enterprises.[30] Creditors operating in competitive markets cannot afford to be passive.

Characteristic Features of Firms in Bankruptcy: Results of a Sample Survey

A comprehensive register of bankruptcies, with information on the different features of firms in various stages of the bankruptcy process, is not available in the Czech Republic. Bankruptcy is dealt with by regional courts and only the very basic legal information (name of the company, address, ownership of the company and its legal form, dates, and the name and address of the bankruptcy administrator) is kept in court registers across the country. So far, the Ministry of Justice and courts have resisted all attempts to create a comprehensive national database. Only the Ministry of Economy has indirectly attempted to collect some aggregate data on the progress of the bankruptcy process, but this data does not include any information on size, assets, liabilities, and other important features of these companies.[31] In the absence of detailed information, we have used a sample survey to investigate the characteristics of firms in bankruptcy.

The Sample and its Composition

We contacted all registered administrators in the areas of Prague and Central Bohemia (eighty administrators in total) and invited them to participate in the survey. These administrators cover two of the eight administrative regions in the country, but about half the total number of enterprises have their head offices located in these two regions. Consequently, we expected to include a wide range of enterprises, differeing in size, ownership, legal form, and industrial activity. Eighteen of those contacted agreed to cooperate; others either did not respond or maintained that their information was of a confidential nature, and therefore they could not help with the survey. In autumn 1995, all eighteen administrators were interviewed in connection with the company they were representing at the time and also asked to complete a questionnaire. In some cases, the questionnaires were left with the interviewees to be completed later and returned by post. Our analysis is based on sixteen of the eighteen questionnaires and interviews which contained sufficient usable information—with the other two excluded for a variety of reasons, particularly for poor or insufficient quantitative information. Because of the way our sample was identified, the survey concentrated on companies in the bankruptcy process, i.e., they had not completed the process at the time of our interviews, although one was indeed through the process soon after our interview. It is possible to identify some of the important aspects of the bankruptcy process by studying this particular sample.

The most noteworthy feature of the bankruptcy process highlighted by our interviewees was the dearth of information, particularly financial, available to the administrators upon their appointment. The reason was relatively obvious: in many cases, the administrators took over when most of the managerial staff had already left the company, some of the owners (in the case of private entrepreneurs) had disappeared, assets had been misused and partially siphoned off, and financial details were either unknown or deliberately destroyed. Only in some cases, where liquidators had been in charge before the bankruptcy filing, were a minimum amount of accounting and financial documents maintained and the disappearance of assets prevented.

The following table summarizes the ownership forms and the activities of enterprises in the sample. Five of the companies, including two agricultural cooperatives, had gone through or were in the process of privatization at the time of filing for bankruptcy.

Table 5.3
Composition of the Sample of Firms in Bankruptcy According to Activity and Ownership

Type	Agriculture	Industry	Trade	Total
State owned	–	1	2	3
Private, of which:		3	7	10
Limited co. (domestic)	–	–	5	5
Limited co. (foreign)	–	1[a]	2[b]	3
Joint-stock co.	–	2	–	2
Cooperative	3	–	–	3
Total	3	4	9	16

[a] With 90% foreign ownership.
[b] One with 100% and one with 80% foreign ownership.
Source: Based on survey results.

Progress of Bankruptcy Proceedings

The firms in the sample had entered the bankruptcy proceedings between 1991 and 1995 and have gone through various stages of this process. As already mentioned, only one firm completed the process in 1995, soon after our interviews. Table 5.4 summarizes the progress of the sample firms since entering the bankruptcy process.

Following the declaration of bankruptcy by courts, all sixteen companies followed the liquidation option of the bankruptcy code. The total absence of any settlement outcome should not come as a surprise since, in the population as a whole too, this option is hardly ever undertaken (see table 5.1). Another feature of the table worth noting is the

Table 5.4
Progress of Bankruptcy Proceedings

Stages of proceedings	1991	1992	1993	1994	1995
First signs of bankruptcy[a]	1	3	5	4	1
Filing for bankruptcy	0	1	5	7	3
Declaration of bankruptcy by courts	0	1	3	7	5
Settlements	0	0	0	0	0
Completion of bankruptcy (through liquidation)	0	0	0	0	1

[a] Not available for 2 firms.
Source: Based on survey results.

length of the proceedings—some companies have been in the process for at least five years. One of the companies completed the procedure in October 1995 but was still not deleted from the Companies Register; another was expected to complete the process by October 1996.[32] The lengthy liquidation process in the Czech Republic compares very unfavorably with that in Hungary which takes about two years (see chapter 6).

Initiation of Bankruptcy Procedures

The bankruptcy proceeding was initiated by liquidators in eight cases, by creditors in seven cases, and by the owner in one case. It may be possible to differentiate between an "orderly" process, most of those filed by the liquidators, and a "disorderly" process, those filed by creditors or owners. In general, administrators dealing with the latter type had access to little detailed information about the financial position of the company and its creditors and faced a much more difficult task. In contrast, those dealing with the former type of bankruptcy already had the list of creditors, liabilities, and assets prepared for them. None of the administrators were former liquidators.

Causes of Bankruptcy

The administrators identified both "formal" and "real" causes of company bankruptcies. Formal causes refer to those stated by the applicant at the time of filing for bankruptcy. However, the administrators often reached the conclusion that other reasons, which the applicants may not have wished to disclose to the court formally, may have accounted for bankruptcy. These are referred to as the real causes. Table 5.5 identifies the causes of bankruptcy for the firms in the sample.

Overindebtedness, i.e., the value of a firm's assets falling short of its liabilities, was identified as the most frequent cause of bankruptcy filings. However, this fact may neither be obvious to others nor come to light easily; in underdeveloped financial markets, the actual value of assets is generally not known to creditors.[33] It is interesting to note that a default on payment was the cause of bankruptcy in only a small number of cases and, within this category, nonbank creditors were more active than bank creditors in pursuing their claims against the debtors. This is a reflection of creditor passivity to which we have already referred. The less active role played by banks in pursuing their claims should not come as a surprise as the incentive of banks to pursue their claims has been rather weak, particularly in the period under considera-

Table 5.5
Formal and Real Causes of Bankruptcy

Formal Causes	No. of Firms	Real Causes	No. of Firms
Over-indebtedness	9	Incompetent management	6
Default on payment to other creditors	4	Secondary payment inability[a]	2
Default on payment to banks	2	Restitution	2
		Departure of qualified employees	1
Others[b]	1	Others[b]	5

[a] The inability to pay its creditors because customers have defaulted on their payment.
[b] Including deception, chain of bankruptcies, etc.

Source: Based on survey results.

tion (see our earlier discussion on creditor passivity). The nonbank creditors, on the other hand, rarely have collateral and feel that filing for bankruptcy may be the only way of recovering at least some of their claims. Another interesting feature of table 5.5 is how the real causes of bankruptcy differ from those stated in the official application to the courts. In particular, the role played by "incompetent management" is highlighted as a major real cause of bankruptcy by a large number of administrators.

Financial Aspects of Bankruptcy Procedures

Once formally appointed, the administrators will publicize the firm's bankruptcy and collect the relevant data on its financial position at the time of the bankruptcy declaration. They would also try to identify and estimate the value of the remaining assets and receivables of the firm. Table 5.6 shows the average values of assets and liabilities for the companies under consideration at the time the administrators took over company affairs.

As already mentioned, many of the administrators maintained that, at the time of their appointment, most high-level personnel with information about the financial position of their companies had left, and that it was thus not possible (or easy) to develop a clear financial picture. In some cases, incompetent or fraudulent personnel had destroyed financial information in order to hide their illegal activities.

While the table indicates that, at the time of filing for bankruptcy, the gap between the average values of liabilities and assets was only about 40 percent, this does not point to the likely rate of creditor satisfaction. Creditors normally receive about 50 percent of collectable receivables,

Table 5.6
Average Values of Assets and Liabilities of Sample Firms at the Time of Bankruptcy Declaration (Kč million)

Assets	**33.01**
of which:	
Receivables	9.09
of which: Collectable receivables	4.70
Liabilities	**54.18**
of which:	
Liabilities to state budget	2.30
Liabilities to suppliers	21.04
Liabilities to banks for credits	10.62
Liabilities to banks for interest	0.77
Liabilities to employees	1.38
Other liabilities	18.07

Source: Based on survey results.

which amounts to a very small share of their claims, and then wait for the liquidation of other assets and the distribution of the net realized value of assets. Given the priority of the state, employees, and collateralized creditors (mainly banks), ordinary creditors will hardly receive anything. In the one case that was completed in October 1995, all that was left for the creditors was the registered capital of the company, a nominal sum, but even this amount has not yet been fully received. This may be one of the ultimate reasons why creditors are not enthusiastic about pursuing a firm to the point of bankruptcy. They are aware that once a firm enters the bankruptcy proceedings, little value may be retrieved upon the completion of the process.

Another interesting feature of Czech firms in the bankruptcy process is the low value of their debts to the state, unlike in the Polish example. This feature confirms the commonly held view that Czech firms in general paid their taxes and other obligations to the state in spite of financial distress. It also reflects the fact that the state had the right to confiscate the firms' unpaid taxes and other dues directly from their bank accounts.

Enterprise Liquidation by Owners

The owners of an enterprise may decide to exit the market by using special provisions governing owner-led liquidation. This type of liquidation is initiated for a variety of reasons, including privatization, restitution, nonviability of the remaining parts of a company after partial privatization, and financial difficulties.[34] The owners (or managers) of a financially distressed company may, of course, embark on the exit process through the Law on Bankruptcy and Settlements, if they so wish. But, as we have already pointed out, until recently there was no legal obligation (or a strong incentive) for them to do so, and consequently the occurence of this type of exit has been rare. The liquidation procedures are particularly suitable for the regulation of the affairs of firms leaving the market for reasons other than financial distress.

The liquidation of state-owned companies is an established procedure going back to the socialist period. Until 1992, liquidation was governed by the provisions of the Economic Code (*Hospodarsky zakonik*) of 1964, last amended in 1990. But with the passage of the Commercial Code (*Obchodni zakonik*), which came into effect on January 1, 1992, the liquidation of state-owned as well as private companies has been conducted according to the new law.[35] In the Czech Republic, unlike some other transition economies, the liquidation process is available only to those entities that are solvent at the time they make the liquidation decision, i.e., they expect to meet the claims of all creditors. The liquidation provisions, therefore, are not open to companies whose liabilities exceed the expected value of their assets—such companies are expected to file for bankruptcy under the Bankruptcy and Settlement Act.

Once the liquidation decision is made, the owner (or the founding body) appoints a liquidator who is charged with the task of selling the assets of the company, either as a whole or piece by piece, and using the proceeds to meet the claims of its creditors.[36] The company's name in the Companies Register is amended by adding to it the suffix "in liquidation," and the liquidator takes over the responsibility for the affairs of the company and the disposal of its assets. The decision to put the company into liquidation and appoint a liquidator is then publicized for the benefit of all interested parties. The liquidator prepares a liquidation plan and, once the plan is approved by the owners, embarks on the process of asset disposal. If the proceeds from the disposal of assets are large enough, the liquidator would be able to complete his task without much difficulty, meeting the claims of all creditors and returning the surplus to the founding body or to the owners. A liquidation report is prepared for the owners that, once approved, enables the liquidator to delete the company's name from the Companies Register.

However, at any point during the liquidation process, the liquidator may realize that the actual or estimated value of assets falls short of the firm's liabilities. This may be completely independent of the company's actions, resulting, for example, from a fall in the price of such enterprise assets as real estate. The shortfall may come to light in the middle of the liquidation process or even after some of the creditors' claims have been met. Whatever the circumstance, once the liquidator realizes that the firm's liabilities exceed its assets, he is obliged by law to file for bankruptcy under the Law on Bankruptcy and Settlements, i.e., to convert from liquidation to bankruptcy. The liquidator will remain in charge until the court appoints a bankruptcy administrator to oversee the liquidation of the firm's assets and the satisfaction of its creditors.

The Implementation of Liquidation Procedures

The liquidation procedure has been extensively used, in conjunction with the privatization program, in the early period of transition. Large companies with complex liabilities and assets often were divided into several smaller units with clear asset and liability structures so that they could be privatized as debt-free (or low-debt) entities. One of these units retained the debts and financially troublesome assets of the original enterprise and remained under state ownership as the so-called "remaining state company" (*zbytkovy statni podnik*). Most of these were wound up through the liquidation process. At other times, although a company was initially chosen for privatization, early analysis had shown that there was little chance of a successful privatization being mounted, and therefore the liquidation proceedings were initiated. Liquidation is in fact a form of privatization whereby the company's assets are often sold or auctioned piece by piece to several private buyers. The main difference is in the destination of the resulting revenues: the revenues from privatization are collected by the Fund of National Property, while the revenues from liquidation are used to meet the claims of the company's creditors, with any surplus (liquidation profit) going to the founding body and eventually to the state.

Although a number of ministries and state organs such as municipalities and district authorities have been involved in the liquidation process, the bulk of state-enterprise liquidations have been initiated by the Ministry of Industry and Trade.[37] Since the beginning of transition, the Ministry of Industry and Trade has been responsible for state-owned establishments in mining, manufacturing (except food processing), trade, and construction activities, i.e., the bulk of state-owned enterprises in the economy. Also this ministry is the only state organization that publishes any information on the liquidation of enterprises under its control. Therefore, given that the Ministry of Industry and Trade covers the vast majority of enterprises entering this process, the data relating to its activities is a fairly close approximation of the total number of liquidations. By the end of 1994, some 256 enterprises under the ministry had entered the liquidation process. Of these, seventy-one completed the process with sixteen filing for bankruptcy. The remaining 185 remained in liquidation, pending the completion of the process.[38]

In so far as enterprises outside the jurisdiction of the Ministry of Industry and Trade are concerned, there is little information on the extent of owner-led liquidations. But the general impression of liquidation specialists is that the number of these liquidations is small. Similarly, there is no centralized information regarding the liquidation of private companies' even though it is estimated that some 10,000 sole proprietorships (very small companies) have been liquidated under these provisions. It is also suspected that some of these companies opt for liquidation as a means of defrauding the Treasury and their creditors.

Shortcomings of the Liquidation Procedures

On the whole, the liquidation process has been progressing satisfactorily, though rather slowly. This is partly due to the fact that, unlike bankruptcy, this process was not a new one introduced during the transition period. The liquidation process had been in existence under socialism, and the founding bodies were acquainted with the process and had probably used it before. Moreover, the liquidator usually takes control of an enterprise that is still an operating entity with employees who are well informed about the company's affairs and, unlike the bankruptcy administrator, he has better access to most of the information necessary for the completion of his liquidation task. Also, unlike the bankruptcy administrator, the liquidator is remunerated more generously and has a stronger incentive to maximize the realized value of assets. A liquidator is paid a monthly salary supplemented by a proportion (ranging from 0.05 percent to 1 percent) of the realized value of assets, subject to a maximum limit.[39] Even though this is more generous than that offered to administrators, the arrangement is still far from ideal because it does not generate a strong motivation to complete the process rapidly. Given that a liquidator may have several commissions at the same time, he will receive a substantial monthly income and will have little incentive to press for the speedy completion of his outstanding cases.

Furthermore, because the expected realized value of assets is never absolutely clear to creditors and even to owners, the liquidator is in a position to keep the firm in liquidation proceedings much longer than necessary by pretending that the value of the firm's assets exceeds that of its liabilities. The uncertainty about the expected value of assets actually gives rise to a major loophole in the liquidation proceedings that provides the liquidator with the opportunity to prolong a case far longer than necessary and treat creditors unequally. The liquidator may be able to continue to dispose of the company's assets and satisfy the claims of some creditors selectively, as long as he believes that the claims of all creditors will eventually be satisfied. Thus, favored creditors will receive some or all of their claims at the expense of other creditors, and the liquidator will continue to draw his monthly salary from the proceeds of asset disposal, postponing the eventual filing for bankruptcy. Early bankruptcy filing would certainly disadvantage the favored creditors and the liquidator. The fundamental problem lies in the fact that the creditors or founding bodies do not know if the realizable value of assets will or will not exceed the volume of liabilities, and the liquidator has no incentive to clarify this question. Except in cases where bankruptcy is obvious, he can always claim that the expected realizable value of assets is greater than the liabilities, and he is thus justified to continue his work.[40] For this reason, liquidators have received much criticism in the press for not widely publicizing their asset disposals widely and for selling the assets under their control to their favorite buyers at low prices.[41]

As in the case of creditor-led bankruptcy, the principal–agent problem involving liquidators may be mitigated by devising an appropriate remuneration formula, which takes into account both the length of the liquidation process and the realized value of enterprise assets, and strengthening of rules governing their actions. Moreover, the agents should be required to provide more information to creditors and owners and be held personally liable for any damages caused to other stakeholders during their period in office.

Another problem contributing to the lengthy duration of some liquidations is that, until recently, tax laws did not allow the write-down of debts by creditors to be treated as losses and written off against their profits, a problem similar to that faced by firms in bankruptcy trying to reach a settlement. This disadvantage has actually worked against any negotiated settlement of liquidation cases, sometimes forcing the liquidator to embark on the bankruptcy procedure. Since August 1, 1995, firms have been enabled, under certain complicated conditions, to write off against their profits some of the losses arising from write-downs. Further clarification and simplification of the rules governing write-downs is still needed.

Characteristics of Firms in Liquidation: Results of a Sample Survey

As with bankruptcies, there is no national register of firms in liquidation with detailed information on the characteristics of firms in different stages of this process. The data from the Ministry of Industry and Trade, to which we have already referred, are available only in a highly aggregated form, and it is not possible to identify the specific features of firms in different stages of liquidation. In order to highlight some of their characteristics, we conducted a survey of a small sample of firms in the liquidation process.

The Sample and its Composition

The population from which we obtained the sample was a group of over 200 firms under the control of the Ministry of Industry and Trade that had entered the liquidation process between 1992 and 1994. These firms were located in Prague, Central and Southern Bohemia, and the regions of Southern Moravia. The liquidators of these firms were invited to participate in the survey, but only fifteen responded positively to our invitation. In autumn 1995, these liquidators were interviewed and asked to complete a questionnaire, which, in some cases, was completed on their own and returned by post. Those companies that did not respond to our request were either unwilling to take part in the research or had already been wound up. As with the survey of firms in bankruptcy, due to the way our sample was identified and the data were collected, the survey, almost by definition, concentrated on companies in the liquidation process, i.e., those that had not completed the process at the time of our interviews. Companies that were liquidated before we attempted to communicate with them were automatically excluded from the sample. Nevertheless, as with the bankruptcy survey, it is possible to identify some important aspects of the liquidation process by studying this particular sample. Table 5.7 summarizes the ownership form and the activity of enterprises in the sample.

Table 5.7
Composition of the Sample of Firms in Liquidation According to Activity and Ownership

	Industry	Trade	Construction	Total
State-owned enterprise	2	11	1	14
Joint-stock co. (100% owned by state)	1	0	0	1
Total	3	11	1	15

Source: Based on survey results.

Of the companies under consideration, ten had gone through some form of privatization—five in small privatization, two by direct sale, two by auction, and one by the voucher scheme—where some parts of the original entity had been transferred to the private sector. Some parts of these companies had also been the subject of restitution claims as we have already mentioned, "remaining state company" parts of the original entity that had stayed under the ministry's control and were being liquidated. The other five companies had not gone through any form of ownership transfer.

Size Distribution of the Sample

Firms in the sample represented a cross section of different sizes, though most of them were remnants of medium to large firms, reflecting the composition of formerly state-owned companies. Although, in practice, many small private companies also go through liquidation proceedings, there is little information on these companies, and our sample did not include any of them. The following table shows the average and range of employment in the sample firms for the 1990–94 period.

Given that firms in our sample began filing for liquidation in 1992, it is clear that they had been undergoing a process of "splitting-off" (and downsizing) in the previous two years. The contraction speeded up

Table 5.8
Employment in the Sample Firms, 1990–94

Year	Average Employment	Range
1990	1535	45–4050
1991	1031	43–3430
1992	292	39–617
1993	164	1–502
1994	6	2–12

Source: Based on survey results.

during the liquidation proceedings, eventually reducing employment to near zero.

Initiation and Progress of Liquidation

All liquidations were initiated by the Ministry of Industry and Trade as the founding body of the enterprises. In four cases, the liquidation was initiated under the older Economic Code and the remaining eleven under the new Commercial Code.

The firms in the sample entered the liquidation process between 1992 and 1994 and have gone through various stages of this process since then. Table 5.9 summarizes the progress of the sample firms since entering the liquidation process. As already mentioned, none of these firms had completed the process at the time of our interviews (autumn 1995), indicating the slow pace of the liquidation proceedings—the average period in liquidation for the firms completing this process being over three years.

It should be noted that the physical liquidation of assets is not the end of the liquidation process. The company's name will not be deleted from the Companies Register until the liquidator has completed a report for the owner or the founding body and the latter has approved this report. The liquidator's incentive to complete the report for the owner and await its approval is not very strong. This is why the number of deletions from the Companies Register is much less than the number of companies where the disposal of assets has been completed. Also, disputes over restitution claims on real estate contribute to the prolongation of the liquidation process. Even if all claims against the company

Table 5.9
Progress of Liquidation Proceedings

Stages of proceedings	1992	1993	1994	1995	1996[a]
Liquidation decision made	8	5	2	–	–
Appointment of liquidation and entry into Companies Register	6	7	2	–	–
Publishing of liquidation decision	5	7	3	–	–
Liquidation plan prepared	6	6	1	1	1
Liquidation plan approved by the founder	5	6	1	1	2
Physical liquidation of assets completed	1	4	1	7	2
Company name deleted from Register				1	
Liquidator filed for bankruptcy				2	

[a] Estimates by liquidators.

Source: Based on survey results.

are satisfied, the liquidation proceedings can not be completed until the restitution claims are settled by a court—a process which also legitimizes the liquidators' prolonged incumbency.

Another point worth noting is that although the liquidators expected to complete most of the cases by 1995 or 1996, as shown in the seventh row of table 5.9, it was clear from the general discussion with the liquidators that the process always takes longer than expected. Therefore, estimates of the time required for the completion of the process should be treated with some caution.

Causes of Liquidation

The liquidators identified several factors as having contributed to the onset of the liquidation process (see table 5.10).

Essentially, the liquidation process had to be initiated for three main, sometimes interrelated, reasons: (1) due to the effects of privatization (and restitution) programs that separated parts of companies for transfer to the private sector; (2) due to a loss of competitiveness, i.e., the inability of firms to cope with new market conditions and a competitive environment; and (3) due to a deteriorating financial position resulting in an inability to meet financial obligations (see below). The case study of Zelenina Terezin (see the appendix) shows how the interaction of these factors resulted in the company's decline and liquidation.

Liquidators

The liquidators were mostly (in thirteen cases) drawn from outside the enterprise, usually from specialized consulting firms. In two cases, members of former management teams (insiders) were appointed as liquidators. This is unusual, particularly in comparison with the practice in

Table 5.10
Causes of Liquidation[a]

Causes	No. of Firms
Privatization of capital assets	6
Financial position of company	6
Loss of competitiveness	4
Restitution	2
Liquidation of founder[b]	2
Others	2

[a] Some respondents identified more than one cause.
[b] The original founder would have been amalgamated into the Ministry of Industry and Trade.
Source: Based on survey results.

established market economies where liquidators are always drawn from outside the company. Given the uncertainty and asymmetric information, the appointment of insiders is likely to increase the costs associated with the principal–agent relationship.

Financial Aspects of the Liquidation Procedures

Before the initiation of the liquidation process, the companies in the sample were generally solvent and, in the last financial year before liquidation, all but one had a positive net worth, i.e., the value of their assets exceeded their liabilities. Moreover, unlike firms in the bankruptcy sample, the liquidators took over these firms as going concerns with most of the information about their activities preserved. Consequently, we can compare the assets and liabilities of these firms more accurately than those in our bankruptcy sample. Table 5.11 shows the average values of assets and liabilities for the companies under consideration in the last financial year prior to the initiation of the liquidation process.

It is clear that, unlike the bankruptcy sample, firms in liquidation start with the value of their assets exceeding their liabilities and the expectation that creditors' claims will be largely satisfied—even though the position may change later during the course of liquidation. Banks followed by suppliers were the main creditors of these companies, with liabilities to the state and employees constituting only a small part of the total liabilities. In spite of the relatively healthy financial status indi-

Table 5.11
Average Assets and Liabilities of Sample Firms in the Last Financial Year Before the Initiation of Liquidation (Kč million)

Assets		**395.67**
of which:		
	Receivables	149.61
	of which: Collectable Receivables	50.33
Liabilities		**314.02**
of which:		
	Liabilities to banks for credits	187.86
	Liabilities to banks for interest	6.36
	Liabilities to suppliers	81.59
	Liabilities to budget	12.19
	Liabilities to employees	1.44
	Other liabilities	24.58

Source: Based on survey results.

cated by table 5.11, the underlying position was precarious and had deteriorated sufficiently during the following year to warrant entry into the liquidation process. The average realizable cash flow (the so-called collectable receivables) is very low in comparison with the average liabilities, giving rise to the speculation that some firms may not be able to convert more of their receivables to cash, and that it may not be possible to compensate all of their creditors; thus, the possibility of liquidators filing for bankruptcy. But, for a variety of reasons, the actual situation has not been as pessimistic as that suggested by the size of the collectable receivables, and it has not become necessary to embark on the bankruptcy alternative in the great majority of cases. First, liquidators can, and always do, negotiate with the creditors with a view to reducing their claims in return for a quicker settlement. With a credible threat of bankruptcy (and a long bankruptcy process with uncertain return at the end) in the background, most creditors would be willing to negotiate a reduction in their claims. In cases of "double collateralization" (which is not very uncommon), where a company has used an asset as collateral with more than one creditor, the creditors' claims become weaker, and they will be even more willing to lower their claims in return for a quicker settlement with the liquidator. Of course, unlike the bankruptcy process, the reduction in claims need not necessarily be proportionate for all creditors, creating the opportunity for favoritism and unfair treatment of some creditors by liquidators. Second, the liquidators do not immediately know how much of their assets can be converted to actual cash and therefore need not file for bankruptcy just because the amount of collectable receivables is very low. Third, given the method of their remuneration, liquidators have a vested interest in prolonging the liquidation process and may therefore argue that they expect to convert a greater part of the assets to cash and meet the claims of all creditors.

Once the liquidation process begins, the liquidator draws up a plan known as the "liquidator's budget", detailing the expected financial outcome of the process, including most importantly the expected realizable cash value from asset disposals and the expected payment to creditors following the negotiations referred to above. Table 5.12 summarizes the liquidators' budgets for the sample companies.

The "average expected value of assets" refers to what the liquidator expects to achieve through the asset disposal process, while the average "recognized liability" refers to the volume of liabilities that has been the subject of negotiated agreement between the liquidator and creditors.

Table 5.12:
Liquidators' Budgets for Sample Firms (expected flows, Kč million)

Assets (average expected value)	**323.5**
of which:	
domestic receivables	147.3
foreign receivables	0.4
movable property	80.2
real estate	95.6
Recognized liabilities (average expected value)	**258.7**
of which:	
collateralized liabilities	90.9
liabilities to the state	10.2
Cost of liquidation	24.4
Net 'profit' of liquidation	10.1
Total expected revenue from liquidation	**293.2**

Source: Based on survey results.

In only two firms, the expected cash value of assets was less than the recognized liabilities, resulting in the eventual filing for bankruptcy.

The penultimate row of table 5.12, "net profit of liquidation," shows the amount left for the owners at the end of the liquidation process. This is a relatively small proportion of the expected realizable value of assets (just over 3 percent) and compares rather poorly with the cost of liquidation (i.e., payment to the liquidator and his related costs), which amounted to 7.5 percent of the expected value of assets.[42] Although the net profit of liquidation is rather insignificant, it should be pointed out that the main purpose of the liquidation of state-owned companies is not to raise funds for the owners but to dispose of the company's assets and to meet the claims of its creditors.[43]

Satisfaction of Claims

While it is not possible to measure the satisfaction rate for different categories of creditors from the above tables, the information from our interviews provides us with an overall picture of creditor satisfaction. In five cases, all recognized claims were fully satisfied, and the same was expected for another four companies in near future. However, two companies had filed for bankruptcy, and the position of the remaining four was unclear at the time of the interviews (autumn 1995).

Concluding Remarks

The creditor-led bankruptcy process and owner-led liquidation procedures covering state-owned enterprises are the main formal mechanisms operating in the Czech Republic. The latter mechanism has been particularly important in the early stages of transition when the bulk of large and medium-sized enterprises were state owned. But with the progress of privatization, the need for state-enterprise liquidations will disappear, leaving the creditor-led bankruptcy process to become the principal vehicle of formal exit for financially distressed firms. Privately owned companies will be able to employ liquidation procedures when they wish to withdraw from a market.

The discussion of the implementation of the two processes and our analysis of two sample surveys have highlighted a number of issues that will be briefly summarized here. First, bankruptcy declarations were comparatively uncommon in the early period of transition in the Czech Republic. The accommodating policies, particularly the postponement of the implementation of the bankruptcy law, the absence of an obligation by managers to declare insolvency and default on debt, and creditor passivity account for the small number of bankruptcies. Second, bankruptcies are increasing rapidly and are expected to become the main form of exit in the near future. There are already indications that banks have become much more prudent in their lending policies (demanding very high collaterals) and more active in pursuing their claims against debtor enterprises. Third, the design of the bankruptcy law is still in need of improvement. A number of design shortcomings have already been dealt with—most recently through the amendments that came to force in June 1966. Further improvements to the bankruptcy law are, however, overdue, particularly in areas such as facilitating conditions for reorganization and reducing the extent of the court's involvement. Apart from the provisions of the bankruptcy law, the government should encourage and assist debtors and creditors to enter informal work-outs.

Fourth, the liquidation of state-owned enterprises has proceeded satisfactorily, with the bulk of the "remaining state enterprises," created during the process of privatization and restitution, liquidated. The liquidation procedures, too, need further improvement, particularly in connection with the remuneration of the liquidators. The legal loopholes that enable liquidators to postpone the declaration of bankruptcy and to treat creditors unequally should be closed. More importantly, the agents should be required to provide more transparent information to creditors and other stakeholders by widely publicizing their program for the disposal of assets and financial information.

Finally, we should briefly highlight the limited processing capacity of the system, arising from the underdeveloped nature of the judicial system and institutions. There are only seven courts across the country (one in Prague and Central Bohemia and six in other regions) handling bankruptcies. The number of judges familiar with the economic and financial aspects of bankruptcy is very limited. At the beginning of 1996, some 450 administrators (280 of them based in Prague and Central Bohemia) were on the court registers and about 500 on the list of liquidators. These figures refer to those who had gone through a training course by the end of 1995, not necessarily to the numbers actually engaged in bankruptcy or liquidation work; in particular, they refer to administrators who are almost certainly involved in other activities.

The human capital involved in the legal process needs continual improvement. The training of judges, administrators, and liquidators in economic and financial matters will play an important role in improving the efficacy of the judicial system. It is also necessary that liquidators and administrators are properly trained and formally licensed as a profession, in much the same way as insolvency practitioners in the United Kingdom or their equivalents in other countries. Liquidators and administrators should belong to a professional organization that provides them with legal and financial support, regulates their activity, and acts as their representative in relation to government organizations. Such an organization may also help in setting up or soliciting professional indemnity insurance for its members. Although these agents are personally liable for their actions and may be sued by stakeholders adversely affected by their decisions, the absence of professional indemnity insurance means that claimants are unlikely to recover their claims from the agents' regular income. Finally, the procedure for the disqualification of agents involved in fraud or malpractice should be introduced urgently and sanctioned by law.

Appendix

Zelenina Terezin: a State-Owned Enterprise in Liquidation

Zelenina Terezin was a fruit and vegetable company engaged in wholesale and retail trade and some processing activities. It had established a wide network linking agricultural cooperatives, with consumers in northern and eastern Bohemia, with its headquarters in Terezin. At the beginning of the transition period, the company had eighteen branches and over 400 retail shops that employed about 1,000 people and had a turnover of Kč 200 million. The transition process led to the break-up of the vertically integrated network of wholesale and retail trade and to the gradual decline of the company. The liquidation process began in March 1993 and was completed in 1997. At times, it seemed that the process might be converted from liquidation to bankruptcy due to the low value of the remaining assets relative to outstanding claims. Five factors can be identified as having been of particular importance in the decline of the enterprise and its lengthy liquidation.

The most important of these factors was the loss of a captive market brought about by small privatization and restitution programs in 1990 and 1991, which led to the privatization of the company's retail shops. A second factor was increased competition resulting from the liberalization of foreign trade, allowing retail shops to diversify their sources of supply and to offer imported fruit and vegetables to their customers. However, the transitional shocks caused by a change in market conditions cannot on their own explain why the firm was eventually forced to exit the market.

Wholesalers with a wide distribution network and significant contacts and facilities have an important place in a modern economy and can survive, profitably, alongside a competitive retail network and alongside foreign competition. Had the company been able to respond to new market conditions by improving the use of its facilities and formulating an effective marketing strategy, it might have survived. After all, even though the retail shops had changed ownership, they could still have retained their links with Zelenina if they had been offered a wide range of supplies at competitive prices. Furthermore, Zelenina itself could have become a distributor of imported fruit, vegetables and other food products. Given that it had freezing, refrigerating, and storage facilities, which many new importers lacked, it could have entered the wholesale market with a good chance of survival.

Thus, three other factors are of particular importance in the decline of this particular enterprise: (1) the inability of management to see, early on in the transition period, the direction of change and the nature of the future market; (2) the absence of real and active ownership interests and the resulting uncertainty; and (3) the loss of skilled employees due to better opportunities elsewhere. By the time the founding body or the nominal owner of the firm, the Ministry of Trade and Industry, felt obliged to intervene by appointing a new director to the management board in late 1992, the company's financial position had already deteriorated, and its losses were mounting. The creditor banks were refusing further credit to the enterprise, and the continuation of its operations was becoming increasingly difficult.

The new director was appointed with the expressed aim of privatizing the firm. In fact, the management board had already submitted a privatization project in mid-1992 so that the enterprise could participate in the first wave of the voucher privatization program, but the enterprise found itself in financial difficulties before its privatization project was approved. In January 1993, the new director together with the rest of the management board recommended the liquidation of the company. At this stage, the company's assets (estimated at Kč 250 million) exceeded its liabilities (approximately Kč 150 million), and a rapid liquidation would have led to the satisfaction of all claimants. But the ensuing liquidation process turned out to be much lengthier than expected. Much valuable time was wasted in procedural delays: a delay in the approval of Zelenina's privatization projects by the Ministry of Privatization of eight months, a delay in receiving confirmation from Ministry of Trade and Industry to liquidate the company of two months, a delay in the registration of the firm's liquidation and its liquidator in the courts of six months, and a delay caused by a dispute between the parliament and ministries over the rights of the latter to approve the direct sale of parts of enterprises in liquidation without parliamentary scrutiny (causing the postponement of all direct sales until January 1994). Such delays not only resulted in increasing debts and accumulated interest but also created an atmosphere of uncertainty under which the disposal of assets was almost impossible. By January 1994, many of the deals negotiated by the liquidator had fallen through and had to be renegotiated because the potential buyers had not been able to withstand these procedural delays.

Some of the claims against the firm were settled during 1994, but the overall settlement process was hindered by the continuous reduction in the value of the enterprise's assets due to the falling prices of land and buildings and by a rise in interest payments. At the same time, the liquidator was unable to secure the agreement of the creditors for a proportionate reduction in their claims followed by a settlement because of an anomaly in Czech tax laws (at the time) that prevented creditors from writing off such losses against their taxable income. By early 1995, the expected value of the firm's assets appeared to have fallen below the value of outstanding claims, and the liquidator was preparing to file for bankruptcy, which would have prolonged the process of asset disposal further and increased the losses to all parties concerned. However, the liquidator believed that changes in the external environment, such as finding buyers interested in the company's assets, might alter the fortunes of the company and those of its creditors. In the course of 1995 and 1996, therefore, she concentrated her efforts on finding suitable buyers for the assets and indeed succeeded in doing so. By early 1997, the agreed claims of all creditors were satisfied, and a small surplus was left for the ministry. It was expected that the company's name would be deleted from the register in August 1997. Of course, it has to be pointed that the liquidator was a major beneficiary of the decision to continue in the search for buyers, as opposed to filing for bankruptcy in early 1995.

Cottex Hronov: an Enterprise in the Process of Bankruptcy

Cottex Hronov was created in 1989 when its predecessor Tepna, a large, well-established textile complex with a good reputation, was broken up into smaller units for the purpose of privatization. It began its operation as an independent state-owned enterprise, with relatively modern plants, equipment, and technology in 1990. The company employed a highly skilled workforce of over 1,700 and had a turnover of Kč 530 million. In the first two years of operation, its performance was satisfactory, operating at a profit and undergoing some restructuring. Before 1989, the former parent company used to export 60 percent of its output to CMEA countries. But with the collapse of the CMEA trading arrangements, Cottex concentrated its efforts on exporting to Western markets. It used the services of a specialist foreign trade company and succeeded in exporting 80 percent of its output to Western markets. Cottex participated in the first wave of the voucher privatization program with 90 percent of its shares exchanged for vouchers by some 2,000 shareholders, individuals, and funds.

The bankruptcy of Cottex was the result of several intertwined factors: (1) a weak mechanism of corporate governance, (2) managerial opportunism, (3) incompetent and negligent management, (4) the lax attitudes of the banking system reminiscent of the soft budget constraint regime that allowed the firm to build massive debts and, (5) the weak and misunderstood bankruptcy procedures.

Although the new company succeeded in absorbing the initial shocks of transition, the incumbent management was unable to sustain the company's early success. The enterprise lacked a unified management and clear orientation and could not withstand the internal conflicts caused by divisions within the management team. A dominant group within the management team pursued self-interested policies to the detriment of the company. The general manager, who had obtained extraordinary powers from the supervisory board to act on its behalf, negotiated credits beyond the ability of the company and used all assets as collateral against bank credits (some were even used twice).

The company registered its first loss in 1992, which increased drastically in 1993. In an attempt to reduce losses and raise funds, the management embarked on a policy of reducing inventories through massive price cuts. The management also severed the firm's links with its foreign trade intermediary and tried to conduct its own foreign trade by operating through a large number of retail outlets and offering them large discounts. The propriety of these discounts to retailers has since then been questioned, particularly in the light of the close relationships between some members of the management team and some retailers, as well as the fictitious nature of a few retailers. It is now clear that at least some of the managers were siphoning off the company's assets (inventories) to retailers with whom they had developed informal associations—the then marketing manager of the firm is now employed by one of the retailers. However, despite the involvement of the police and Interpol, no charges have been brought against any of the former employees, and the fictitious retailers have not been traced.

Cottex provides a typical example of opportunistic behavior by managers facilitated by a weak corporate governance mechanism—both characterizing the early stages of transition. Indeed, in the final half of 1993, there was no corporate governance structure at work. The Fund of National Property was more concerned with overseeing the voucher privatization scheme than with the affairs of one of its several thousand companies. Despite being alerted by the firm's supervisory board in May 1993, the fund did not have the time, resources, or will to intervene in the affairs of one company. The new owners (individuals and privatization investment funds) had not received their shares and could not intervene; in fact, they did not attempt to act even after they received their shares. The absence of the influence of owners in the crucial pre-privatization period was the most fundamental cause of the company's bankruptcy. Of course, the willingness of creditors to extend additional credit to the firm without investigating its credit worthiness facilitated the management's pursuit of their disastrous policies.

By 1993, the management's behavior had become increasingly negligent as well as incompetent. With the volume of debt reaching twice the value of assets, banks eventually refused to extend further credit to the firm, triggering a process that led to the dismissal of the general manager by the supervisory board in July 1993. Then one of the firm's smaller creditors filed a petition for default on the payment of Kč 1.5 million, thus setting in motion the initial stage of the bankruptcy process. Neither the company nor its management consultants could utilize the breathing space provided by the three-month legal protection period to find a solution to its problems. Thus in December 1993, the regional court initiated the bankruptcy process, appointed an administrator, and put the company under his supervision.

The appointment of an administrator, the identification of creditors, the formation of a creditors' committee, and the search for a buyer for the company as a whole took nearly a year. Although a potential buyer was found, the banks involved in the process were not willing to provide him with the necessary credit. The creditors' committee, made up of several banks and three of the largest creditors, rejected the piecemeal sale of the company's assets. This is hardly surprising given that the minimum price tag placed on the firm by the court would not cover even half of the firm's liabilities or even its debt to banks. In January 1995, the value of the firm's assets (as determined by the court) stood at Kč 250 million, and its liabilities at Kč 540 million.

The banks were ambivalent about the disposal of the firm's assets. On the one hand, they wished to sell the enterprise in one piece in order to maximize the income from asset disposition; on the other hand, they were not prepared to facilitate this sale by providing some form of credit for a potential purchaser. The most likely explanation for this ambivalence is that the banks were waiting for the government to intervene by writing off some of the company's debts. Nonbank creditors represented on the creditors' committee had no interest to settle either. With banks having used all assets as collateral, the nonbank creditors would not have received anything from the proceeds of the settlement.

Given the banks' position and the difficulties of disposing of the company as a whole, the court's minimum price for the firm was eventually lowered and the piece-by-piece sale of assets, expected to take two to three years to complete, was contemplated and discussed by the administrator in January 1995. In fact, this provided additional incentive for the potential buyer(s) to wait as long as possible in order to gain a maximum advantage.

The plan to sell the assets piece by piece was changed later in 1995 when a Malaysian company (Hulaon) appeared on the scene as an interested buyer. After lengthy negotiations, Hulaon purchased the company as a whole and soon restarted the production process, employing most of the former employees. The price paid by Hulaon and the extent to which creditors' claims were satisfied have not been disclosed. Cottex Hronov's name has been erased from the register of companies. The lengthy bankruptcy process led to the dissatisfaction of the administrator who felt he had spent far too much time on this project. He maintained that this would be his first and last administratorship!

Having entered the bankruptcy procedure, the main problem facing Cottex was the absence of strong incentives for creditors and the administrator to complete the process speedily so that the social cost of bankruptcy is minimized.

References

Aghion, P., O. Blanchard, and R. Burgess. 1993. The behavior of state firms in Eastern Europe: Pre-privatization. Working paper no. 12 (October). London: European Bank for Reconstruction and Development.

Blejer, Mario I. and Fabrizio Coricelli, eds. 1995. *The Making of Economic Reform in Eastern Europe: Conversations with Leading Reformers in Poland, Hungary and the Czech Republic.* Aldershot: Edward Elgar.

Brom, K. and M. Orenstein. 1994. The privatized sector in the Czech Republic: Government and bank control in a transitional economy. *Europe-Asia Studies* 46, no. 6: 893–928.

Capek, A. and P. Mertlik. 1996. Organizational change and financial restructuring in Czech manufacturing enterprises 1990–1995. Prague: Czech National Bank, Institute of Economics. Mimeographed.

Carlin, W., J. Van Reenen, and T. Wolfe. 1994. Enterprise restructuring in the transition: An analytical survey of the case study evidence from Central and Eastern Europe. Working paper no. 14. London: European Bank for Reconstruction and Development.

Deloitte Touche Tohmatsu. 1995. Central and Eastern Europe bankruptcy and restructuring: Czech Republic, Slovak Republic. Report for USAID. Washington, D.C.: Deloitte Touche Tohmatsu.

Drabek, Z., K. Janacek, and Z. Tuma. 1994. Inflation in the Czech and Slovak Republics, 1985–1991. *Journal of Comparative Economics* 18, no. 2 (April): 146-74,

Estrin, S. and P. Hare. 1992. Firms in transition: Modelling enterprise adjustment, Working paper no. 89. London: London School of Economics, Centre for Economic Performance.

Franks, J., K. Nyborg, and W. Torous. 1995. A comparison of US, UK and German insolvency codes. Occasional paper (May). Washington, D.C.: World Bank, Private Sector Development Department.

Hashi, I., J. Mládek, and A. Sinclair. 1996. The process of exit in the Czech Republic 1990–1994. *Studies and Analyses* 75. Warsaw: Center for Social and Economic Research.

Hlavacek, J. and Z. Tuma. 1993. Bankruptcy in the Czech economy. Prague: Charles University and the Center for Economic Research and Graduate Education. Mimeographed.

Mitchell, J. 1993. Creditor passivity and bankruptcy: Implications for economic reform. Chap. 7 in *Capital Markets and Financial Integration,* edited by C. Meyer and X. Vives. Cambridge: Cambridge University Press.

Mládek, J., and I. Hashi. 1993. Voucher privatization, investment funds and corporate governance in Czechoslovakia. *British Review of Economic Issues* 15, no. 37 (October): 67–96.

Organisation for Economic Cooperation and Development (OECD). 1991. *Economic Surveys: Czech and Slovak Federal Republic 1991.* Paris: Organisation for Economic Cooperation and Development.

Sak, P. B. and H. N. Schiffman. 1994. Bankruptcy law reform in Eastern Europe. *The International Lawyer* 28, no. 4 (winter): 927–50.

Tichy, Lubos. 1994. The bankruptcy code of the Czech Republic. In *Corporate Bankruptcy and Reorganization Procedures in OECD and Central and Eastern European Countries.* Paris: Organisation for Economic Cooperation and Development.

Tuma, Z. and J. E. Dotson. 1995. Privatization byproducts: Firms with changed property and liquidations. *Privatization Newsletter of the Czech Republic and Slovakia,* no. 30 (January): 1–3.

Varanese, J. B. and A. Westphal. 1994. Debt for equity: The Czech Republic's swapping for survival game. *Survey of East European Law* (April).

Notes

We are grateful to the administrators and liquidators who participated in the surveys reported in this chapter. Special thanks are due to Ing. Anna Klosova for her continued cooperation and support.

1. During 1990, of course, a number of other important measures, such as the reduction of food subsidies, the unification of exchange rates combined with a sharp devaluation of the commercial exchange rate, important legal reforms, and the small privatization program had been implemented. For a discussion of different aspects of the Czech transformation program, see Drabek, Janacek, and Tuma (1994); Blejer and Coricelli (1995).

2. Throughout this chapter, we use the abbreviation Kč for Czechoslovak Koruna for the period prior to 7 February 1993 and Kč for Czech Koruna for the period following the seperation.

3. For details of these measures and their impact, see Hashi, Mladek, and Sinclair (1995): 11-4; Brom and Orenstein (1994); OECD (1991).

4. Informal work-out arrangements are not uncommon in the Czech Republic—they are reached by negotiations between the debtor-firm and banks and other creditors and may also involve the imposition of certain conditions on the debtor. But such agreements are not always known to outsiders and are not usually reported in the financial press; therefore, they are difficult to investigate. This is, of course, not true of the most important informal exit mechanism led by owners and managers, i.e., downsizing, which is discussed separately in chapter 4.

5. For a detailed discussion of the Czech bankruptcy code, see Hlavacek and Tuma (1993); Tichy (1994); Sak and Schiffman (1994); Varanese and Westphal (1994). Throughout this chapter, the term "bankruptcy" refers to the overall legal process of dealing with financial distress initiated by creditors and pursued through the court system. The term covers both "settlement," which is the equivalent of reorganization, and "liquidation," which is the process of winding up the firm.

6. For the similarities between the 1991 law and the Austrian and German codes, see Tichy (1994): 96; Sak and Schiffman (1994): 929.

7. The term "liquidator" refers to the person overseeing the liquidation of a state-owned enterprise according to separate procedures that will be discussed later.

8. The deposit is also expected to discourage creditors from filing unnecessary applications (wasting the court's time), as a means of putting pressure on debtors.

9. This provision was introduced in the 1993 amendments to the bankruptcy law. The protection period may, under special circumstances, be extended by another three months. This limited period may also be used by some debtors to negotiate with their creditors and reach an agreement that can then be presented to the court as a settlement plan. The 1996 amendments restricted the use of this period to companies with over fifty employees. There is no stay of claims and no priority for new credits during this period.

10. The administrator is selected from a list kept by each regional commercial court, according to his specialization and the case under consideration. The list is compiled using recommendations from the Ministry of Justice, municipalities, bar associations, and other official organizations. The selection procedure was clarified and improved by the 1996 amendments.

11. Since the 1996 amendments, the meeting of the Creditors Commitee has been publicized by announcements in the official commerical bulletin (*obchodni vestnik*) and the court's notice boards.

12. The "ordinary settlement" provisions are not, strictly speaking, part of the bankruptcy law but may be embarked upon in conjunction with bankruptcy procedures. During the procedures, the rights of the management are somewhat restricted: the debtor is not allowed to take independent legal action that might affect the interests of its creditors. Neither the debtor nor the creditor is allowed to propose a declaration of bankruptcy in the course of a settlement.

13. See the case study of Cottex Hronov, a company under bankruptcy proceedings, in the appendix.

14. For example if the settlement impairs the rights of secured creditors or if there are doubts about the real intentions of the management of the bankrupt firm.

15. Tichy (1994): 84–5.

16. In 1994, for example, there were six cases of settlement, but four of them were unsuccessful, leaving only the two cases shown in table 5.2.

17. This shortcoming was eventually recognized and the obligation by all those "who can represent the company" to file for bankruptcy in the event of overindebtedness was introduced from June 1, 1996 (paragraph 68 of the 1996 amendments). In terms of our discussion, the absence of an obligation to declare insolvency remains a major cause of the small number of bankruptcy filings in the period under consideration.

18. The liquidation process for state enterprises (discussed below) has always included the declaration obligation. Here the liquidator in

charge is obliged by law to file for bankruptcy as soon as he discovers that liabilities exceed the expected value of assets.

19. For a discussion of the factors motivating the managers in the early transition period, see Aghion et al. (1993); Carlin et al. (1994); Estrin and Hare (1992).

20. The situation may be further complicated if the court attempts to establish the "honest intention" of the bankrupt firm, as required by law. In the absence of strict criteria, this provision will either act as an impediment to a settlement or will have to be ignored.

21. The creditors of a state enterprise in liquidation were also subject to the same bias and, therefore, were less motivated to reach an agreement with the liquidators. This bias was partially removed by the 1995 amendments (593/1995).

22. Franks, Nyborg, and Torous (1995): 32. One example of the restrictive nature of the role of courts is that they set the minimum price at which the assets of the bankrupt firm should be sold. It is not possible to sell the assets below the minimum price unless the administrator goes back to the court and asks for a reduction—this is what usually happens in practice.

23. It was initially thought that the payment of fees at the end of the bankruptcy process would motivate the administrator to complete his work speedily. However, it soon became clear that the fees were too small to serve as a source of motivation and that other factors also contributed to the slowness of the process.

24. This point was highlighted in a recent report commissioned by USAID (see Deloitte Touche Tohmatsu (1995): 4) and also emphasized in our own case study of an enterprise in bankruptcy (see the case of Cottex Hronov in the appendix to this chapter).

25. For a comprehensive discussion of creditor passivity, see Mitchell (1993).

26. Indeed, the Czech National Bank (CNB) embarked on rescue and support operations for potentially failing private banks even as late as 1996. The program, officially estimated to cost Kč 100 billion (unofficially Kč 240 billion), involved the transfer of the nonperforming loans of participating banks to the state-owned Konsolidacni banka, in return for a greater supervisory control by the CNB. For details, see *Central European Business Weekly,* October 25–31, 1996.

27. This was particularly important in the preprivatization period when banks were in the process of preparing their privatization project. Of course, it should be pointed out that all Czech banks were required

to review their debt portfolio and make appropriate provisions for bad debts before privatization. But this requirement did not fundamentally affect the view that a bank's net worth would be reduced by the bankruptcy of its debtors.

28. For a discussion of interconnections between banks and PIFs, developed in the course of the voucher privatization scheme, see Mládek and Hashi (1993).

29. The state is still a major shareholder of large Czech banks and financial institutions. It owns the whole of Konsolidačni banka and, on average, about 40 percent of the shares of most major banks.

30. Capek and Mertlik (1996): 45.

31. The data is actually prepared for the Ministry of Economy by a private company that collates the information gathered from different regional courts.

32. Initially, it seemed that the duration of bankruptcy would be very short for this company, only eleven months, but in practice, events turned out differently. After the administrator's final report was approved by the court, it became clear that the case had to remain open because the former owner was unable to pay his personal liability of Kč 100,000. The court then agreed to payment by Kč 10,000 installments to start from April 1996. Therefore, the bankruptcy process remains incomplete and the company's name is still on the register until the payment of the final installment.

33. It is conceivable that this value may not be known even to owners, but the managers usually have a fairly accurate picture of their assets, though it may not be in their interest to share this knowledge with others.

34. At other times, an enterprise may be liquidated because of a particular decision by the government that follows a specific policy measure and has nothing to do with the financial position of the enterprise. The decision to close small coal mines or bring to an end prefabricated housing construction meant that certain companies were no longer needed—even though these companies had a satisfactory financial status.

35. The new Law on State-Owned Enterprises (no. 77/1997), containing provisions for the liquidation of these companies, passed this year. The ministries and other founding bodies will have to decide, within six months, whether the liquidation of their companies will be carried out under the new law or under the current commerical code.

36. Liquidators need to have a university degree and must successfully complete a short training course of approximately three weeks before receiving their certificate.

37. The Ministry of Agriculture, for example, was involved in the liquidation of food-processing enterprises and agricultural cooperatives. The latter group was especially prominent as it included cooperatives that did not complete their transformation through the relevant legal procedures within the specified time period and, by law, had to be liquidated.

38. Tuma and Dotson (1995): 3.

39. The tariff in the Ministry of Industry and Trade, which accounts for most of the liquidations, is a monthly salary of Kč 15,000–20,000 and a maximum limit of Kč 150,000 on the proportion of the realized value of assets.

40. The liquidator's decision may of course be challenged in courts but in most cases, given the uncertainty and information asymmetry, a challenger has little chance of success.

41. See, for example, Tuma and Dotson (1995): 3. Our own case studies confirm the view that liquidators are subjected to offers of bribes as well as threats of violence, by both creditors and potential buyers of assets.

42. This compares very favorably with the remuneration of bankruptcy administrators in the United Kingdom, which amounts to 5 percent of the realized value of assets.

43. For private companies, however, the situation is different, and the net profit of the process is important for owners. This, *ceteris paribus*, will ensure that a better monitoring mechanism will be in place for the liquidation of private companies.

6

Hungary's Bankruptcy Experience, 1992–1993

Cheryl W. Gray, Sabine Schlorke, and Miklós Szanyi

As policy makers in both transition and developing economies look for policies and processes to spur enterprise restructuring, they should take a close look at Hungary's experience with bankruptcy reform in 1992 and 1993.[1] Although other countries have adopted innovative restructuring processes, Hungary's experience with formal bankruptcy law is indeed unique in the post-socialist world.[2] Hungary adopted a tough new bankruptcy law in late 1991 that took effect on January 1, 1992. The law required the managers of all firms with arrears over ninety days to any creditor to file for either reorganization or liquidation within eight days (the so-called "automatic trigger") and provided a rather sympathetic framework for them to do so. The law immediately resulted in a wave of filings, with some 3,500 filings in April 1992, after the ninety day "grace" period covered by the law, and over 22,000 filings in 1992–3 (table 6.1). This level of filings was far beyond the expectations of policy makers when the law was adopted.

Although the level of activity has been enormous, detailed information on how the bankruptcy process has actually worked in Hungary has been scarce. Many views—both positive and negative—have been put forward regarding the particular impact of the law on enterprise restructuring and its general impact on economic growth, but these preparations have been supported by very limited reliable data. This study helps to fill this vacuum by providing detailed data on a randomly selected stratified sample of actual cases filed in the first two years after the enactment of the law. These data are supplemented with information obtained in numerous interviews with judges, liquidators, and firms involved in the bankruptcy process to give an overall picture of the process in practice during the first two years of its implementation.

Bankruptcy law plays at least three important roles in market economies. First, it provides ailing firms with an orderly means of exit. Second, it shifts the control of assets toward creditors and helps to real-

Table 6.1
Hungarian Reorganization and Liquidation Processes, 1/92 through 12/93

	Reorganization	Liquidation
Filings	**5156**	**17133**
Of these:		
State-owned enterprises	492	1820
Cooperatives	965	2768
Business entities	3762	12545
(of these limited liability companies):	(2959)	(8927)
Of these approximate %		
with over 300 employees	6%	a
51–300 employees	24%	a
50 or fewer	70%	a
Status as of 31/12/93		
Closed	4627 (90%)	b
with agreement	1250 (27%)	
reversion to liquidation	1377 (30%)	
administrative completion	2000 (43%)	
Pending	529 (10%)	

[a] Data not available

[b] Over 10 000 liquidation cases were completed by the courts in 1992 and 1993, but these included cases filed in earlier years under the previous law. Furthermore, over three-fourths of those completed cases were "administrative completions," i.e. cases withdrawn or rejected on administrative grounds rather than completed on the merits. Only a very small number of the 17133 cases filed in 1992 and 1993 were completed within the two years mandated in the law.

Source: Hungarian Ministry of Finance.

locate assets to better uses through a combination of restructuring and liquidation.[3] Third, it promotes the flow of credit in an economy by protecting creditors and serving as a final stage of debt collection. These first two roles work together: The threat of exit spurs restructuring, and the impossibility of restructuring spurs exit. The bankruptcy process should ideally be able to discriminate between unviable firms and potentially viable ones that can be saved through restructuring. For enterprises able to cover operating costs out of current revenues but unable to cover debt service, reorganization provides an avenue to restructure debt burdens and thus continue operation. The process may promote such restructuring formally, as in the Hungarian reorganization procedure, or through informal debtor–creditor work-outs undertaken to avoid formal bankruptcy. Firms unable to cover even operating costs are clear candidates for exit unless fundamental operational restructuring can be achieved via reorganization.

In their emphasis on preserving jobs and production, policy makers in many transitional countries focus on these first two roles for bankruptcy law, and these roles are also the main focus of this chapter. However, the third role is at least as important for economic growth. A well-designed bankruptcy process takes control over financially distressed firms before all assets have been misused or dissipated, and it gives creditors the information and power to direct the use of the remaining assets to maximize the potential for debt recovery, either by improving the firm's performance via reorganization or by liquidating the firm and satisfying the claims of creditors, to the extent possible out of sale proceeds. By thus giving creditors the confidence that debts can be collected, bankruptcy processes (and collateral laws prior to bankruptcy) facilitate the role of banks and other creditors in funding and monitoring investment in an economy and in exerting influence over enterprise managers. Without the ability to collect debts, banks will refuse to lend at all or lend only to those clients they know well, thereby becoming peripheral players in both resource allocation and corporate governance, or they will turn to the state for support when loans turn bad. Thus, bankruptcy legislation is an important complement to, not a substitute for, disciplined macroeconomic policies and privatization and the hard budget constraints and corporate governance possibilities they create.

Considering these various roles, the major questions to be addressed below include the following:

1. What types of firms entered reorganization and/or liquidation in Hungary in 1992 and 1993, and why?
2. How cumbersome were these processes in practice?
3. What direct effects did these processes have on the restructuring of problem firms, on the exit of problem firms, on the privatization of enterprises, on the building of institutions?
4. What were the roles of the various actors in these processes?
5. Has the process served reasonably well as a debt-collection mechanism for creditors?
6. Considering the answers to the above questions, how can the process be improved?

As will be described in detail below, the outcome of the process is decidedly mixed. While the bankruptcy process indisputably spurred institution building in the courts, the trustee profession, and the banks and may have succeeded broadly in separating viable from unviable firms, it did little to further either deep restructuring or the exit of ailing firms.

The Legal Framework for Hungarian Bankruptcy

The Hungarian bankruptcy law of 1991 replaced earlier legislation adopted in 1986 and provided Hungary for the first time with a modern legal framework quite similar in structure to the American bankruptcy regime, albeit with the addition of the controversial automatic trigger. Debtors could file for either reorganization or liquidation, while creditors could file for liquidation only. If debtors filed for reorganization, the incumbent management could stay in place, and the firm received automatic relief from debt service and asset foreclosures for three months (extendible by a further one month). During this three-month period, the management of the firm was supposed to develop a reorganization plan and present it to the firm's creditors. Unanimous approval by all creditors was required for the plan to be adopted; otherwise the case reverted automatically to liquidation. A firm with a successful plan could not file again for bankruptcy for at least three years. Trustees' and creditors' committees were not required in reorganization cases but could be organized at the discretion of creditors. New borrowing during reorganization did not receive priority over existing debt.[4]

The liquidation process provided for in the 1991 law was also in line with international norms. It provided for a liquidator to be appointed once the court reviewed and decided to proceed with a case. The liquidator was supposed to notify creditors, draw up a list of assets, sell the assets, and divide the proceeds among creditors in order of priority—liquidation costs first, followed by creditors secured by mortgage, other creditors, and finally equity holders.[5] The entire process was supposed to be completed within two years. The law set compensation levels for liquidators and trustees, and regulations adopted concurrently with the law provided an annual licensing procedure for liquidators, setting out minimum capital requirements and professional qualifications.

Numerous important changes were made to the law in September 1993, drawing ostensibly from the first one and a half years of experience with the 1991 law. The unanimous creditor approval requirement was considered too tough, so it was replaced by a requirement of creditor approval by one-half the number and two-thirds the value of outstanding claims. The automatic three-month stay on debt service was considered too generous and easy to abuse and was replaced by a discretionary stay that required the same level of creditor approval within fifteen days from the date of filing.[6] Liquidators' compensation was considered too low and was increased. To stem the unanticipated flood of cases, both the automatic trigger and the automatic reversion of failed reorganizations to liquidation were eliminated. Finally, trustees were made mandatory in all reorganization cases. Further amendments to the law in May 1997 increased the reporting requirements of liquidators and the role of creditors' committees in overseeing them.

After the passage of the 1993 amendments, the number of reorganization cases declined dramatically (figure 6.1). There are several likely reasons for this decline. First, the 1993 amendments removed both powerful carrots (the automatic stay) and powerful sticks (the automatic trigger), and the trustee requirement increased the costs and introduced potentially undesired outside controls into the process.[7] Furthermore, the end of 1993 also saw the introduction of a new out-of-court workout process called "debtor consolidation" into the Hungarian scene. While a description of this process is beyond the bounds of this chapter, suffice it to say that debtor consolidation could well have been seen by many debtors and creditors as a substitute for reorganization under the bankruptcy law.[8] Finally, the general economic conditions of Hungary improved in 1994, and many of the worst firms may well have already been included in the flood of cases in 1992–3.

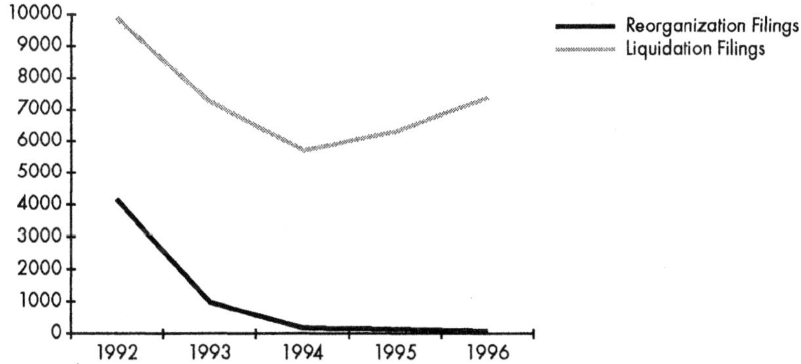

Figure 6.1: Filings Under the Hungarian Bankruptcy Law

Source: Hungarian Ministry of Finance.

The Bankruptcy Sample

To gain insight into many of the questions raised above, we undertook a survey of 117 bankruptcy cases filed between April 1992 and September 1993. All were covered by the unamended 1991 law. They were filed in one of three courts: Budapest, where approximately one-third of all Hungarian cases were filed in 1992–3; Pest County; or Debrecen, a more rural location. The sample was limited to manufacturing firms and was stratified both by process and by size (see table 6.2). With regard to process, the sample was stratified to favor completed reorganizations (sixty-three cases) while still having a substantial number of liquidations, whether cases transferred from reorganization (twenty-eight) or those filed as liquidations (twenty-two); four cases were filed as reorganizations but withdrawn before completion. With regard to size, the sample was stratified to include both small and large firms on a roughly equal basis. Large firms were defined either as firms taken from a list of Hungary's 603 largest loss-making firms in 1992,[9] or as firms not on that list but with assets worth over 100 million forint (approximately $1.25 million in 1992). It should be noted that because the sample of large firms was taken from the list of lossmakers, the financial performance of the large firms in our study is likely to have been worse than a random sample of large firms that filed for bankruptcy. Actual cases were chosen at random, subject to these stratification criteria and to the willingness and ability of firms to participate.[10] Data for each firm were collected both from court files (on average about one-quarter of all data) and from interviews with managers and/or liquidators.

Table 6.2
The Sample of Firms in Bankruptcy, by Process and Size of Firm, Hungary 1992 (number of firms)

Process	Large firms	Small firms	Total
Completed reorganization agreements	36	27	63
Transfers from reorganization to liquidation	14	14	28
Liquidation filings	10	12	22
Withdrawals	0	4	4
Total	60	57	117

Source: Authors' calculations.

Sector and Ownership

Table 6.3 shows the resulting breakdown in the sample by sector and by ownership, two variables not controlled in the stratification. The sectoral distribution is broad, with a somewhat heavy representation by firms in the machinery and equipment sector. Ownership patterns support the prior expectation that larger firms tended to be state owned while smaller firms tended to be private. Table 6.4 shows the basic indicators for large and small firms at the time of filing for bankruptcy.[11] Large and small firms had on average 625 and thirty-seven employees, respectively. While their overall level of debt, both long and short term, as a share of the reported book value of assets was similar and on aver-

Table 6.3
Sectoral Distribution and Type of Ownership of Sample Firms, 1992
(number of firms)

Firm distribution	Large firms	Small firms	Total
Sector			
Transport equipment	0	9	9
Electronics and medical equipment	2	1	3
Machinery and equipment	19	19	38
Metals, plastics, and chemicals	14	9	23
Paper, wood, and printing products	5	7	12
Textiles, apparel, and leather	12	7	19
Tobacco and food	8	5	13
Total	60	57	117
Firm ownership			
State agency	29	6	35
State	13	7	20
Majority state owned	1	2	3
Majority privatized	2	0	2
Fully privatized	4	0	4
Private, established domestically	4	33	37
Private, established as a joint venture	3	4	7
Private, established by foreign parties	1	0	1
Cooperative	2	4	6
Other	1	1	2
Total	60	57	117

Source: Authors' calculations.

Table 6.4
Characteristics of Firms at Time of Filing (generally end-1991)

Mean of:	Large firms	Small firms	Total
Number of employees	625	37	344
Total assets (book value) in million forint	1142	88	605
Total debt as percentage of total assets	145	147	146
bank debt	58	12	34
payables to suppliers	43	65	54
government debt	9	19	14
After-tax profit (loss) as percentage of total assets	-33	-9	-21

Source: Authors' calculations.

age very high (146 percent), large firms tended to have a much larger share of bank debt and a somewhat lower share of debt to suppliers and the government.[12] Both had a large residual of unclassified debt.[13]

Reasons for Financial Distress

Reported external reasons for prebankruptcy financial distress in small and large firms are shown in figure 6.2.[14] While firms report a wide range of external reasons for financial distress, a decline in the domestic demand for the products produced by the firms appears to have been more important for large firms, which is not surprising given that many were state-owned firms producing goods that were obsolete or uncompetitive in the transition environment. Unfavorable relative changes in

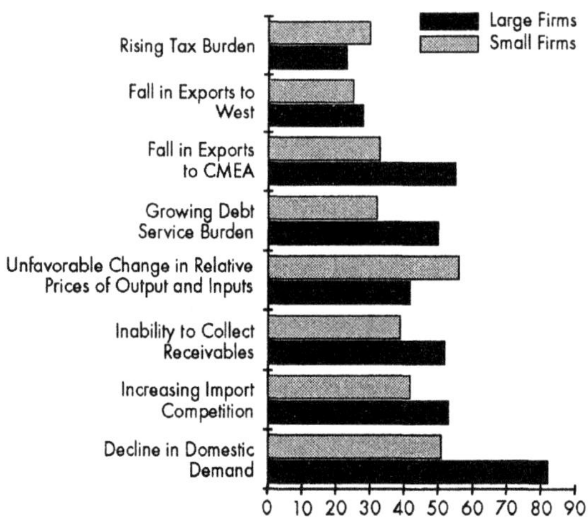

Figure 6.2: Reasons for Financial Distress

Source: Authors' calculations.

output and input prices and high tax burdens appear to be somewhat more important for smaller (mostly private) firms. In contrast to a common opinion in Hungary, a decline in exports to the CMEA, while important for both groups, was by no means the primary reason for financial distress in this sample of firms. Of course, internal reasons for financial distress, such as weak management or poor accounting, are also likely to be very important in many cases but were not readily measurable in this survey.

The Bankruptcy Process in Action

What Type of Firm Enters Reorganization and/or Liquidation?

The enormous number of bankruptcy filings in April 1992 is a clear indication of the effect of the automatic trigger that was introduced in the 1991 law. The survey also highlights this effect, as over 95 percent of the firms in the sample noted the trigger as the immediate impetus for its filing.[15] Under the trigger, a firm could file for either reorganization or liquidation, and one goal of the survey was to find out how firms taking these various routes differ.

Table 6.5 shows key financial indicators at time of filing for three categories of firms—those who exited the reorganization process with successful agreements, those whose reorganization cases were transformed into liquidations, and those whose cases were filed initially as liquidations. These figures indicate that the outcomes of the bankruptcy regime appear to have had some degree of rationality even as early as 1992. The debtors in the transformed cases were in much greater debt to all types of creditors than the debtors with accepted reorganization plans. The former also had greater losses than the latter. Furthermore, debtors in transformed cases not only had fewer assets overall, but a higher percentage of their assets were inventories and receivables. By contrast, debtors with accepted reorganizations had more cash, real estate, and machinery—assets that are more likely to have a positive market value.

These data suggest that the reorganization process did have some success in separating viable from unviable firms. While undoubtedly an important conclusion, this interpretation should nevertheless be tempered by impressions of the process gathered by the authors during out-

Table 6.5
Financial Distress in the Sample Firms at the Time of Filing for Bankruptcy, 1992

(percentage of total assets) **Indicator and process**	**Large firms**	**Small firms**
Debt		
Completed reorganization agreements	70	104
Transfers from reorganization to liquidation	302	245
Liquidation filings	188	148
After-tax profits		
Completed reorganization agreements	-23	-3
Transfers from reorganization to liquidation	-54	-25
Liquidation filings	-34	-26

Source: Authors' calculations.

side interviews of managers and liquidators from 1992 to 1994. These impressions suggest two other possible reasons for the differences between accepted and rejected reorganizations—both of which imply that the latter were perhaps never intended to succeed. First, the 1991 law quickly and dramatically altered both the legal framework for bankruptcy and the responsibilities placed on the managers of bankrupt firms. It is very likely that many managers did not immediately understand the new law and its requirements and thus filed for reorganization when they should have filed for liquidation. Second, it is widely believed in Hungary that some managers of state-owned firms have spun off or otherwise diverted valuable state-owned assets, whether fixed assets, labor, or intangibles (such as contracts and goodwill), to subsidiaries or private firms. Furthermore, owners and/or managers of private firms can also direct valuable assets to other uses (or foreign bank accounts), leaving only "shell" firms to enter reorganization and/or liquidation. In an environment with poor information and underdeveloped "watchdog" institutions, it is exceedingly difficult to prevent such activity.[16] The extent of asset diversion is unknown and impossible to measure,[17] but its occurrence on a significant scale in Hungary is generally accepted.[18] Many of these reorganization filings may have been undertaken by managers who had previously diverted valuable assets and were biding their time before liquidation.[19] In sum, while some of the transformed cases may represent serious yet ultimately unsuccessful attempts to restructure, it is the authors' belief that many represent either cases of managerial misunderstanding or cases of the prebankruptcy diversion of assets.

Turning to liquidations, one can see from table 6.5 that firms in liquidation also had higher levels of debt and greater losses than firms with accepted reorganization agreements, and their assets were also more concentrated in receivables and inventories. Again, the process appears to have pushed the worst firms into liquidation, although again prefiling value diversion in both large and small—i.e., public and private—firms probably played some role in creating the financial distress in certain cases.

How Cumbersome are these Processes in Practice?

The flood of bankruptcy cases filed in 1992 and 1993 undoubtedly put a strain on Hungary's judicial institutions. There were only eight bankruptcy judges in the Budapest court in 1992, handling over 15,000 cases. It is perhaps somewhat surprising, therefore, to note that over 60 percent of the reorganization cases filed in 1992 were completed the same year, and that over 95 percent of the cases filed in 1992 and 1993 were completed by the end of 1993 (see table 6.1). Survey data on the average time required for various stages of the reorganization process (table 6.6) further support the conclusion that the process was not unduly slow. The average time required for an agreement to be finalized was approximately eight months for both large and small firms. On average the debtors presented their reorganization proposals about six weeks after the court's decision to proceed or about eighteen weeks after filing. The period of negotiation between the presentation of the first plan and the final resolution of the reorganization case averaged another four months. Unsuccessful cases, particularly those involving large firms took somewhat longer than successful ones, although virtually all cases were completed within one year of filing.

A major reason why reorganization cases could proceed quite quickly, despite their huge numbers, was the low level of substantive involvement by courts and trustees. Once a case was approved by a judge to proceed (which took on average about three months, indicating the degree of overload in the courts), the judge had little substantive involvement.[20] The process was managed by the debtor and its creditors, and in this decentralized mode the process could proceed quite rapidly. It is interesting to note that in none of the ninety-five reorganization cases in the sample did the parties choose to involve a trustee in the

Table 6.6
Time Requirements for Reorganization Cases

	Completed reorganizations		Cases transferred from reorganization to liquidation		All	
Average time in days between:	**Large firms**	**Small firms**	**Large firms**	**Small firms**	**Large firms**	**Small firms**
Filing and the court decision to proceed with the case	80	66	107	104	87	79
Court decision to proceed with the case and the submission of the first reorganization plan	39	48	55	30	43	42
Submission of the first reorganization plan and the final court decision	119	110	152	127	126	114
Total[a]	238	224	314	261	256	235

[a] The total number is not an exact measure of the average duration of the bankruptcy process, because the underlying number of cases changes from subperiod to subperiod above.

Source: Authors' calculations.

process. This could be because of the extra expense involved combined with the fact that trustees had to be selected from a preapproved list that might not have corresponded to the parties trusted by the creditors. It could also simply reflect the relative passivity of creditors during this period (see discussion below.) This lack of demand for trustees brings into question the reasonableness of the 1993 amendment to require a trustee in bankruptcy cases.

The quickness of the reorganization process was not, however, characteristic of liquidation cases in the sample (see table 6.7). Only one of the fifty liquidation cases in the sample had been completed by late 1994: that is, within the two years required by law. The average time between filing and the first disposition of assets was about thirteen months, and even this amount of time is significantly underestimated because only about one-half of the firms had sold any assets when the survey was conducted.

A major cause for delay in the liquidation process, particularly in cases originally filed as liquidations, was the court's slowness in appointing a

Table 6.7
Time Requirements for Liquidation Cases

	Cases transferred from reorganization		Cases filed as liquidations		All	
Average time in days between:	**Large firms**	**Small firms**	**Large firms**	**Small firms**	**Large firms**	**Small firms**
Filing or transfer from reorganization and the appointment of a liquidator	46	179	350	225	183	200
The appointment of a liquidator and the formal notification of creditors	14	37	35	35	24	36
The formal notification of creditors and the first disposition of assets	200	133	304	134	244	133
Total time until first disposition of assets[a]	260	349	689	394	451	369

[a] The total number is not an exact measure of the average duration of the liquidation process, because the underlying number of cases changes from subperiod to subperiod above.

Source: Authors' calculations.

liquidator. This step alone took over seven months for small cases and almost a year for large cases.[21] While this delay is perhaps not surprising, given the flood of over 10,000 liquidation cases in 1992 alone, it almost certainly had serious costs in some cases because of the vacuum of supervision and the opportunities for further asset diversion during the interim period.

It is interesting to note that courts took far less time to appoint liquidators in cases transformed from reorganization, particularly those cases dealing with large firms, than in cases originally filed as liquidations. This could be because the court's previous exposure to these firms during the reorganization phase gave the court (and the liquidators) the information and incentive to move quickly once the reorganization failed. Indeed, in the case of large companies the total elapsed time between the initial filing for reorganization or liquidation and the first disposition of assets in a liquidation was no longer for those firms that went through reorganization than for those that did not.

Who is in Control of these Processes?

A key to understanding the likely impact of bankruptcy in Hungary is to understand who controls the reorganization and liquidation processes. The greater the control wielded by one party (be it debtor or creditor) over a process, the more likely that process is to benefit that particular party. In advanced market economies, where information is relatively plentiful and open and judicial processes are relatively well developed, bankruptcy is typically a complex balancing act between numerous competing interests, all of which quite actively defend their own interests. In transition economies, however, the situation is quite different. Information is far more costly, and judicial processes—even notions of "due process" and "fiduciary responsibility"—are far less developed. As a result, some parties may have neither the means nor the power to defend their interests effectively. Furthermore, some of the parties to bankruptcy proceedings may not have strong incentives to collect debts aggressively. For example, state-owned firms or state-owned banks may be more inclined to turn to the state for compensation than to pursue debt collection through official legal means. (This is particularly true if there is a history of repeated bank recapitalizations, as in Hungary.)

Figure 6.3 presents indicators of the relative amount of participation of various parties in reorganization and liquidation. It is clear from this data that managers tended to be the most powerful figures in reorganization proceedings, generally controlling the process, and that liquidators had virtually total control in liquidation cases, often with managers still in active roles. Banks and other creditors were sometimes active, sometimes passive, but virtually never in control of either process. Interestingly, banks do not appear to have been significantly more active than other types of creditors, whether trade creditors or government creditors. Another more general indicator of the relative lack of involvement of banks, particularly compared with their very active role in bankruptcies in advanced market economies, is the very low percentage of cases (approximately 3 percent) filed by banks through 1993 (table 6.8).

The relative inactivity of creditors, particularly banks, is likely to be due to several reasons. First, creditors in Hungary, as in other transition economies, may lack the information and expertise to understand what is at stake and to actively oversee debtor management and/or liquidators. There is certain to be a learning curve in this as in other areas of commercial development in these countries. Our cases, all of which were filed

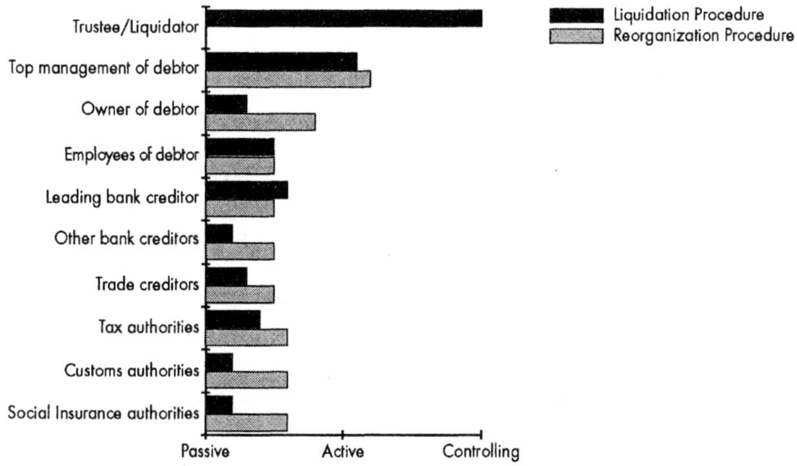

Figure 6.3: Who Controls the Bankruptcy Process for Large Firms?
Source: Authors' calculations.

in 1992, were perhaps on the early end of that learning curve. Furthermore, many of the watchdog institutions that can help provide information to creditors—such as accountants, credit-rating services, securities regulators, or the press—are in their infancy in transition economies.[22] Second, creditors may lack the incentive to be strong debt collectors, particularly if they are state owned (as all the large banks have been until 1995 in Hungary) and perhaps expect future state assistance (as Hungarian banks repeatedly received between 1991 and 1995). Third, creditors often express doubt to this day that they can recover anything in the process. While this is understandable in the case of liqui-

Table 6.8
Who Filed Liquidation Cases in Hungary in 1992–93?

	Percentage of Petitions filed by:
Bank creditors	1.5%
Government creditors (tax, social security, customs)	13%
Other trade creditors, liquidators, and conversions from reorganization	18%
The firm itself	67.5%
Total	100%

Source: Hungarian government statistics.

dation, given the power of liquidators to prolong the process and the priority given to liquidation costs over creditors' claims (see below), it is not clear why the reorganization process is seen as so unfavorable to creditors. Indeed, under the legislation in place in 1992, any creditor had the power to force firms into liquidation by refusing to agree to the reorganization plan (given the unanimous agreement requirement and the automatic reversion to liquidation), and thus on paper the power of creditors was very strong. This strong formal power lends further credence to the importance of the first two explanations noted above.

What is the Direct Effect of the Reorganization Process on Enterprise Restructuring?

The fundamental challenge of transition is enterprise restructuring, and the core question in this research is what effect the Hungarian bankruptcy process has had on restructuring in Hungarian firms. The effects on restructuring can be direct and/or indirect. Indirectly, the mere fact that bankruptcy became so widespread in 1992 probably spurred greater financial discipline in transactions among firms. While evidence appears to point to improvements in financial discipline with regard to inter-enterprise transactions,[23] perhaps for this as well as other reasons, this study did not attempt to assess these indirect effects. It did attempt to assess, however, the direct effects of the process on restructuring by studying the contents of reorganization plans and the changes in firm behavior and performance during and after bankruptcy (whether reorganization or liquidation).

Financial Reorganization

The contents of the financial reorganization plans of the ninety-one cases of successful and unsuccessful reorganizations in the sample are summarized in figure 6.4. The data point to the relatively unsophisticated nature of the final plans. The overwhelming majority of accepted reorganization plans provided for either an extension of loan maturity, generally of one-half to two years, and/or a write-off of debt principal, including capitalized interest arrears of about 13 percent in the case of bank debt and 20 to 30 percent in the case of debts to the government and suppliers. About one-third of accepted plans provided for some partial immediate debt repayment, of widely varying amounts, while 21 percent provided for a reduction in interest rates. Six of the sixty-three accepted agreements provided for debt–equity swaps by one or more

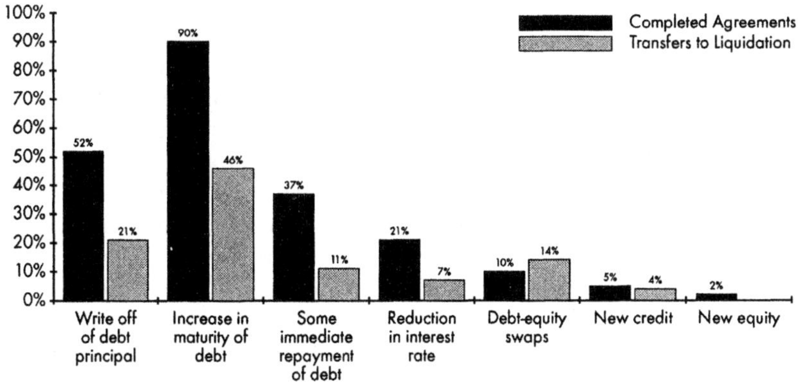

Figure 6.4: Contents of Reorganization Agreements: Financial Restructuring

Notes: Percentage of Restructuring. Plans with the Provision

Source: Authors' calculations.

types of creditor, although there is evidence that most were never implemented. Only three of the sixty-three plans provided for new credit, and only one provided for new equity.[24] Overall, agreements for small firms contained fewer concessions than agreements for large firms, perhaps not surprisingly given their less onerous financial condition at the time of filing.

It is clear from Figure 6.4 that proposed plans in unsuccessful reorganizations (i.e., those transformed into liquidations) contained fewer provisions overall than plans in successful cases. However, if a provision was included, its magnitude was often greater than in the case of successful agreements. The paucity of provisions further supports the conclusion discussed earlier that many of these cases were not filed with the intention to succeed in the first place. The relatively higher magnitude of these provisions may point to the likely absence of serious negotiations in many rejected cases.

Operational Reorganization

Most of the firms in the survey agreed or undertook steps to downsize during the reorganization period, as indicated in figure 6.5. Whether or not formally included in the reorganization plan, almost two-thirds of all firms with successful plans agreed or undertook steps to reduce employment, typically by one-quarter to one-third, and almost one-third agreed or undertook steps to sell assets or parts of the firm.[25] The filing of bankruptcy was not necessarily the primary reason for such downsizing. Many of the firms were already downsizing before bankruptcy, as were many other firms that never entered bankruptcy, and may well have continued in any case. At a minimum, however, it is clear that bankruptcy did not provide a safety valve to stop downsizing, as may have occurred in Poland—see chapter 8. Only 6 percent agreed or undertook steps to change top management, and only 3 percent (or two out of sixty-three firms) committed to new investments or changes in the membership of the companies' overseeing boards of directors.

As in the case of financial plans, the operational restructuring plans were far less ambitious in the cases of unsuccessful reorganization, with fewer than one-half as many firms committing to or undertaking changes as in the group with successful outcomes. Again, this is likely in part to reflect less commitment to real restructuring, and in some cases greater prebankruptcy value diversion, in this subset of firms.

In sum, an analysis of the reorganization plans of firms that successfully emerged from Hungary's reorganization process indicates that they had significant, albeit rather unsophisticated, content. Hungary's processes were primarily focused on short-term debt relief and continued downsizing and generally did not envision new investment, new management or innovation. Creditors were clearly not imposing radical

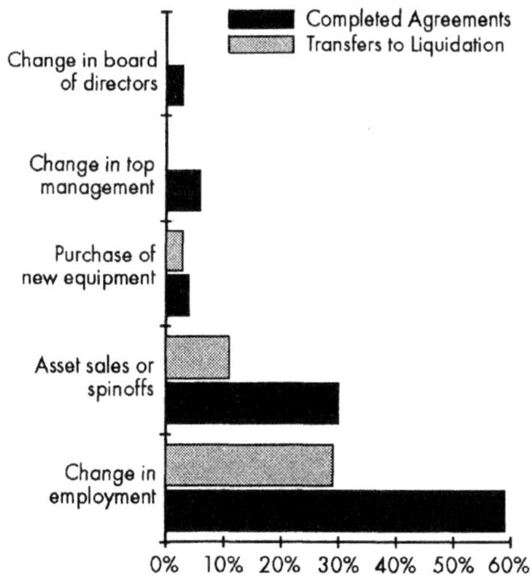

Figure 6.5: Operational Restructuring during Reorganization

Note: Percentage of firms that agreed to or undertook change.

Source: Authors' calculations.

changes on these firms, and control over firms' assets was not shifting to new agents.[26]

Initial Outcomes of the Reorganization Process

What happened to the firms that emerged from the reorganization process with agreed plans? Outcomes to mid-1994, on average about two years after filing, are shown in table 6.9. Over 90 percent of the firms—89 percent of the large ones and 96 percent of the small ones—were still in operation in mid-1994. The large firms had made greater changes than the small ones since their emergence from reorganization, which perhaps reflects a worse starting position. Over 70 percent of large firms reported having significantly reduced employment, 40 percent having sold major assets, and 34 percent having changed top man-

Table 6.9
Initial Outcomes of "Successful" Agreements (as of late 1994)

	Percentage	
	Large	**Small**
Percentage of firms that were still in operation	**89**	**96**
Restructuring: percentage of firms that:		
—made new investments	14	7
—sold major assets	40	11
—had access to new bank credit	17	11
—changed top management	34	26
—significantly reduced employment	71	48
—made major changes in production profile	14	7
Financial performance: percentage of firms that:		
—improved financial performance	49	63
—expected to make a profit in 1994	31	63
—anticipated having to file for bankruptcy or liquidation again in 1994 or 1995	31	11
Of firms that improved their financial performance, percentage reporting:		
—more favorable price structure for outputs and inputs	5	15
—higher sales volume	74	40
—lower interest payments	16	0
—improved repayment rate on receivables	37	35
—improved inventory management	74	55
—reduced material expenses	74	40
—reduced wage bill	37	40

Source: Authors' calculations.

agement. Only about one in seven, however, reported having made major changes in their production profile, having made new investments or having had access to new bank credits. About one-half reported improved financial performance, and about one-third expected to make a profit in 1994. However, another third expected to have to file for reorganization or liquidation again.

If one looks at the reported reasons for improved performance in firms reporting overall improvement, the major reasons were higher sales and reduced input costs. Lower interest payments were relatively unimportant despite the financial reorganization agreements. Perhaps these firms reduced debt liabilities but not necessarily actual debt service, if they were previously unable to service all of their debt.[27] Although relative magnitudes are similar for small firms, the overall percentage of firms that reported change is about one-half that of large firms. Yet their financial performance was somewhat stronger, probably reflecting less serious financial distress prior to bankruptcy.

In sum, postreorganization performance appears to be primarily a story of belt tightening combined in many cases with higher sales volume and better financial performance. Innovative restructuring appears to have been rare, as indicated by the low percentage of firms that reported major changes in their production profile. Yet perhaps two-thirds of the firms that entered the process expected to survive, and one-third were reportedly already profitable in 1994. Taken together with the institutional strengthening engendered by the process, this is arguably a story of real, albeit perhaps modest, success.

What is the Direct Effect of the Liquidation Process on Enterprise Exit?

The original design of the bankruptcy law was envisioned as providing two avenues for ailing firms: reorganization and liquidation. However, it is clear both from the results of this study and from numerous discussions with liquidators and other involved parties that the liquidation process does not necessarily result in exit. Of the fifty cases of liquidation in our sample, including twenty-two originally filed as liquidations and twenty-eight transferred from reorganization, only one case (that of a small firm), had been completed by mid-1994, a date that fell approximately at the end of the two-year deadline under the law. About 40 percent of the firms in our sample were still in operation some two years after the original filing date (table 6.10), and the great majority of these had remained under the same management that existed before the firm filed. Larger firms, particularly those transferred from bankruptcy, were more likely to remain in operation than smaller firms. Furthermore, the overall percentage of workers expected to maintain jobs with the subsequent users of assets was about one-third for larger firms and slightly less for smaller ones.

Table 6.10
Outcomes of Liquidations to Late 1994

	Transfers from Reorganization		**Liquidation Filings**	
	Large	**Small**	**Large**	**Small**
Percentage of firms operating as a going concern during liquidation	57%	23%	40%	33%
Percentage of firms remaining under existing management after liquidation filing	44%	11%	30%	29%
Percentage of claims expected to be recovered by:				
Workers	100%	60%	62%	64%
Secured creditors	46%	41%	23%	26%
Unsecured creditors	17%	2%	9%	6%
Percentage of workers maintaining jobs with subsequent user of assets	36%	11%	36%	33%

Source: Authors' calculations.

In essence, there appear to have been three broad types of firms involved in the liquidation process in 1992 and 1993: "shell" companies, which had few if any assets when liquidation was filed; small firms (mostly private), which were quite easy to liquidate and thus were often closed quickly; and larger firms (mostly state owned) with significant assets, which were rarely closed completely during a liquidation proceeding.

Why did so many firms continue in operation during the liquidation process, despite the fact that it was originally designed as an exit process? Data from the survey and from related interviews support the view that liquidators in large part saw their role as restructurers and privatizers, rather than as simply liquidators. Liquidators worked closely with the management of the debtor firm and tried to find purchasers of the companies in whole or in part, while preserving as many jobs as possible. One reason why this strategy was so common is the structure of compensation for liquidators. As long as the firm continued in operation, the liquidator was entitled to a fee of 2 percent of gross receipts; if assets were sold, liquidators were entitled to 5 percent of the sales price. Furthermore, the costs of liquidation included any costs incurred to keep debtor firms in operation during the liquidation process. The costs could include, for example, the fees of consultants hired to assist the liquidator on debt service or new borrowing to finance restructuring.[28] These costs had top priority, even above secured mortgage liens. Clearly there were financial incentives for liquidators to keep some firms in operation.

While it is perhaps good news for some Hungarian workers and some parts of the Hungarian economy that the wave of liquidation did not lead to more forced exits, it is not necessarily good news for creditors or for firms seeking credit. Creditors reported that they had very little influence over the decisions of liquidators. Although the percentage of claims expected to be recovered by creditors (see table 6.7) was not low by international standards (even though expectations were likely to overstate eventual recoveries in these cases), banks generally claimed in interviews that in reality they expected to recover very little and anticipated any recoveries to be delayed by years while the liquidator negotiated as painless a restructuring and sale as possible.

It is interesting to note that although the number of reorganization cases dropped dramatically after late 1993, reorganizations were indeed still occurring, but through the liquidation process. This indeed became a major route for the restructuring of state-owned firms in Hungary. What the system lacked then, and still lacks, is an efficient and dependable exit process that creditors can rely on as a final stage in debt collection. The weakness of exit together with the problems arising from foreclosure on collateral at earlier stages of the debt-collection process almost certainly raise the cost of credit in Hungary.

What is the Effect of Bankruptcy on Privatization and Institution Building?

Although bankruptcy may not be an efficient exit mechanism for firms in their entirety, it has been an important avenue for privatization and the "recombination"[29] of existing assets in the economy, either as parts of firms or merely as individual assets. Indeed, the bankruptcy law was probably one of the main stimulants of privatization in the Hungarian economy in 1992 and 1993. Not only did the formal processes of reorganization and liquidation involve significant sales of assets, but the mere existence of these processes created incentives for managers to spin off valuable assets into new entities, often partially or wholly privately owned, while leaving liabilities in problem firms to enter bankruptcy. Furthermore, in the case of state-owned firms, the liquidation process appears to be as much a privatization procedure as one involving exit, as liquidators have put enormous efforts into finding private buyers for viable parts of these firms.

Perhaps most important of all has been the impact of the bankruptcy process on institutional development in Hungary. The process has stimulated the development of a cadre of professional trustees and liquidators with in-depth knowledge of the techniques of financial and organizational restructuring. Hungary has been willing to license both foreign and domestic firms as liquidators, and the foreign participation has brought outside knowledge and expertise into the picture. Foreign participation has also led to an increase in the number and commercial expertise of judges and in the sophistication of banks' understanding and approach to debt collection. Such learning by doing, even if it is fraught with problems and mistakes in the early stages, may be the only way to build the important institutions of a market economy.

Conclusions

Several broad conclusions can be drawn from the data and discussion presented above. First, the bankruptcy process appears to have had some degree of economic logic in 1992 and 1993. Better firms were more likely to enter and emerge successfully from the reorganization process, while worse firms were more likely either to fail during reorganization or file straight for liquidation. Furthermore, although the reorganization plans and related negotiations between debtors and creditors were not as sophisticated as one would find in advanced market economies, these plans did appear to address some core issues—debt restructuring, debt relief, and, in some cases, operational downsizing. There was scarce evidence of deep restructuring or of management change—a clear indication that the process was less than ideal. But the process was not a meaningless exercise with economically irrational or counterproductive results, nor did it result in the immediate forced closure of potentially viable firms. Given that Hungary's bankruptcy experiment was the first of its kind in the transition world, one can perhaps interpret this as a modest success.

Second, the experiment also supports the view that judicial reorganization need not be slow and costly. The first wave of reorganizations was handled surprisingly quickly, particularly considering the sheer number of cases, the novelty of the process, and the shortage of trained judges. This relative quickness is largely attributable to the decentralized design of the process. Once a case was approved by the court to proceed, the court had little role. The strict time limits laid out in the law also probably helped in assuring a relatively speedy resolution of cases.

With regard to speed and cost, it is very possible that the amendments of 1993 took a turn in the wrong direction by requiring the appointment of a trustee, chosen from the list of licensed liquidators, in all reorganization cases. Such a requirement made the process more bureaucratic and expensive. If creditors believe a trustee will help represent their interests, they should have the option of appointing one, as provided in the 1991 law, but this need not be a requirement. Indeed, if the creditors are not motivated to look after their interests, it is unlikely that a trustee will do it for them effectively.

Third, the major delays in the process in our sample occurred not in reorganization but rather in liquidation. Much of this delay was attributable to slowness in the appointment of liquidators to cases, and this delay led to significant opportunities for asset diversion, as discussed below. However, some of the delay was also attributable to the fact that liquidation was to a large extent perceived by all parties more as reorganization than as pure liquidation. This became even more true after late 1993, when the number of reorganization cases steeply declined—i.e., when liquidation appeared in effect to have replaced reorganization as the primary restructuring process. Interviews with liquidators and firms confirmed that many if not most liquidators saw themselves as active restructurers, representing first of all the interests of employees or the public rather than the interests of creditors. Virtually all real firms (as opposed to shells or firms with minimal assets, of which there were plenty) stayed alive during the liquidation process as the liquidator looked for ways to privatize their viable parts. While this may have been good for restructuring and privatization, it was not necessarily good for creditors, who felt powerless and unrepresented. In the end, this lack of a viable creditor-led exit and debt collection mechanism harms firms because it increases the cost and reduces the flow of credit in the economy.

It was noted earlier that one important reason that liquidators took their time was the structural basis of their fees. The Hungarian government should consider a change in the fee structure so that liquidators' fees consist only of a fixed percentage (whether 5 percent or another figure) of proceeds from the final sale of assets. This rather simple change could have a major impact on the process, speeding it up without sacrificing the incentive to save viable firms and better aligning the interests of the liquidators with those of the creditors.

Fourth, although the bankruptcy process displayed some economic logic, one should not assume that it operated as a similar law would in a market economy. The incentives of creditors to pursue debt collection aggressively are not yet as strong in transition economies, such as Hungary, as in advanced market economies. In the case of banks, for example, these incentives were compromised by successive bank recapitalizations between 1991 and 1995, which encouraged banks to turn to the state for assistance rather than depend primarily on the pursuit of problem debtors.[30] Not only are creditor incentives somewhat weak, but the watchdog institutions that one takes for granted in advanced market economies—such as accountants, lawyers, judges, credit-rating services, bailiffs—are still in their infancy. Thus, creditors find it extremely difficult to gather the information with which to defend their interests even if they are motivated to do so. The result is that bankruptcy processes (and what happens immediately before them) appear to be controlled to a far greater extent by debtor management in Hungary and other transition economies than in advanced market economies.

What does such managerial control imply for the outcome of the bankruptcy process? In essence, it implies that these managers and to some extent the debtor firms they manage will gain more than they would if the process were better monitored and controlled by creditors. A likely source of gain in Hungary appears to have been asset or other value diversion or value stripping prior to bankruptcy. Valuable assets were transferred to separate firms prior to filing (and the records disappeared so the transfers were not traceable by creditors, trustees, or liquidators), leaving the less valuable assets and the liabilities to enter the bankruptcy process. Interviews undertaken by the authors indicated that such asset diversion may have been quite common in 1992 and 1993, for both state-owned and private firms, although the survey was unable to capture this phenomenon on a wide scale which is not surprising, given the secretive nature of such transfers. Creditors could also have been involved in asset diversion by colluding with the debtor firm to transfer assets and thus repay that particular creditor prior to bankruptcy at the expense of other creditors. In advanced market economies, such transfers in anticipation of bankruptcy are void or voidable by the trustee. They are by law also voidable in Hungary, but liquidators reported tremendous difficulty obtaining the necessary evidence, due in large part to the underdevelopment of the watchdog institutions.

It is not easy to control asset diversion, but certain policy steps can certainly help. The major need is to strengthen the incentives of creditors to monitor the process closely and to improve their capacity to do so. This can be assisted, not only in Hungary but also in other transition and developing economies, through:

1. collateral and bankruptcy laws that clearly put secured creditors first in priority of recovery, even above costs of the proceedings;
2. streamlined court and bailiffs' procedures that lower the costs of foreclosure on collateral;
3. formulas for the compensation of liquidators that align their incentives clearly with those of creditors;
4. bankruptcy regulations that require the appointment of a liquidator immediately after a case is filed, to eliminate a long period between filing and approval during which incentives for value diversion are at their peak;
5. regular reporting requirements for liquidators and trustees, such as those included in the 1997 amendments to Hungary's law, that increase the transparency of activities;
6. strong banking privatization and reforms that reduce banks' ties to the state and thus their expectation of state subsidies;
7. strong macroeconomic discipline and enterprise privatization that reinforce the incentives of trade creditors to actively pursue collection of their debts;
8. avoidance of repeated bank recapitalizations, bad loan carveouts, or informal work-out processes that may be seen as backdoor avenues for state subsidization of debtors or creditors.

Finally, one must recognize that developing the institutions of a market economy, particularly the watchdog institutions referred to earlier, is a massive task and necessarily takes time. It will be greatly facilitated, however, if tight macroeconomic discipline leads to hard budget constraints, and thus firms and banks demand these institutions because they no longer view the state as their automatic safety net in times of financial distress.

Was the Hungarian experience a success? Was the automatic trigger that set it off a good idea? The answer depends profoundly on one's expectations. On the one hand, the Hungarian bankruptcy process in

1992–3 was nowhere near as efficient or effective as bankruptcy experience in advanced market economies. This was inevitable, given the distortions in incentives and the weakness of institutions in the transition setting. On the other hand, it was a start in the right direction. The controversial automatic trigger jump-started a process that helped change perceptions and stimulated needed institution building. This mechanism strengthened financial discipline among firms and furthered asset privatization and the building of a new profession of trustees and restructuring experts.[31] Such a trigger is clearly not needed in mature market economies with diligent creditors and was arguably too draconian, even in Hungary.[32] But an artificial trigger may nevertheless be useful in the very early stages of transition to help make bankruptcy a working reality and a viable option for creditors and debtors. The Hungarian bankruptcy experience should not be discarded but rather should be strengthened through strong and broad complementary market reforms.

References

Baer, Herbert L. and Cheryl W. Gray. 1996. Debt as a control device in transition economies: The experiences of Hungary and Poland. In *Corporate Governance in Central Europe and Russia,* edited by Roman Frydman, Cheryl W. Gray, and Andrzej Rapaczynski, Budapest: Central European University Press.

Dewatripont and Tirole. 1994. *The Prudential Regulation of Banks.* Boston: MIT Press.

Stark, David. 1996. Recombinant property in East European capitalism. In *Corporate Governance in Central Europe and Russia,* edited by Roman Frydman, Cheryl W. Gray, and Andrzej Rapaczynski, Budapest: Central European University Press.

Szanyi, Miklós. Market exit in Hungary, 1990–1994. Working paper. Center for Social and Economic Research (CASE), 1996.

Szanyi, Miklós, 1995. Liquidity Crisis and Bankruptcy Procedures in Hungary, OECD *Trends and Policies in Privatization,* 11, No. 2.

World Bank. 1996. *From Plan to Market.*World development report.

Notes

1. For the purposes of this chapter we use the term "bankruptcy" for the entire framework and "reorganization" and "liquidation" for the two specific procedures provided in the law. This differs from the Hungarian terminology, which uses the term "bankruptcy" to refer to the specific reorganization procedure rather than the broader overall framework.

2. The Polish bank-led conciliation process is an oft-cited alternative work-out process. For an empirical analysis of its short-term impact, see chapter 8.

3. The role of bankruptcy law in altering control rights over a firm is the subject of much recent literature in corporate finance. For further discussion and references, see Baer and Gray (1996).

4. In contrast, financing during reorganization is granted top priority under the U.S. Chapter 11 procedure. However, the situation may not be entirely analogous, as there are much tighter controls on asset disposition and cash flow during reorganization under Chapter 11 than in the Hungarian case. Thus, some Hungarian firms may have been able to "finance" their reorganizations, to the extent new financing was needed, through sales of unneeded assets rather than new bank loans.

5. Liens other than mortgages on real property had no priority over unsecured credit.

6. This creditor-approval requirement made it difficult if not impossible in most cases for debtors to obtain such relief from debt service, because creditors would not be likely to approve such a moratorium without seeing a viable reorganization plan.

7. Liquidators are licensed by the state and are not always considered by creditors to represent their best interests.

8. For a description, see Szanyi (1996) or Baer and Gray (1996).

9. We wanted to sample heavily from this list, which represented Hungary's biggest problem firms. It we had not stratified the sample to favor large firms, a totally random sample would have contained overwhelmingly small firms.

10. Approximately 40 percent of firms approached for the study agreed to participate.

11. All financial data cited in this study should be regarded as approximations. Data on assets, liabilities (particularly residual equity), and income are all questionable given the enormous deficiencies in accounting in the transition environment. However, because the extent

of accounting deficiencies within individual firms is unlikely to be correlated with other independent variables used in this analysis, we believe that the overall findings of the study (which depend on relative comparisons among different categories of firms rather than absolute magnitudes) are unlikely to be seriously compromised by such accounting deficiencies.

12. The firms in our sample were worse off financially than the average firm in bankruptcy, as is evident from a comparison of these numbers with data on bankruptcy cases collected by the Hungarian Central Statistical Office (CSO). According to the CSO data, the average debt/asset ratio of firms that filed for reorganization in 1992 was .57, well below the average for firms in our sample. We are indebted to Prof. Mark Schaffer for providing us with the CSO data.

13. In addition to credit from other parties (for example, owners or affiliated firms), some of this unclassified debt could well be misclassified suppliers' credits — for example, arrears to utilities. Little of it is likely to be bank credit.

14. The results shown in figure 6.2 summarize both prebankruptcy numerical data and subjective judgments reported in the questionnaire.

15. Only six firms, all of them liquidation cases, did not cite the automatic trigger as the impetus for filing. The other main reason cited was an attempt or threat by creditors to foreclose on collateral or otherwise collect debt. A total of sixteen firms cited this second reason (ten of which also cited the automatic trigger).

16. This is not unique to Hungary. Similar value stripping is widely reported to occur in Bulgaria, Ukraine, and other transitional economies that have been slow to privatize state assets. It can also be widespread in privatized firms if nonmanagerial shareholders have little ability to monitor managerial behavior (as in Russia). See World Bank (1996).

17. The survey attempted to get at the question of prebankruptcy asset diversion by asking numerous and varied questions on the topic. Only a small number of firms reported major asset transfers in the three years prior to filing. However, this is a variable that managers may choose to hide and that liquidators may not have information about, and thus significant underreporting is likely.

18. See, for example, Stark (1996).

19. These managers could have filed directly for liquidation, but filing for reorganization first resulted in an automatic three-month delay. Such delay might have been helpful, for example, in avoiding a subse-

quent investigation of prior asset transfers by liquidators, who have the legal right to void transactions occurring within one year of liquidation filing.

20. Such approval depended in most cases on the judge's finding that required information had been submitted with the filing.

21. This finding is probably somewhat biased by the large share of sample firms handled by the Budapest Court. This court was thought to be the most overloaded and thus the slowest in the country at that time.

22. For a further discussion of the institutions needed to support a market economy, and how they develop in transition settings, see World Bank (1996).

23. See, for example, Szanyi (1996). The improvement in interenterprise financial discipline was not necessarily matched by an improvement in the discipline imposed on firms by banks or government creditors during this period. See Baer and Gray (1996).

24. The absence of new credit is not surprising, given that the Hungarian law gives no priority to such financing.

25. Although the operational changes were reported in the survey questionnaires to be part of the reorganization plans, it is likely that in many cases they were undertaken simultaneously but were not formally included in the plan.

26. Recent literature in corporate finance stresses the importance of changing control rights over firm assets in times of financial distress. However, a number of authors, including Dewatripont and Tirole (1994), have suggested that control rights should not necessarily be shifted when an economy is subject to a systemic shock, since poor management did not lead to the bankruptcies. Rather, work-out processes are needed that keep control over productive assets in the hands of those who know how to use them. Such reasoning could arguably apply in the case of Hungary and other transition economies.

27. Even if actual debt service does not decline substantially, debt reduction may nevertheless lead to greater operational efficiency if it resolves the debt overhang problem.

28. Thus under law new financing during liquidation received better treatment (i.e. top priority among claims) than new financing under reorganization (discussed earlier).

29. This concept is taken from Stark (1996).

30. Baer and Gray (1996).

31. For further analysis of its impact on financial discipline, see Szanyi (1995).

32. Even if a trigger is adopted, ninety days is almost certainly too short, given that it barely exceeds average payment periods in advanced market economies.

7 Classical Exit Processes in Poland: Court Conciliation, Bankruptcy, and State Enterprise Liquidation

Cheryl W. Gray and Arnold Holle

A change in incentives and risks faced by enterprises and their managers lies at the heart of the transition in former socialist economies. Financial discipline needs to replace soft budget constraints, and the entry of new competitors and exit of loss-making firms needs to become the rule rather than the exception. Only through financial discipline can product and capital markets impose market discipline on managers, and only through entry and exit can markets select the most efficient producers.

The goal of this chapter is to examine how classical exit processes work in Poland, a country at the forefront of the move to a market system. A thorough study of exit processes should look not only at firms that exit but also at those that do not exit the market. Indeed, one issue we examine is how Polish firms slated for downsizing or closure differ from those selected—by the market or by administrative or political mechanisms—for survival.

Our study of exit processes is part of a larger study of bank and enterprise reform adopted by the Polish government in 1993, the Enterprise and Bank Restructuring Program (EBRP).[1] The goals of the EBRP were to rehabilitate and lay the groundwork for privatizing seven of the nine commercial banks that had been created out of the National Bank of Poland in 1989 and to restructure and privatize, under the banks' command, a group of financially troubled state enterprises. The program required the banks to establish work-out units and to take action by March 1994 to recover loans classified as doubtful or loss as of the end of 1991 (the so-called base portfolio). Several resolution paths were stipulated in the law. By the end of March 1994 (later extended to the end of April), each bank was required to take action so that each firm with a loan in the base portfolio met one of the following criteria: (1) the debtor had been fully servicing its debt for at least the last three months; (2) a court or bank conciliation agreement had been concluded; (3) the debtor had been declared bankrupt; (4) liquidation had been initiated under the Privatization Law (i.e., privatization is pending) or under the law on SOEs (i.e., the enterprise is being shut down); or (5) the debt had been sold on the fledgling secondary debt market.

The first path, a return to debt service, was the only one that did not envision exit and was intended essentially for healthy firms. The second, court or bank conciliation, was intended for potentially viable firms that could be successfully restructured through one of these two formal work-out processes. Court conciliation was a little-used work-out process in existence since 1934. Bank conciliation was a new and more flexible bank-led work-out process introduced by the EBRP to be available to banks and ailing firms for three years. The last path, sale of the problem loans on the secondary market, was intended to foster the transfer of debt to parties with a greater willingness or ability to put pressure on the firm to repay.[2]

The two remaining resolution paths were more focused on exit than on restructuring. The third path, bankruptcy under Poland's 1934 bankruptcy law, envisioned the closure of the troubled firm under the direction of the court and the distribution of its remaining assets to creditors. In theory, the firms in the worst financial state—that is, those with debts exceeding assets and with a liquidation value higher than the firm's value as a going concern—should enter bankruptcy. The fourth path, liquidation, differed from the third in that it was supposed to be available only to solvent firms (those whose assets exceeded their debts). Liquidation under the privatization law was merely a form of ownership change, while liquidation under the state enterprise law envisioned closure of the firm under the direction of the founding body.

We examine below three formal work-out and liquidation paths laid out in the EBRP—court conciliation, bankruptcy, and state enterprise liquidation. (Chapter 8 looks at bank conciliation.) We also look briefly at the two other paths in the EBRP, repayment and sale of debt.

Sample Distribution: Resolution Paths and Banks

This chapter is based on a survey of seventy-seven firms that went through at least one of five resolution paths—court conciliation, bankruptcy, state enterprise liquidation, repayment, and sale of debt. These seventy-seven firms are part of a larger stratified sample of 139 firms drawn from the pool of firms with debt to a bank larger than Zl 1 billion classified (based on the results of a 1992 audit of the banks) as doubtful or a loss as of year-end 1991.[3] In the case of the seven banks that remained in state hands, this is the pool of firms and debts—the latter defined as the "base portfolio"—covered by the EBRP. For Wielkopolski Bank Kredytowy (WBK) and Bank Slaski, the two banks slated for early privatization, the names of firms and size of the overall bad loan portfolio were not available to the authors. For the seven state-owned commercial banks, the base portfolio included 787 firms with loans totaling about Zl 16 trillion, or $1.43 billion.

The overall sample of 139 firms includes 130 firms from the seven state-owned banks and nine from the two privatized banks. The sample of 130 constituted about 17 percent of the total number of firms in the base portfolio of the state-owned banks. It was stratified to include some firms from each bank and at least ten firms in each resolution path, with a special concentration on bank-led conciliation cases. Cooperatives, companies in the defense industry, and a few intensely political cases were excluded from the sample. To the extent possible, cases were drawn at random subject to these criteria.[4] Because it is difficult to find data and interview subjects in completed bankruptcy and liquidation cases, our sample for these two resolution paths is composed primarily of cases that are still ongoing.[5]

Table 7.1
The 139-Firm Sample by Resolution Path

Resolution path:	Share of 787 enterprises in "base portfolio"	Number of enterprises in sample	Share of sample	Number of banks from which cases were taken
Repayment / good clients[a]	40%	22	16%	6
Bank conciliation	23%	62	45%	8
Court conciliation	2%	10	7%	4
Sale of debt	8%	10	7%	7
Liquidation	5%	12	9%	5
Bankruptcy	17%	23	17%	8
Other	5%	0	0%	–

[a] There are three different groups of debtors in this category: Some debtors had not been late on their payments before 1992, but were categorized as bad debtors in order to increase the amount of the recapitalization. Another group paid their debt back in full, and a third became current on their payments.

Source: Authors' calculations.

The 787 firms in the base portfolio of the seven state-owned banks and the final sample of 139 firms are broken down by resolution path as shown in table 7.1. We oversampled for bank conciliation cases—in terms of number but not in amount of bank debt[6]—because we wanted to study that process in depth. We undersampled for good clients, which are by far the largest EBRP group in terms of numbers. The percentage of cases in our sample from other resolution paths is similar to the overall percentage in the EBRP universe.

With regard to bank coverage, cases in all resolution paths were taken from at least four banks to try to get as broad and representative a view as possible of the EBRP program in Poland. However, there was some concentration in certain banks that were more cooperative than others. The breakdown by bank of the 139-firm sample, the twenty-two firms that repaid or became current on their loans, the sixty-two conciliation cases, and the fifty-five cases in other resolution paths is shown in table 7.2. Six banks are well represented in the 139-firm sample; from fourteen to thirty-two cases were drawn from each, representing from 12 to 46 percent of their total EBRP cases. Three banks are clearly underrepresented, with only six cases, two cases, and one case, respectively.

Table 7.2 also categorizes the nine banks into two groups based on their financial condition in 1993, when final decisions were taken on the resolution paths of most base loans and conciliation agreements began to be negotiated. Our sample of seventy-seven cases in paths other than bank conciliation is divided approximately equally between weaker and stronger banks. Our assessment of the financial condition is based on four indicators: (1) risk-weighted capital adequacy in 1993, when the agreements were being negotiated; (2) the change in risk-weighted capital adequacy in 1991–93; (3) the percentage of the 1991 loan portfolio rated as doubtful or loss; and (4) the change in percentage of loan portfolio rated as doubtful or loss in 1991–93 (see appendix 7.1). In our view, those banks that had adequate capital in 1993 or a relatively smaller 1991 bad loan portfolio to be worked out, or which had already shown an ability to improve either or both, were better placed to tackle the work-out effort successfully. The two privatized banks were automatically included in the category of strong banks. They were the first banks to be privatized, both because their situation in 1991 was clearly better than that of the other banks and because they were viewed to have better risk assessment and bad loan work-out skills. The three banks classified as weak had dim prospects for privatization in the near

Table 7.2
Distribution of Base Portfolio (787) and Sample (139)

	Financial condition[a]	Number of enterprises in base portfolio	Number of enterprises surveyed	Number of enterprises that repaid or became current	Number of enterprises in bank conciliation	Number of enterprises in other resolution paths
Bank 1	weak	72	14	1	7	6
Bank 2	weak	69	32	6	11	15
Bank 3	weak/ adequate[a]	158	19	5	8	6
Bank 4	adequate/ strong[a]	111	32	3	18	11
Bank 5	strong	146	6	0	5	1
Bank 6	strong	N.A.	14	3	8	3
Bank 7	strong	100	2	0	2	0
Bank 8	strong	131	19	4	3	12
Bank 9	strong	N.A.	1	0	0	1
Total		787	139	22	62	55

[a] Banks 3 and 4 are in the middle in our consolidated measure of financial condition. Bank 4, the stronger of the two (with a much higher capital ratio and more improvement in its capital position and loan portfolio), has been classified with the strong banks for purposes of our analysis. Bank 3 (which had an extremely high level of bad debts in 1991) has been classified with the weak banks.

Source: Authors' calculations.

future and were to be consolidated with Pekao S.A., the former savings bank for hard currency, under a plan signed into law on July 16,1996.

We would like to emphasize that the assessment of a bank as strong or weak does not necessarily reflect the quality of its management. The regional allocation of portfolios to banks made risk spreading particularly difficult for bank managers. The various banks inherited portfolios of differing qualities and clients with diverse prospects, and they operated in regional economies with varying growth potentials. In the words of one bank manager: "A commercial bank with a substantial loan portfolio can only be as good as the financial standing of its clients."

Characteristics of Sample Firms

Sectoral Distribution

Overall, the decision for a firm to enter bank conciliation or one of the other resolution paths does not appear to have been heavily affected by the sector in which it operated. Figure 7.1 shows a breakdown of the

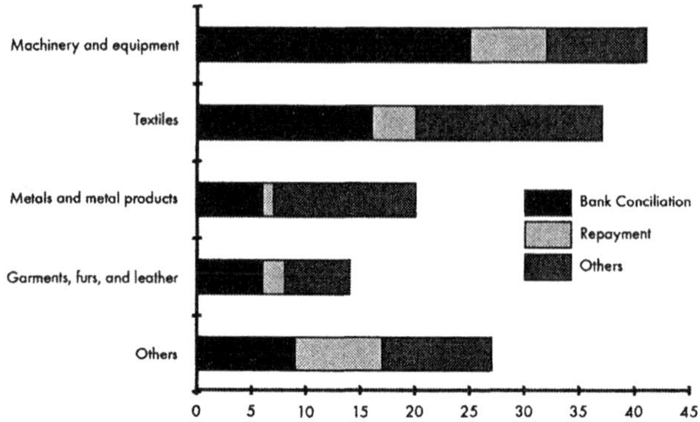

Figure 7.1: Sample Distribution According to Industry Type
Source: Authors' calculations.

139-firm sample into three broad groupings: the sixty-two that entered bank conciliation, the twenty-two that repaid or became current on their debt, and the fifty-five that entered other resolution paths. While there is a significant concentration of all three among two broad sector groupings—textiles, machinery and equipment—all sector groupings have firms in each samples. Bank conciliation is somewhat more common for firms in machinery and equipment and somewhat less common for firms in metals and the residual "other" category.

Amount of Debt

Table 7.3 divides the base portfolio among resolution paths. While only 23 percent of firms entered bank conciliation, they accounted for 46 percent of the base portfolio. Enterprises in other resolution paths had far lower levels of bank debt on average—between Zl 9 billion and Zl 17 billion per firm, compared with Zl 41 billion for firms in bank conciliation.

Profitability and Employment

Figure 7.2 shows the average operating profits in 1991 and 1992 and the average number of employees of the firms entering different resolution paths.[7] These two variables are significant explanatory variables for the path selected.[8] Firms entering bank conciliation were on average more profitable in 1991–92, with average operating profits of 1 percent, than firms in other paths. Those entering liquidation or bankruptcy

Table 7.3
Share of Debt by Resolution Path for all 787 EBRP Firms

Resolution path	**Share of 787 firms (in number)**	**Share of base portfolio (in value)**	**Average debt owed to main bank (end-91)—in bln Zl**
Repayment/good clients	40%	20%	15.1
Bank conciliation	23%	46%	41.1
Court conciliation	2%	1%	13.8
Sale of debt	8%	7%	16.8
Liquidation	5%	2%	9.4
Bankruptcy	17%	10%	12.1
Other	5%	4%	13.8

Source: Authors' calculations.

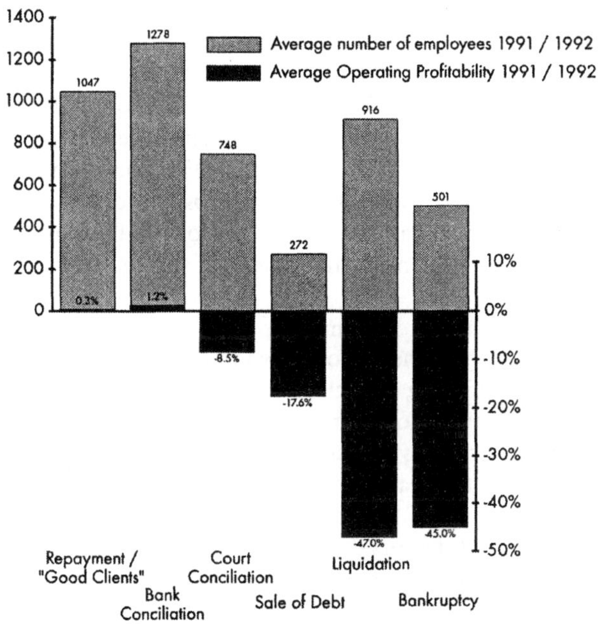

Figure 7.2: Average Operating Profitability and Number of Employees

Source: Authors' calculations.

were the least profitable, with average operating profits of -47 and -45 percent, respectively. Firms entering bank conciliation also had on average more employees (almost 1,300 per firm) than firms in other paths. Those entering bankruptcy had the fewest employees (other than the small number of firms whose debt was sold), but had still been quite large in 1991–92, with about 500 employees on average. In essence, the work-out routes captured firms that either had reasonable prospects for successful work-out or were large enough to make a political impact. This result is encouraging and shows that the process may have roughly succeeded in separating viable from unviable firms.

Reasons for Financial Distress

The causes of financial distress in the sixty-two enterprises entering the bank conciliation process differed little from those in the seventy-seven enterprises going into different paths. The most commonly cited cause of financial distress—named by almost nine out of ten firms in both groups as one of the three most important causes and by almost one-half as the most important—was declining domestic consumption of the goods they produced. Indeed, total domestic consumption of the major product of the seventy-seven firms declined on average by more than 40 percent between 1989 and 1991. The second most commonly cited cause, which affected about one-half of all firms, was an inability to collect receivables. A decline in exports to CMEA markets affected about one-third of the firms and was cited as the most important cause by one-fifth of the firms. One-quarter to one-third of the firms noted increasing import competition, increasing prices of inputs, or rising tax burdens as important.

These answers confirm that many of the firms in our sample were severely affected by the general downturn in the Polish economy in 1990 and 1991, either suffering a decline in sales themselves or having customers who were unable to pay their bills. A smaller but still significant percentage were affected by structural changes specifically attributable to transition, including the realignment of prices, increasing import competition, and declining CMEA exports. While it is often hard to differentiate between these two factors—recession verses transition-related structural change—in practice, one might expect those firms citing structural reasons for their financial distress to have a lower likelihood of eventual recovery. No significant differences in reasons for financial distress appear to exist, however, between the firms in our sample that entered work-out processes and those that repaid or were slated for closure.

Structure of Enterprise Debt

Figures 7.3 through 7.6 give a snapshot of the structure of debt in seventy-three of the seventy-seven firms that entered resolution paths other than bank conciliation.[9] Although overall debt levels did not rise sub-

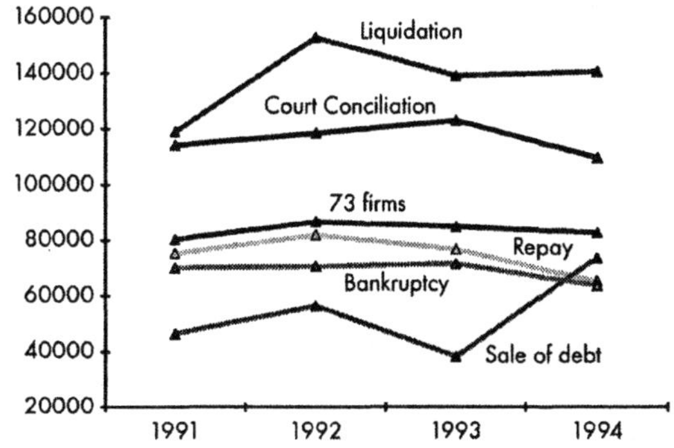

Figure 7.3: Average Debt by Resolution Path (million real 1991 Zl)

Source: Authors' calculations.

stantially in real terms in the early 1990s for firms in most resolution paths (figure 7.3), the size of the debt relative to assets (figure 7.4) and the structure of the debt (figure 7.5) both changed dramatically. As a share of total assets, total debt rose on average from 65 percent in 1991 to 157 percent in 1994. Most of this increase reflected a decline in the real value of assets, due both to the shedding of assets and to inadequate indexing for inflation.[10] With regard to the structure of debt, bank debt and payables to suppliers fell both in real terms and as a share of total debt, while government debt skyrocketed by both measures. Taxes and social insurance payables to the government more than doubled in real terms from 1991 to 1993. As a share of total assets, they increased from

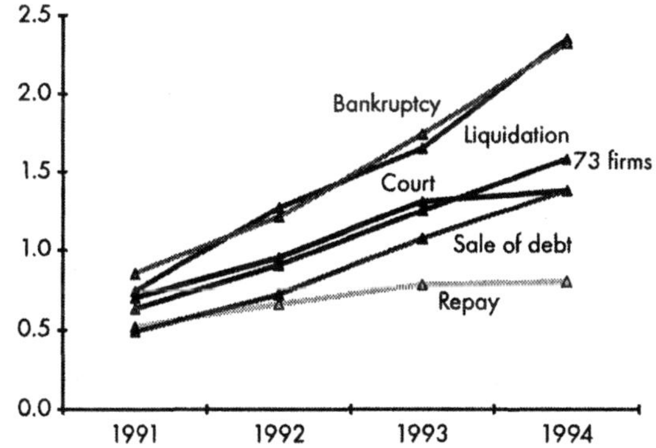

Figure 7.4: Debt as a Share of Total Assets

Source: Authors' calculations.

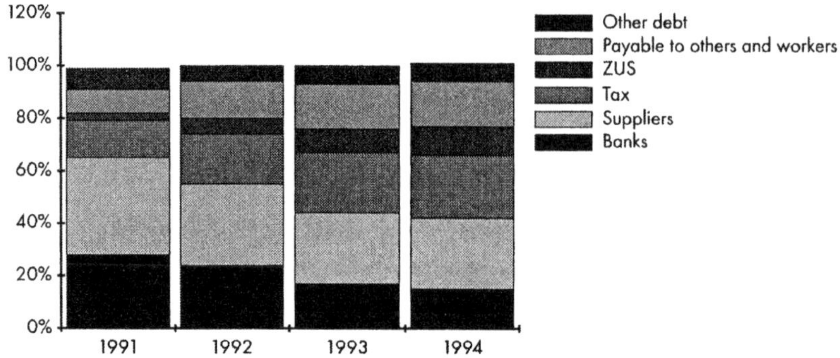

Figure 7.5: Debt Structure by Type of Creditor (73 firms)

Source: Authors' calculations.

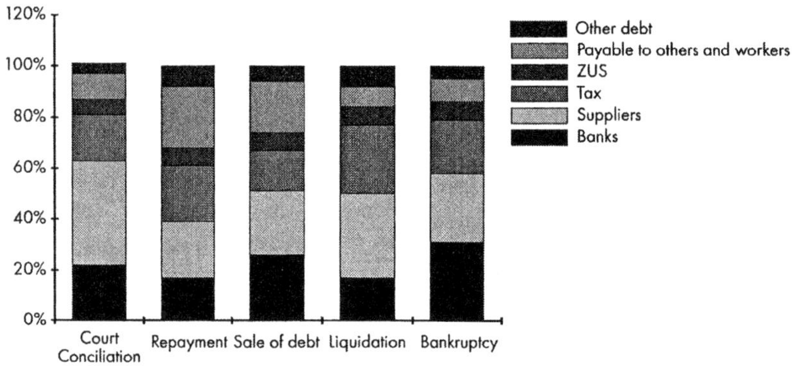

Figure 7.6: Debt Structure at End-1992 by Resolution Path

Source: Authors' calculations.

Table 7.4
Identity of Largest Creditor (66 cases)

	1991	1993
Banks	19	12
Suppliers	35	22
Tax	5	20
ZUS	0	1
Other	7	11

Source: Authors' calculations.

12 percent in 1991 to 44 percent in 1993. In sixteen cases, the government (the tax office and ZUS, the social security agency) replaced banks

or suppliers as the largest creditor (table 7.4). At least 70 percent of these payables consisted of overdue tax and social insurance arrears.[11] The structure of debt did not vary dramatically among firms in the various resolution paths other than bank conciliation (figure 7.6), although banks were somewhat more prominent in bankruptcy cases, and suppliers were more prominent in court conciliation cases.

These trends support the findings of other studies that indicate that suppliers are among the first creditors to begin imposing hard budget constraints on firms in transition.[12] As the suppliers themselves are squeezed by market pressures and cut-offs in subsidies, they begin to require payment in cash before goods are shipped. State-owned banks also tighten their lending when subject to macroeconomic and market discipline. The biggest remaining source of softness in firms' budget constraints during the early stages of reform is likely to be the government, which has great technical and political difficulty collecting tax and social insurance payments and thereby forcing financial discipline on problem firms.[13]

Court Conciliation

Court conciliation (sometimes called "arrangement") is a work-out process that dates from 1934. It was adopted simultaneously with the bankruptcy law of that year, and was designed to provide an alternative to liquidation for ailing firms that were able to restructure their debts with their creditors and thereby continue in business.

Court conciliation is a rather inflexible process when compared with more modern reorganization processes in mature market economies, and the Poles adopted the bank conciliation process in 1993 in part to avoid the inflexibility of court conciliation.[14] A party can apply for a court conciliation only if it ceased to pay debt service "due to reasons that are exceptional and independent of it . . . and insolvency is due to circumstances over which [it] had and could have had no impact."[15]

Work-outs under court conciliation exclude secured creditors and government creditors (such as tax and social security offices), and thus they cover only trade creditors and bank creditors (to the extent they are not covered by, or choose to forego, security interests). Because the procedure was designed to provide debt relief, the law envisioned only financial terms in the restructuring agreement; operational conditions—such as changes in employment, investment, or management—were not expected, although they presumably could be included if all parties agreed. Any agreement must be approved by a two-thirds majority, in terms of the value of claims, or four-fifths for write-offs greater than 40 percent. Finally, only parties attending the proceedings are allowed to vote on the proposed agreement. It may be difficult for a debtor with many creditors to assemble the required majority in one place for the vote.

Once the debtor applies for court conciliation, the court must decide within two weeks whether to proceed. If it decides to open a case, the judge appoints a judge-commissioner and a reorganization trustee. Incumbent management stays in control of the firm, supervised by the trustee, but must obtain permission from the judge-commissioner for all business activities outside normal operations. Secured creditors can be barred from foreclosing on assets if such foreclosure would hinder reorganization, and all creditors are barred from filing for bankruptcy or accepting debt repayments outside of a conciliation agreement.

The Process in Action

Court conciliation lay on the books virtually dormant throughout the socialist period. It was brought to life in 1990, and filings expanded rapidly in 1991 and 1992. However, only a small share of applications led to actual conciliation cases, as most were either rejected by the court or settled out-of-court (table 7.5).

Table 7.5
Applications for Court Conciliation in Poland, 1990–92

	Applications	Procedure opened	Rejected applications
1990	2	1	0
1991	76	8	8
1992	688	98	73

Source: Polish Ministry of Finance.

Our sample had ten cases of court conciliation. Of these cases only two were initiated before bank conciliation was adopted as an alternative process on February 3, 1993. It is interesting that court conciliation continued to be used even after bank conciliation emerged as a feasible alternative. The application for conciliation was filed by the debtor. It appears that creditor pressure triggered the filing in about one-half of the cases, while the other half were filed because the debtor hoped to get debt relief or additional working capital (table 7.6).

Table 7.6
What Triggered Court Conciliation? (in number of firms)

	Most important reason	One of the three most important
Attempts or threats by creditors to foreclose on collateral	3	4
Inability of debtor to obtain additional working capital	2	6
Pressure by founding organ to deal with creditors	0	1
Threat by creditor(s) to sell their debt	1	5
Other (debt relief)	3	3
Other (creditor pressure)	1	1

Source: Authors' calculations.

The actual process of conciliation was quite rapid. Our ten cases took on average about six months from initiation to agreement and another nineteen days for the agreement to take effect. Of the cases that were not appealed, court conciliation took only about 15 percent longer than bank conciliation from initiation to effectiveness.[16] These question the view that court conciliation is necessarily too slow—a major rationale behind the adoption of the bank conciliation process.

In almost all cases, two or three creditor groups were formed for the purpose of negotiation. Small creditors, which held only 2–3 percent of the debt, usually formed a separate group. In contrast to bank conciliation, small creditors in court conciliations were more inclined to vote in favor of proposed agreements than large creditors. While this might be expected, given that they generally received better treatment, small creditors did not react similarly in bank conciliations, perhaps because they distrusted the objectivity of a process controlled by another creditor. In only one of our ten cases was a creditors' council created to monitor the implementation of the agreement, and in practice it is unclear who (if anyone) conducts such monitoring. Although government claims are not included in court conciliation agreements, seven of our ten firms negotiated separate agreements with ZUS (the social security agency).

Financial and Operational Outcomes

What were the outcomes of conciliation in our sample of cases? Our survey was conducted on average about two years after the agreements were signed. It is possible to gauge early impacts, although clearly the story is still unfolding in many of these firms. In terms of financial restructuring, court conciliations provided only for debt relief—either write-offs or reschedulings (table 7.7). There were in practice no debt–equity swaps or new credits as in some bank conciliations. Of the two forms of debt relief, court conciliation agreements had fewer write-offs (on average about 30 percent of debt) than bank conciliation agreements (on average about 60 percent, as discussed in chapter 8). Small creditors received bigger write-offs than large creditors, but the difference was not as marked as in bank conciliations. However, reschedulings in court conciliations were more generous. On average they gave a

Table 7.7
Financial Conditions in Court Conciliation Agreements

Condition	Weak banks		Strong banks		All banks	
	No. of cases	% of debt in conciliation	No. of cases	% of debt in conciliation	No. of cases	% of debt in conciliation
Write-off						
—large creditors	6	30%	1	37%	7	31%
—small creditors	6	8%	2	21%	8	12%
—one category	0		1	80%	1	80%
Increase in maturity of debt: No. of days between when agreement took effect and:						
Large creditors						
—first payment	6	340	3	328	9	336
—last payment	6	1780	3	1424	9	1662
Small creditors						
—first payment	5	149	3	192	8	165
—last payment	5	777	3	405	8	637
One category						
—first payment	0		1	457	1	457
—last payment	0		1	1188	1	1188
Immediate partial repayment						
—large creditors	0	0	0	0	0	0
—small creditors	1	3%	0	0	1	3%
—one category	0	0	0	0	0	0
Debt–equity swap	0	0	0	0	0	0
New equity	0	0	0	0	0	0
New bank credit	0	0	0	0	0	0

Source: Authors' calculations.

grace period of six months for small creditors and seven months for large creditors, more than 50 percent longer than under bank conciliation. The rescheduled loan period was some two years for small creditors and four and one-half years for large creditors, 100 percent and 50 percent longer, respectively, than in the case of bank conciliations. *Indeed, if one computes the net present value of the rescheduled loans for all classes of creditors, it appears that both processes yielded very similar benefits for debtors: about two-thirds of their debt was effectively erased in both processes.*

In contrast to bank conciliation, there is no evidence that enterprises indebted to weak banks were treated more leniently than those indebted to strong banks. Indeed, the opposite was true in our sample, although its size is too small to draw exact conclusions. Also in contrast to bank conciliation, our regression results point to a significant positive relationship between the extent of write-offs and two other variables—the operating profitability of the firm and its level of indebtedness.[17]

In terms of operational outcomes, the results of our small sample are disconcerting. Only in two of the ten cases did it appear at the time of the survey that the rescheduled debt would be properly serviced. The other eight firms continued to face difficulty in debt service. Two had subsequently folded and two more were trying to conclude a bank conciliation agreement when they were interviewed in mid-1995; of the other four, three were trying to find other means of debt relief and in one case bankruptcy proceedings had begun. Although reported gross and net profit margins had improved as firms were allowed to record debt write-offs as income,[18] average operating profits as a share of operating revenues of the ten firms had fallen from -8 percent in 1992 and -7 percent in 1993 to -10 percent in 1994(figure 7.7). Clearly the performance of most firms had not improved as a result of the court conciliation.[19]

In sum, the court conciliation process is inadequate as currently designed, primarily because of its inflexibility—its exclusion of debt to government, its total emphasis on financial rather than operational restructuring, its high majority voting requirements (particularly in the case of large write-offs), its requirement that creditors be present to vote, and other provisions. But it is not fatally flawed. In a sample of ten cases it worked surprisingly speedily as a debt reduction device, although apparently less effectively as a restructuring tool. With amendments in design and greater resources devoted to monitoring agreements, combined with continued efforts to spur market-oriented behav-

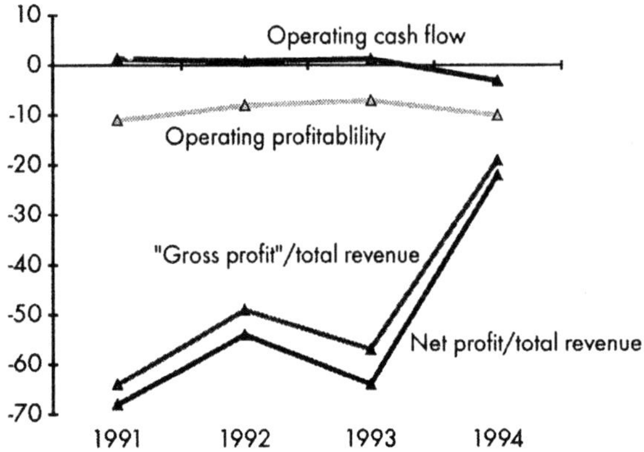

Figure 7.7: Profit Measures for Firms in Court Concilliation

Source: Authors' calculations.

ior in banks, the court conciliation process could become a reasonable formal work-out process for firms in financial distress.

Bankruptcy

The Polish bankruptcy process, originally adopted in 1934 and amended in 1990, is modeled on pre-war European statutes and is designed as a liquidation process for insolvent firms.[20] A creditor, owner, or manager of a firm can petition the court for a declaration of bankruptcy.[21] The judge is generally supposed to open the case if the petition is complete and if the company has sufficient assets to cover procedural costs.[22] The judge then appoints an official trustee, who takes over management of the firm's assets. All debts immediately fall due, and all creditors are asked to file their claims. The trustee can continue to keep the firm in operation during bankruptcy if needed to preserve the value of company assets. The trustee creates a balance sheet for the company and publishes a detailed list of debts. Interest stops accruing, except on secured debts, once bankruptcy is declared. Most set-offs of claims are no longer allowed, and the trustee can prohibit any new foreclosures on collateral. The district court sets the level of remuneration of the trustee based on a recommendation of the bankruptcy judge.[23] The bankruptcy judge can appoint a creditors' council to help manage and dispose of assets and must do so if 20 percent of creditors so request.

The law as it is now designed has several major deficiencies. First and perhaps foremost, the priority list discourages active involvement by nongovernment creditors in the bankruptcy process because the list makes it difficult for banks and other creditors to recover anything.[24] Creditors often express the view that the government always comes first. In fact, if the government and procedural costs do not consume the entire estate, it is likely that employees' claims will. Second, even with little expectation of recovery, creditors are asked to pay between 5 and 13 percent of the value of their debt as an advance payment of court fees.[25] A third deficiency is that the law provides few means for a trustee or judge to void fraudulent transactions made by managers or owners prior to the bankruptcy filing.[26] Fraudulent transactions are indeed thought to be common, and the legal system must find a way to identify and punish them if the bankruptcy process, or indeed any debt collection process, is to be credible.[27]

The Process in Action

The number of bankruptcy petitions to Polish courts grew steadily in the early 1990s (figure 7.8). Although most petitions were considered by the courts, it appears that more than one-half were rejected, in most cases because the petitions were incomplete or assets insufficient to cover costs. Given the poor treatment of secured creditors under the

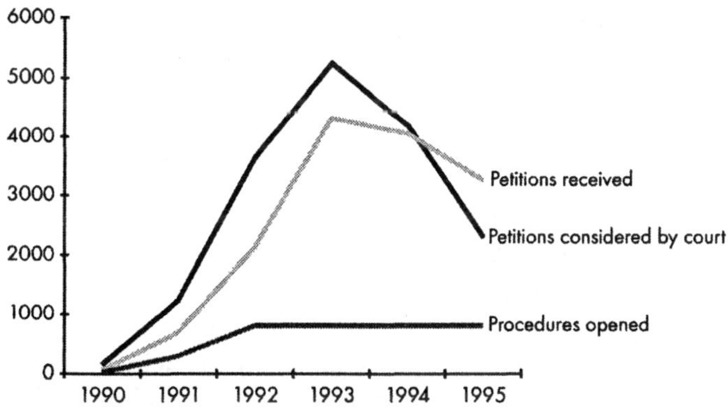

Figure 7.8: Bankruptcy Petitions and Cases by Year, 1990–96

Source: Polish government statistics.

rules of priority and the requirement for creditors to deposit money for costs up front, it is not surprising that about two-thirds of all cases appear to have been filed by the debtor.[28]

The implementation of the law is severely hampered in Poland, as in all transition settings, by institutional weakness. The courts are understaffed, underfunded, and undertrained, and they lack support from related professions—such as trustees, accountants, lawyers, bailiffs, investigators, and prosecutors—that provide critical information-gathering and enforcement functions in more established market economies. A 1993 study of eighty bankruptcy petitions found that the proceedings were started and completed as expected, with assets divided among creditors, in only fifteen cases.[29] The other petitions were either rejected because of incomplete information or lack of funds to cover costs or were withdrawn. The study concluded that, while some of the cases were legitimate instances of economic downturn, many were fraudulent in nature. Most assets with any value had been sold or otherwise disappeared before the petition for bankruptcy was filed or considered by the court. However, investigations of possible crimes were extremely rare, presumably in large part because of the absence of resources or information to prosecute cases.

Our 139-firm sample contained twenty-three enterprises in bankruptcy, which owed debts to eight of the nine commercial banks. As noted in figure 7.2, these firms were in considerably worse shape than the other 116 firms, with average operating losses of nearly 50 percent of sales in 1991 and 1992. Creditors were not as passive against these enterprises as against those that entered bank or court conciliation proceedings. In nineteen of the twenty-three cases, debt collection had already been taken before the filing of the bankruptcy petition. The date of filing in our sample ranges from June 1991 to April 1994. Eight cases were filed before the EBRP law was adopted on February 3, 1993, and six cases were filed in April 1994, just before the EBRP's extended deadline for dealing with base portfolio debt. Four of the twenty-three had previously been in state enterprise liquidation.

Our sample is split evenly between filings by the debtor and filings by creditors. The debtor filed in nine cases and its founding body, representing the state treasury as owner, in three. Five cases were filed by a bank creditor, five by a supplier, and one by the tax office. Creditor filings in our sample are much higher than average, in part because of the linkage of our cases with the EBRP and the requirement that banks take action to resolve bad debts in EBRP firms.

The filing was protested in three cases, twice by the debtor and once by the founding body. The filing of a protest does not appear to have held up the process significantly. On average, the court opened the bankruptcy proceeding three months after the bankruptcy petition was filed; only one case was severely delayed, languishing for fourteen and a half months before the court opened the proceeding. A trustee was appointed in all cases immediately. In all but one case, the judge appears to have selected the trustee independently; in the exception the choice of trustee may have been influenced by incumbent management. On average, the trustee filed a first report after three months and made the first disposition of assets a few days later.

Only two of the twenty-three cases had been completed at the time of our survey (on average, more than two years after the court decision to proceed). Trustees in the other twenty-one cases were asked how long they expected their cases to take in total. Two thought their cases could be completed within two years, eleven expected the process would take two to three years, and eight thought they needed at least three years. If these expectations are accurate, the average length of a bankruptcy case would be about three years. The most commonly cited reasons for delays were unclear ownership rights, particularly of real estate (mentioned by thirteen firms), and the lack of buyers for assets (mentioned by fourteen firms).

Financial and Operational Outcomes

Although the phenomenon is much less marked than in Hungary (see chapter 6), even in Poland it appears that liquidation through the bankruptcy process can be an avenue for enterprise restructuring in certain cases. Eighty percent of our sample of firms continued to operate as a going concern after bankruptcy had been declared, but only for one year on average. Five of twenty-three were still in operation when the firms were surveyed in mid-1995. From 1992 to 1994, those firms had seen sales revenues fall by 14 percent (after accounting for inflation), real operating profits fall by 78 percent, and employment fall by 38 percent, but wages for remaining employees had risen by 25 percent in real terms. Three firms expected improved operating results in 1995, two even anticipated an increase in profits. One company in particular did so well that it settled with its creditors in a bankruptcy conciliation, emerged from bankruptcy, and is now operating under its old management.

A major function of bankruptcy is to transfer control over assets to new agents, or to new private agents in the case of transition economies. Three-quarters of the assets that had been sold, leased, or transferred by the time of our survey had indeed gone to unaffiliated private parties. In nineteen of the twenty-three cases, the trustees had attempted to sell all or part of the firm as a going concern, and it appears that roughly 40 percent of the fixed assets of these firms will survive.

The major losers in Polish bankruptcy are creditors, even secured creditors, because of the many claimants with higher priority. The trustees interviewed in the study anticipated that gross recoveries from asset sales would equal on average about 25 percent of the value of assets on the opening balance sheet. A full 80 percent of these recoveries were expected to be consumed by bankruptcy expenses and severance payments to workers. In all but one case, employees' severance claims were expected to be fully satisfied (table 7.8). Nevertheless, banks were expected to receive nothing in ten cases and be fully compensated in none. Suppliers, in the lowest priority class, will recover nothing in three-quarters of all cases and on average were expected to recover roughly 7 percent of their claims.

Bankruptcy is in theory one mechanism through which control rights over a firm shift to creditors in times of financial distress. As seen in Figure 7.9, creditors have more involvement in bankruptcy than in state enterprise liquidation, but the level of involvement is still less than that of debtor management.

What do these results say about the functioning of the Polish bankruptcy system? Like court conciliation, the process is faulty but not fatally flawed. A change in the order of priorities, which began with the pas-

Table 7.8
Schedule of Creditor Satisfaction in Bankruptcy Cases
(Percentage of Claims Satisfied)

Lowest creditor group at least partially satisfied:	**Employees**	**Social insurance**	**Government**	**Banks**	**Suppliers**
Employees (N=1)	70%	0%	0%	0%	0%
Social Security and Government (N=9)	100%	32%	25%	0%	0%
Banks (N=6)	96%	39%	34%	21%	0%
Suppliers (N=6)	100%	92%	87%	43%	24%
Average percentage of claims satisfied	98%	49%	43%	17%	7%

Source: Authors' calculations.

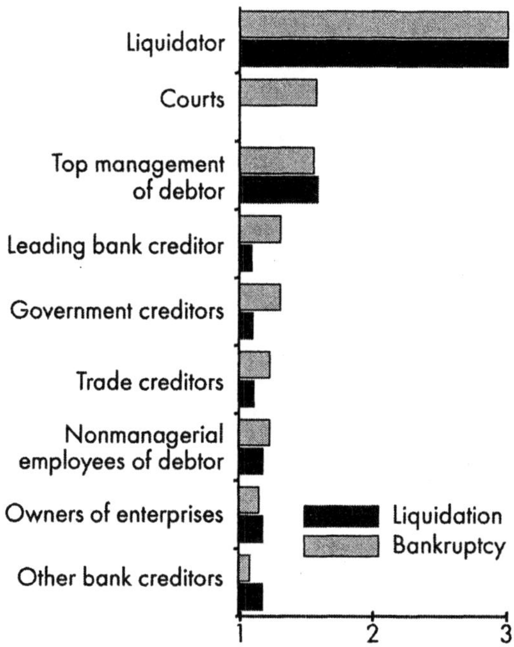

Figure 7.9: Average Involvement of Various Creditor Groups
1 = Passive; 2 = Active; 3 = Controlling
Source: Authors' calculations.

sage of the new collateral law in 1996, will help. In addition, a major effort is needed to build institutional capacity in the courts, the trustee profession, and related investigative and prosecutorial arms of the government in order to detect and punish fraud in the bankruptcy process. Poland has a beginning on which to build, but much remains to be done.

State Enterprise Liquidation

Article 19 of the Polish State Enterprise Law provides for the liquidation of state-owned companies.[30] Although this law, adopted in 1981, is a legacy of the socialist legal system, there is no evidence of Article 19 having been used before transition began in 1990. Under Article 19, creditors may initiate the liquidation of a state-owned borrower by petitioning the governmental entity charged with exercising ownership control (the founding body), or the founding body may initiate the procedure with the authorization of the Ministry of Privatization and the Ministry of Finance. The law specifies several criteria that justify—but do not require—a liquidation filing, including inability to pay the obligatory dividend to the state treasury and negative after-tax earnings. Only companies that are still solvent are in theory eligible for this procedure. However, many of the companies in liquidation prove to be insolvent, and many ultimately end up in the bankruptcy courts.

Liquidation is a process controlled by owners and managers. The founding body appoints a trustee charged with drawing up a balance sheet and list of liabilities and selling off the assets in whole or in part. There are no restrictions on who may serve as liquidator, and appointment of the incumbent manager as the liquidator has reportedly been quite common. Creditors have means to influence the process. Nevertheless, they may prefer Article 19 liquidation to bankruptcy because the costs of realizing collateral are lower and because liquidation affords an opportunity to neutralize the superpriority of state claims.

The Process in Action

Liquidation under Article 19 has been widely used in Poland since 1990, with almost 1,300 firms having entered the process and about 57 percent of these having completed it or been moved into bankruptcy (table 7.9). Data on 853 cases filed in 1990–92 indicate that about three-fourths of the cases are relatively small firms (under 200 employees), and only 9 percent are large firms (over 500 employees).[31]

As can be seen from table 7.9, the number of petitions for liquidation per year declined after 1991. This probably reflected both the turnaround in the Polish economy and the likelihood that the worst firms had already exited. However, the number of liquidations converting to bankruptcy was quite steady. This could signal a realization by liquidators that some firms that filed for liquidation had insufficient assets to cover their debts; alternatively, in the absence of careful oversight by creditors, liquidators or managers could conceivably have diverted some assets of firms in liquidation to new owners, leaving state entities to enter bankruptcy with debts and few assets.

Although the number of new petitions fell and the number converting to bankruptcies remained steady from 1991 to 1995, the backlog of unfinished cases grew every year. At the beginning of 1996, almost 600

Table 7.9
Liquidations Started and Completed between 1990 and 1995[a]

Year	Petitions	Refused	Accepted	Completed liquidations	Bankruptcy filings
1990	58	0	20	0	0
1991	538	24	512	22	18
1992	314	15	322	80	127
1993	237	13	228	108	143
1994	160	4	155	101	25[b]
1995	60	4	52	21	[128][c]
Total	1367	60	1289	332	441[d]

[a] Meller (1996) citing data from the Ministry of Privatization.
[b] By September 1994.
[c] By inference for the period October 1994 to end 1995.
[d] Blaszczyk, 1995.

open cases—already in process over two years on average—still remained to be resolved.

Three previous surveys—covering twelve, twenty-six, and twenty-two firms, respectively[32]—looked at the liquidation process in action. The first two looked primarily at what happened to the assets of liquidated firms. They found that most assets were sold, if possible, at auction; moveables were quite easy to sell, real estate much harder. Although discounts were often large, many of the assets were eventually put to use in new private firms, and many employees were able to keep their jobs with the new owners. Creditors were likely to be the major losers in the process. No clear schedule existed in most cases for satisfying debt claims, and many irregularities occurred—aggravated by the fact that liquidators were in most cases the managers themselves.

The third survey, of twenty-two firms, looked at a sample of liquidations of relatively small Warsaw-area firms. In contrast to the earlier studies, this survey found few examples of liquidators having a prior relationship with the company.[33] Creditors did not initiate the liquidation in a single case; all cases were initiated by the founding body or company management. In stark contrast to our results (see below), creditors were fully satisfied in fifteen of the twenty-two cases in this survey. It is possible that the outcomes of these twenty-two cases were significantly better than average outcomes from liquidation in the country as a whole. Not only were all twenty-two in the Warsaw area, where the administrative infrastructure for liquidation is better, but most companies were service rather than manufacturing firms and were relatively small (with sixty-eight employees on average). We doubt that the conclusions of this prior study—that liquidation is a better option for creditors than bankruptcy—apply in the country as a whole.

Our sample includes twelve cases of state enterprise liquidation. With average operating losses of over 60 percent in 1991 and 1992, these firms were in worse financial situation than firms in any other resolution path. They were also the first to be dealt with. Liquidations began on average in July 1992,[34] more than eight months before the average starting date of bankruptcy cases and about a year and a half before the average start of bank conciliation cases. Despite their terrible condition, the enterprises entering liquidation had seen very little pressure from creditors. Only one-sixth had been subject to any action to collect debt prior to the beginning of liquidation—a far lower proportion than firms in other resolution paths. Perhaps this is explained by their early starting date, as creditor passivity was most marked in the beginning years of transition.

Our sample confirms that liquidation is a debtor-driven process. Of the twelve cases in our sample, managers of the debtor firm filed the petition for liquidation in eight cases, the workers' council of the debtor firm filed in three, and the founding body in one. Although respondents reported various reasons for filing for liquidation rather than bankruptcy (table 7.10), none of the twelve firms was fully servicing its debts at the time of filing. This, together with the small role played by the founding body in initiating cases, strongly suggests that liquidation has in practice been an alternative mechanism to deal with insolvent com-

Table 7.10
Reason for Placing Firm in Liquidation Rather than Bankruptcy (number of cases)

Reason	**Most important reason**	**One of the three most important**
Firm was servicing all its debts	in no case	in no case
Firm had high net assets	2	4
Creditors expected to receive more under liquidation	2	6
Creditors wanted to restructure firm	2	6
Management wanted to restructure firm	3	6
Other	2	2

Source: Authors' calculations.

panies, rather than what it was originally intended to be—a means for the state to close insolvent state enterprises.

Our survey reinforces the conclusion of earlier studies that creditors have no real influence over the process. Liquidators were appointed quickly, on average three days after liquidation proceedings began. In three-quarters of all cases, the debtor chose the liquidator; in the remaining firms, the founding body controlled the selection. In no case did creditors influence the choice of liquidator.

The liquidators in our sample were able to move much faster at the beginning of the process than the trustees in our sample of bankruptcy cases, perhaps because liquidators knew the companies better. Liquidators filed a first report in fifty-one days on average, more than a month faster than bankruptcy trustees. The first disposition of assets occurred eight and a half weeks into the process, as compared to fifteen weeks in bankruptcy cases. But the liquidation process then slowed down, and on average our liquidation cases are expected to take longer to finish than our bankruptcy cases. The five completed cases in our sample took on average more than three years to complete.[35] Liquidators in the seven unfinished cases expect their companies to be in liquidation for four years and eight months on average—more than 50 percent longer than average bankruptcy cases. Why is the process ultimately so slow? Eleven of twelve liquidators cited the lack of buyers for assets, and six cited confusion in ownership rights, particularly of real estate. The compensation formula for liquidators may also play a role because compensation is on a flat-rate monthly basis and is not tied to revenues from asset disposition. Liquidators have little incentive to complete the process.[36]

What happens in the interim? Four-fifths of our firms (the same proportion as in bankruptcy) continued to operate after liquidation had begun, and one-half were still in operation when the firms were surveyed in mid-1995—on average three years after filing. From 1992 to 1994, sales had fallen 49 percent in real terms in these firms, and operating profits (also after accounting for inflation) had fallen by 11 percent. Employment had fallen by 45 percent, but real wages per employee for those still employed had risen by 76 percent.

Outcomes

Liquidation is in part a process of privatization, whether of firms or of their assets. Liquidators tried to find buyers of parts of the firms in three-quarters of our cases. It appears that nearly 40 percent of our firms' fixed assets will survive as part of a going concern. Insiders of the firms appear to be in subsequent control of about 20 percent of the assets sold, leased, or transferred by these firms by mid-1995. That is roughly twice the level of insider privatization as under bankruptcy. As in bankruptcy, the majority of assets (64 percent) were subsequently controlled by nonaffiliated private parties.

While liquidation may be an important avenue for privatization, creditors are the big losers. They are recovering very little from liquidation in our sample of firms. Liquidators expect gross revenue from asset disposition to equal on average 19 percent of the value of assets on the opening balance sheet. But in eight of our twelve cases for which data are available, liquidation expenses and severance payments are estimated at double this amount—some 38 percent of the opening book value. Banks are expected to recover only 6 percent of the value of their claims on average,[37] and suppliers only 3 percent (table 7.11). In two-thirds of our cases, bank creditors and suppliers are expected to receive nothing.

In sum, while state enterprise liquidation is on paper a means for government owners to close solvent companies, it appears in practice to be used more commonly as a means for debtor management to bypass bankruptcy and maintain control over the disposition of assets of insolvent firms. Because it impedes the ability of creditors to recover their debts, the process undercuts the potentially important governance role that creditors can play—and do play in mature market economies—over firms in financial distress.

Table 7.11
Schedule of Creditor Satisfaction in Liquidation Cases
(Percentage of claims satisfied)

Lowest creditor group at least partially satisfied:	Employees	Social Insurance	Government	Banks	Suppliers
Employees N=3	93%	0%	0%	0%	0%
Social Insurance N=1	100%	10%	0%	0%	0%
Government N=4	100%	13%	11%	0%	0%
Banks N=1	75%	12%	10%	12%	0%
Suppliers N=2	100%	100%	100%	13%	15%
Average percentage of claims satisfied	96%	25%	23%	7%	3%

Source: Authors' calculations.

Other Resolution Paths

The other two resolution paths taken by some firms in our sample are repayment and sale of debt. As noted earlier in figure 7.2, firms in our sample that repaid their debt or became current on debt service had on average over 1,200 employees and zero profits in 1991–92, while firms whose debt was sold were generally small and unprofitable (with average profts of -18 percent).

Repayment

Twenty-two of the firms in our sample were classified as having either fully repaid or become current on their debt to their lead bank. When we took a closer look, we found that four of these firms had in fact never been in arrears,[38] and thus only eighteen actually fit the category (fourteen having repaid in full and four having become current on debt service). Some of these eighteen firms repaid as early as 1992, others not until the summer of 1994. On average, it took approximately six months to clear arrears, starting from the date that payments to the lead bank were resumed. About 80 percent of the amounts repaid went for principal, 20 percent for interest. Repayments were all in money rather than in equity or assets.

While the lead bank was repaid in full, other creditors did not fare as well. Of the eighteen firms, four cleared no arrears to trade creditors and eleven cleared them only in part. Five cleared no arrears to government creditors, and nine cleared them only in part.

When asked how they obtained the funds that financed the repayment, five of the eighteen firms cited new loans from banks or other creditors as the most important source. Although lead banks were not allowed by law to give new credit to firms with debt in their base portfolios, other creditors were not legally barred from extending new credit. If this same ratio of 5:18 were to hold for all firms that repayed, this would imply that eighty-seven firms paid back old loans with new loans—arguably not the intention of EBRP. Two firms disposed of assets to pay back their loans, one received cash support from government, and the other seven cited operating profits (i.e. retained earnings) as the most important source of funds for repayment.

The eighteen firms that repaid were not only better than other firms in our sample at the beginning of the process, but they have fared somewhat better since. Sales revenues rose on average by 1 percent in real terms from 1992 to 1994, and operating profits rose 15 percent. The level of outstanding debt dropped by 18 percent. Employment in those firms fell on average by 22 percent during those two years, and the average wage rose 68 percent. This is the only resolution path in our sample with firms that report rising sales and profits.

Sale of Debt

In theory, sale of debt is an interesting and innovative alternative to traditional routes of debt collection. It allows banks to rid themselves of problem debt without resorting to costly negotiations or judicial procedures and to put it in the hands of firms or individuals better able to deal with it. There are several hypothetical reasons why such parties might want to purchase bad debt from banks. First, they may be more willing or able than banks to collect the debt. Second, they may be customers of the debtor firm who can use such debt to pay for goods and services. Third, they may wish to swap the debt for equity and take control of the debtor firm. Under any of these scenarios sale of debt can increase financial discipline and improve corporate governance in debtor firms.

In practice, however, sale of debt was perhaps the least successful path of EBRP. Banks had little incentive to sell their debt. One reason involved taxes: the losses on such sales (that is, the difference between the book value and sale price) were not deductible from income for tax purposes, while write-offs of debt under other forms of restructuring were deductible. Thus, a sale of debt for 40 percent of its book value (a high price in such markets) would cost the bank as much as a 100 percent write-off of bad debt. Another disincentive was the strong aversion to debt sales by debtors: if the bank thought any continuing relationship with the client was even a remote possibility, they would find it difficult to take a step so disliked by the client.

Not only were the incentives of banks weak, but so were those of potential purchasers. Purchasers faced the same problems as banks with debt collection—slow judicial procedures and low legal priority under collateral and bankruptcy laws. In addition, the ability to use debt to pay for purchases from debtor firms was extremely limited in practice; although debt could be sold without the consent of the debtor under Polish law, the purchaser of the debt could not use it to pay for goods and services provided by the debtor without the latter's consent. Finally, as noted earlier, the automatic approval for debt–equity swaps envisioned under EBRP was blocked in practice by the Ministry of Privatization, making it unlikely that purchasers could gain control of debtor firms.

Our sample included ten cases of debt sale. Only six were successful sales; the other four were unsuccessful attempts. Although the motivations behind the successful cases were not entirely clear, indications are that three were attempts by employees or competitors to get control via debt–equity swaps, one involved a customer who wanted to use the debt to pay for purchases from the debtor firm, one was a purchase of debt by the local government as a form of subsidy, and one was a buyback of debt at a discount by the debtor itself (not allowed by law but difficult to stop in practice). On average the bank took three and a half months to complete the sale and received 23 percent of the face value of the debt (with a range from 7 to 59 percent in the six cases). Our survey and related interviews with banks and firms confirmed the view that debt sales are not yet easy to use or widely accepted alternatives to more conventional debt collection routes in Poland.

Summary and Conclusions

The Enterprise and Bank Restructuring Program adopted by the Polish parliament in early 1993 provided numerous avenues for banks to resolve their bad loan problems. This chapter has looked at three traditional exit processes—court conciliation, bankruptcy, and state enterprise liquidation—and has briefly touched upon debt repayment and sale of debt as alternatives under EBRP. Chapter 8 surveys the innovative bank conciliation (i.e. work-out) process.

From a broad perspective, many aspects of EBRP appear positive. The program was innovative in design and was implemented without fraud or corruption. It was an important catalyst in spurring creditors to take action against bad debtors, and there appears to have been rough economic logic in the division of firms among resolution paths. Better off and/or larger firms tended to repay their debt or enter bank conciliation, while weaker and/or smaller firms tended to go into bankruptcy or liquidation.

Looking in greater detail, the traditional exit processes appear to have worked but with many flaws. Our sample of ten court conciliation cases were concluded in about six months on average—about the same as the time required in our bank conciliation cases (see chapter 8). Firms in court conciliation received smaller debt write-offs but greater extensions in debt maturity than firms in bank conciliation. On a net present value basis, the extent of debt relief under the two processes looks similar. In contrast to bank conciliation, the extent of write-off in our court conciliation cases was positively correlated with two other economic variables: the operating profitability of the firm and its level of indebtedness. With regard to outcomes, the subsequent performance of firms in court conciliation did not improve, and in eight of ten cases, they continued to have problems servicing their debt.[39]

Poland's bankruptcy and related legislation has had major weaknesses in design and implementation, most notably the low priority given to secured creditors, the institutional weakness of the bankruptcy courts and related professions, and the difficulty that judges and trustees have had in identifying and curbing fraudulent behavior. Bankruptcy is inevitably a slow process, and in our sample of twenty-three cases, the process was expected to take on average at least three years. Creditors have little involvement in the process, although still more than in state enterprise liquidation. They expected to recover very little of their original claims in our sample of cases (on average 17 and 7 percent for banks and suppliers, respectively), but again, still more than in state enterprise liquidation.

Neither bankruptcy nor court conciliation as currently designed give creditors sufficient control over firms in financial distress.[40] Both could work much better if redesigned, however, and if supported by institutional development in the courts and related professions and by better systems of collateral and debt collection more generally. Court conciliation could be redesigned in several ways to increase flexibility. Government claims could be included in the process. A lower majority could be required for approval of a work-out agreement—not varying with the extent of debt write-offs proposed. All creditors could be allowed to vote, whether or not present. And more financial and operational restructuring options could be available for inclusion in restructuring agreements. Creditors' rights under bankruptcy could be strengthened by ensuring that secured creditors have first priority, by reducing up-front fees, and by giving courts and trustees greater powers and resources to uncover and punish fraudulent transactions. Any improvements in design need to be complemented by strong economic policies that give banks and other creditors powerful incentives to use these debt-collection mechanisms.

State enterprise liquidation is perhaps the most problematic of the three formal processes. It is almost entirely controlled by debtors. In most cases debtor management chooses the trustee—and in some cases even serves as trustee. In our sample of twelve cases, state enterprise liquidation is proving to be significantly slower than bankruptcy. Firms continue in operation far longer than in the bankruptcy process, and more assets eventually end up under the control of managers and employees of the original firm. It appears that the process, though on paper designed for solvent firms, is often used in practice as a way to get around bankruptcy and keep debtor management in control of assets for as long as possible. Creditors are the big losers: they have no power and in our sample of cases were expected to recover almost nothing (6 and 3 percent for banks and suppliers, respectively). The loophole of state enterprise liquidation needs to be closed if the other formal processes are to work as intended. This form of liquidation should be strictly limited to solvent firms; if this is not feasible, the process should arguably be eliminated altogether because of the abuse it invites.

The EBRP included a nonbureaucratic market-based alternative to these formal processes—sale of debt. In practice, however, it appears to have played a very limited role. Few sales were attempted and even fewer concluded. Tax disadvantages and debtor antipathy appear to have undercut banks' incentives to sell, and the difficulty of using debt to pay for purchases or swapping debt into equity appears to have undercut potential purchasers' incentives to buy. While a secondary market for debt can in theory be an effective and nonbureaucratic means to increase financial discipline in problem firms, it will take some time—and probably a change in tax and other rules—to build such a market in Poland.

The EBRP also allowed firms to repay or become current on debt and thereby avoid other resolution paths. A large number of firms (about 40 percent) did repay. In our eighteen sample cases that repaid arrears (the other four in the category never having been in arrears), almost 40 percent appear to have used retained earnings to repay, while 28 percent appear to have borrowed new money to pay back old debt.

When looking at the Polish experience, and that of Hungary and other transition economies as well, one could well argue that policy makers should focus on improving traditional and broadly applicable exit and work-out processes, rather than adding new ones for selected subsets of firms. The traditional processes—formal and informal work-out processes and bankruptcy—are needed in any case. Judges need not be heavily involved in all aspects of these processes (in the case of work-outs, more decentralization is generally better), but some oversight by courts is arguably needed to insure due process in the treatment of all parties. Special alternatives for selected firms—whether bank conciliation in Poland, debtor consolidation in Hungary, or enterprise jails elsewhere—tend to suffer from the same general problem: they lead those firms to expect lenient treatment and thereby create a moral hazard that may stall further restructuring. Our survey has buttressed our belief that Poland has neglected its traditional processes, in part because of its emphasis on bank conciliation. Now that bank conciliation has expired as an option, Polish authorities should shift their energies to improving the fundamental tools of debt collection and corporate governance.

Appendix 7.1
Data Used for Bank Categorization

	Category	Equity as a share of risk-weighted assets, 1993[1]	Change in equity as a share of risk-weighted assets 1991 to 1993	Bad loans as a share of loan portfolio 1991	Change in bad loans as a share of loan portfolio 1991 to 1993
Bank 1	weak	-1.2%	-14,0%	31%	+13%
Bank 2	weak	-4.4%	-3.2%	high	large increase
Bank 3	weak/adequate	-6.6%	+2.6%	60%	-38%
Bank 4	adequate/strong	8.5%	+5.1%	41%[a]	-4%[a]
Bank 5	strong	21.2%	+17.9%	41%	-13%
Bank 6	strong	strong	privatized	low	privatized
Bank 7	strong	6.6%	+8.3%	28%	-10%
Bank 8	strong	10%[b]	strongly positive	28%	-3%
Bank 9	strong	strong	privatized	17%	privatized

Underlying data:
[a] Data not available for 1991; 1992 data used instead.
[b] Data not available for 1993; 1992 data used instead.

	Category	Equity as a share of risk-weighted assets, 1993[2]	Change in equity as a share of risk-weighted assets 1991 to 1993[3]	Bad loans as a share of loan portfolio 1991[4]	Change in bad loans as a share of loan portfolio 1991 to 1993[5]	Total
Bank 1	weak	1	1	2	1	5
Bank 2	weak	1	1	1	1	4
Bank 3	weak/adequate	1	2	1	3	7
Bank 4	adequate/strong	3	3	1	2	9
Bank 5	strong	3	3	1	3	10
Bank 6	strong	3	3	3	3	12
Bank 7	strong	3	3	2	3	11
Bank 8	strong	3	3	2	2	10
Bank 9	strong	3	3	3	3	12

Rankings:
1 Excluding recapitalization bonds received at the end of 1993.
2 Negative = 1; Positive up to 10% = 2; Positive of 10% or more = 3.
3 Decrease = 1; Increase up to 5% = 2; Increase above 5% = 3.
4 Over 40% = 1; 20–40% = 2; Below 20% = 3.
5 Increase = 1; Decrease up to 10% = 2; Decrease of 10% or above = 3.

Source: Authors' calculations.

Appendix 7.2
Logistic Regression Results

A logistic regression was run to test the significance of operating profitability and number of employees in explaining the resolution paths taken by the 139 firms in our sample. The coefficients and their chi-square values are indicated below. The positive coefficients for operating profit and number of employees for paths 1 and 2 indicate that firms with higher operating profits or more employees are clearly more likely to repay or enter bank conciliation than to "exit" via bankruptcy or state enterprise liquidation. The high chi-square values and low P-values confirm that these two variables are highly significant. The chi-square and P-values for path 3 are lower, indicating that there is not a highly significant difference between the firms that enter court conciliation and those that exit. (The coefficient for operating profit has a P-value just over 10 percent, however, making it marginally significant.)

Resolution Path:Values relative to bankruptcy/liquidation
(chi-square, P-values in parentheses)

	1: Repayment/good clients (relative to 1)	2: Bank conciliation (relative to 1)	3: Court conciliation (relative to 1)
Intercept	-.77[a] (2.86, .091)	.05 (.02, .895)	-1.49[b] (6.08, .014)
Operating profit (EBIT)	5.75[b] (10.81, .001)	6.33[b] (19.83, .000)	2.95 (2.70, .101)
Number of employees 1992	.001[a] (3.72, .054)	.001[b] (6.55, .011)	.001 (1.20, .273)

[a] P-value less than 10 percent.
[b] P-value less than 2 percent.

Source: Authors' calculations.

Appendix 7.3
Comparing Poland's Two Formal Work-out Processes

	Bank Conciliation	**Court Conciliation**
Legal basis:	Law of February 3, 1993	Presidential Decree of October 24, 1934, as amended in 1990
Valid until:	March 18, 1996	Indefinitely
Pertains to:	Majority state-owned companies	All businesses
Application made by:	Debtor	Debtor
Application made to:	Bank holding at least 20% of the debt of the debtor; 10% if that debt is larger than one billion old zloties	District Court of the debtor
Liabilities excluded:	Social insurance (ZUS), wage claims, personal withholding taxes payable by firm, secured creditors	All those excluded in bank conciliation plus taxes, fines and fees to government authorities
Secured creditors:	Can either take part in agreement or accept security in full satisfaction of their claim.	Same
List of creditors in theory put together by:	Debtor	Debtor
List of creditors in practice put together by:	Bank	Judge
Restructuring plan in theory prepared by:	Debtor	Debtor
Restructuring plan in practice prepared by:	Bank	Unknown
Debt–equity swap:	Encouraged	Allowed
Voting:	All creditors, whether at meeting or not	All creditors at meeting, minimum 50% for quorum
Required majority:	Creditors with 50% of claims; tax office has to vote with lead bank	Creditors with two-thirds of claims, or four-fifths if write-off larger than 40%
Effectiveness:	After signature from Ministry of Privatization	After court approval
Supervision by:	Creditors' council	Trustee
Chosen by:	Creditors' assembly	Creditors' assembly
In case of non-compliance:	Bank can either reimburse other creditors for their losses or apply to court for agreement to be unwound	A creditor or the trustee can apply to the court, which can then hold a trial to unwind the agreement

Source: Authors' analyses.

References

Baer, Herbert and Cheryl W. Gray. 1996. Debt as a control device in transition economies: Evidence from Hungary and Poland. In *Corporate Governance in Central Europe and Russia*, edited by Roman Frydman, Cheryl Gray, and Andrzej Rapaczynski. Budapest: Central European University Press.

Brol, Jan. 1993. Upadlosc i postepowanie upadlosciowe w swietle praktyki sadowej, in: Report from the Conference on Insolvency Proceedings, Popowo, Poland, November 15–20. (Summary published in *Rzeczpospolita. Pathologia w bankructwach.*)

Coates, Richard and Arlene Mirsky. 1995. Restructuring and bankruptcy in Central and Eastern Europe. Deloitte Touche Tohmatsu International.

Dabska, Luiza. 1995. Polish bankruptcy law and its application. ACE project on the process of enterprise exit in the transition to a market economy. Case Institute, Warsaw. Mimeographed.

Fan, Qimiao and Mark Schaffer. 1993. Government financial transfers and enterprise adjustments in Russia, with comparisons to Central and Eastern Europe. Working paper no. 394.

Groszek, Mieczyslaw et al. 1993. *Restrukturyzacja Finansowa Przedsiebiorstw i Bankow*. Warsaw: Komentarz, Elinex.

Groszek, M. and S. Ciesla. 1993. Liquidation and bankruptcy—regulations, experiences, results: The case of Poland. Warsaw: Polish Development Bank. Mimeographed.

Meller, Michael. 1996. Liquidation of state-owned enterprises in Poland. Paper presented at conference, Ownership Transformation and Restructuring Processes in Central and Eastern Europe, April, 11–12, Warsaw.

Sak, Pamela Bickford and Henry N. Schiffman. 1994. Bankruptcy law reform in Eastern Europe. *The International Lawyer* 28, no. 4.

Szlezak, Andrzej. 1993. Polish bankruptcy and reorganization law. Warsaw: Soltyszinski and Partners. Mimeographed.

Notes

1. For a more in-depth description of the EBRP, see chapter 8.

2. It was possible for firms to go through more than one resolution path. A firm could, for example, go from state enterprise liquidation into bankruptcy, or from court conciliation into bank conciliation (but not vice versa), and possibly then into bankruptcy or liquidation.

3. The other 62 firms in the 139-firm sample went through bank conciliation. For a description of the origin—both date and type—of the debts of the 139 firms to the banks, see chapter 8.

4. The selection was random in six banks for which the authors had access to a complete list of their base portfolios. The other state-owned commercial bank and one privatized bank chose the sample. The other privatized bank did not cooperate in the study.

5. It is not clear a priori whether the selection of primarily ongoing cases creates a bias and, if so, whether the bias is toward better or worse firms. We believe there is not likely to be a strong bias either way.

6. If measured in size of bank debt, the bank conciliation sample is representative. Firms in the bank conciliation process owed 46 percent of the debt to banks in the base portfolio.

7. Size of debt is to some extent a proxy for size of the firm and is therefore correlated with number of employees.

8. See appendix 7.2 for logistic regression results. This pattern holds for both strong and weak banks.

9. Debt data were unavailable for the other four firms. For detailed debt data on firms in bank conciliation, see chapter 8.

10. Revaluation of assets during this period was allowed several times, with the extent of revaluation being largely at the discretion of firm management.

11. We do not know the exact break-down between current and overdue payables for all categories of taxes for all years. Of debts to the tax office and the social insurance agency at year-end 1993, 28 percent of payables were current and 72 percent were overdue (43 percent for more than one year). Because payments to ZUS were in general more likely to be made than payments to other tax agencies, an estimate that three-quarters of tax liabilities were in arrears appears reasonable.

12. See, for example, Fan and Schaffer (1993).

13. The decision which creditor to pay can be an important one in financially distressed companies, sometimes handled personally by the Chief Executive. A number of managers in the survey expressed person

al gratitude to the head of the local tax office, without whose help the enterprise would not have survived.

14. See appendix 7.3 for a comparison of the two processes.

15. Groszek (1993). The enterprise must have been operating for three years, have maintained adequate bookkeeping, and have not been in bankruptcy or prior conciliation within the past five years.

16. Our sixty-two cases of bank conciliation took on average 118 days from initiation to agreement, and on average forty-nine more days until effectiveness because of the need to obtain approval from the Ministry of Privatization (chapter 8). In the case of bank conciliation, many agreements were at least partially negotiated before the process officially began, while this is much less likely to have occurred in court conciliation. Thus, it is possible that the two processes were in practice equally rapid.

17. The dependent variable Y was the percentage of total base portfolio debt that was written off. The best-fitting regression equation produced the following statistics for three dependent variables:

	parameter	est.t-statistic	P-value
EO91 (1991 operating profits)	0.390	2.3	5.10
DA91 (1991 debt/assets ratio)	0.434	3.4	5.04
DUMMY (1=weak bank)	-.116	-1.9	0.15

Two other dependent variables—number of employees and number of days agreement was reached before April 30, 1995—were insignificant.

18. The practice of recording write-offs as income-inflated profit margins in firms subject to bank conciliation as well. See chapter 8.

19. It should be noted, however, that even in the U.S. some 90 percent of Chapter 11 cases eventually end up in liquidation. Saving even 10 percent of firms—and a significantly higher percentage of large firms—could arguably be viewed as success.

20. The bankruptcy process does provide the possibility of a conciliation agreement among unsecured creditors, if priority creditors can be fully satisfied and if the firm submits a financial restructuring plan approved by two-thirds of these creditors in value of claims and one-half in number agree. A survey in 1993 found only one instance when such conciliation procedure had been used in the course of bankruptcy (Brol, 1993).

21. Managers are by law required to file a bankruptcy petition within two weeks from the "debtor's failure to pay his debts" or they become

personally liable to the creditors for any losses arising from failure to file (Groszek and Ciesla, 1993). A 1993 study found that this provision was violated regularly, with no consequences for firm managers (Brol, 1993). It is unclear whether any attempt has ever been made to hold a manager liable for failure to petition.

22. The court has significant discretion as to whether or not to initiate a bankruptcy proceeding. Before deciding to initiate a case, the court can hold hearings and request testimony from the debtor, creditors, and other interested parties, and, in the case of state enterprises, from the workers' council, the founding Ministry, and the State Treasury (Coates and Mirsky, 1995).

23. Remuneration generally ranges between 2 and 20 times the average salary in Poland per case (Coates and Mirsky, 1995). The trustee also receives reimbursement for all expenses.

24. The priority given to secured creditors in bankruptcy was extremely confusing (Baer and Gray, 1996) until the passage of the new collateral law in late 1996. The bankruptcy law provides that secured creditors should be satisfied first, but subject to the rules on priorities of mortgages and liens laid out in the Polish Code of Civil Procedure. Pursuant to the Code of Civil Procedure, prior to 1996, secured creditors came far down in priority, below procedural costs, payments to employees, taxes, and rents due on government-owned property. Furthermore, the government had an automatic lien over all property of any party in arrears to the government (for taxes, social security payments, or customs duties). This lien need not have been written or formalized in any way to have priority. Since most problem debtors had large arrears to the government, this automatic lien severely impinged on the security provided by any other liens. Finally, non-bank secured creditors were at an extreme disadvantage, because all bank loans, whether or not secured, had priority over other creditors, even if the latter were secured.

According to the bankruptcy law, once claims secured by collateral are satisfied, the remainder of the assets (and any excess of proceeds from the sale of secured property over the value of secured claims) become the bankruptcy estate. This estate is then used to satisfy creditor claims in the priority specified in the bankruptcy law itself. According to this latter bankruptcy-specific priority, bank and trade creditors come behind: (1) the costs of the proceedings (which include all amounts due to the court, the receiver, and employees for wages, severance payments, etc.), (2) taxes, and (3) social security contributions.

25. Szlezak (1993).

26. The law provides only that gifts made within six months prior to filing can be voided. It does not extend to sales or other types of contract (even if they contain an element of gift through underpricing). There is also opportunity to void fraudulent transactions made prior to filing, but such a process is extremely difficult to implement because it requires proof of intent to defraud. Furthermore, in 1970 a number of actions, such as intentionally reducing the value of a creditor's claim by paying back selectively or not keeping adequate accounting records, were decriminalized, and this made it more difficult for judges and trustees to detect and void prior fraudulent actions.

27. Brol (1993); Sak and Schiffman (1994); Coates and Mirsky (1995).

28. In 1991 and 1992, 67 and 60 percent of all cases, respectively, were filed by the debtor firm itself. (Groszek and Ciesla, 1993).

29. Brol (1993).

30. This should not be confused with Article 37 of the Privatization Law, which provides a privatization route called "privatization through liquidation". Privatization through liquidation is not an exit process in our meaning of the term and is not included in our study.

31. Groszek and Ciesla (1993).

32. Meller (1996).

33. The phenomenon of the manager being appointed liquidator may have been more common in 1991 and 1992 than in later years.

34. The earliest liquidation filing in our sample was in June 1991, and the latest in January 1995.

35. The quickest was a little faster than two years, the longest took four years almost to the day.

36. In the prior study, of twenty-two Warsaw cases, liquidators were paid on average 9 to 16 million zloty per month, a multiple of what bankruptcy trustees typically receive.

37. If the average bank creditor recovers 6 percent of outstanding claims four and a half years after the beginning of the process, the net present value of the creditor's recovery is 2.2 percent of its face value on the day the liquidation procedure began.

38. These three were presumably included in the base portfolio either by mistake or to shore up the amount of the recapitalization.

39. Although it is still early to judge outcomes, initial indications are that firms in bank conciliation may not have seen much improvement either.

40. Both appear more successful as avenues to transfer control over assets to new (see chapter 8) private parties.

8 Poland's Bank-Led Conciliation Process

Cheryl W. Gray and Arnold Holle

Poland is one of the fastest-growing economies in Central and Eastern Europe. In 1990 the government implemented a strong macroeconomic reform program that liberalized most prices, devalued and made the zloty partially convertible, and eventually cut inflation. Although the government did not move as rapidly on privatization, Polish state enterprises were forced to react to declining subsidies,[1] new competition from imports, a collapse in traditional trading structures, and the government's stated commitment to eventual privatization. State enterprises reduced their workforces, shed unnecessary assets, worked harder to collect overdue receivables, and took other steps to try to stay in business in the new environment.[2]

Although state enterprises did begin the painful process of restructuring, many were heavily burdened by growing debt. Some debt was inherited from socialism, but for most firms the debt originated in the early days of reform. Firms looked to bank credit to address immediate liquidity problems—some managers believing that this reform effort would be short lived like previous ones. While banks had some incentives to refuse, in practice it was easier for banks to provide further working capital and not force firms into liquidation. By late 1991, it was clear that, for macroeconomic reforms to be sustainable, they needed to be accompanied by strong banking reforms that would sharply reduce the flow of bank credit to problem firms.

In early 1993, more than a year after the debt problem was clearly identified, the Polish government adopted perhaps the most far-reaching programs of banking reform yet undertaken in any transition economy. The Enterprise and Bank Restructuring Program (EBRP) attacked the problem on many fronts. It included short-term policy directives to curtail indiscriminate lending and longer-term policies to change the fundamental incentives of banks. Policy was not the only focus: the program also addressed some issues of organization and skill enhancement within selected departments in the banks as well as the legal processes for debt workouts.

The Bank Conciliation Procedure

One of the most innovative features of the reform program was the introduction of a new process—the bank conciliation procedure—for bank-led work-outs of problem firms. This process has received wide acclaim from participants and observers both within and outside Poland.[3] This chapter looks carefully at how the bank conciliation process has functioned in practice by studying both its procedural aspects and its initial impact on enterprise restructuring in a representative sample of firms.[4] Although a few studies have summarized the outcomes of the process in some detail at the aggregate level,[5] none have yet presented firm-level data.

The bank conciliation procedure is a work-out process similar to formal work-out processes in other countries, such as Chapter 11 in the American bankruptcy code or the bankruptcy procedure in Hungary (see chapter 6). From a public policy perspective, these procedures are intended to promote the reorganization of firms whose value as going concerns exceed their liquidation value. Such firms, for example, may have assets (such as specialized machinery or unique trademarks) that have little value in alternative settings. Through reorganization, a problem debtor tries to negotiate a reduction in immediate debt-service requirements as a means to keep the firm alive. In return for the reduction in debt service, creditors may insist on partial payments, equity stakes, or fundamental changes in the size or functioning of the firm in order to increase their chances of future repayment of the remaining debt.

Poland's bank conciliation procedure was designed as a temporary process to bypass some of the shortcomings of its existing judicial debt work-out procedure, the law on "Arrangement Proceedings" (or "court conciliation"). The latter (see chapter 7) dates from 1934, although significant amendments were made in 1990, and is extremely inflexible. The bank conciliation procedure shifts power from the courts and the borrower to the banks. Banks are empowered to negotiate work-out agreements with problem debtors and force them on dissenting creditors, provided creditors representing over 50 percent of the value of outstanding debt agree. A firm can apply for the procedure to its leading bank creditor, as long as that creditor holds 20 percent of that firm's debt, or 10 percent if the amount is at least 2 billion zlotys. The parties then negotiate whether to pursue this route or opt for one of the other choices provided under EBRP.

Borrowers and/or certain creditors acquire several potential advantages if they opt for restructuring under bank-led conciliation rather than judicial conciliation. First, the process is likely to be somewhat less cumbersome because the courts are not involved except to hear an appeal against an agreement. Second, the rules of priority change. The treasury loses its superpriority and the social security office, secured creditors, and unpaid workers remain outside the agreement and thereby retain their security (and thus their implicit priority).[6] Third, the ability of small creditors to block agreements is more limited because a smaller voting majority is required for an agreement to be approved.

Fourth, responsibility for monitoring the restructuring program is explicitly delegated to the lead bank. If the lead bank does not terminate the agreement when the restructuring plan is violated, it becomes liable for any additional losses incurred by the other creditors.

Fifth, the range of potential outcomes is broader under bank-led conciliation. For example, creditors may exchange debt for equity. The designers of EBRP hoped that debt–equity swaps would be a central feature of many bank conciliation agreements, allowing debtors immediate relief from debt service while also facilitating their privatization, once the banks themselves were privatized.[7] Finally, if the conciliation agreement is declared void, any concessions are unwound, and the original debt claims of all creditors are reinstated. This gives the borrower and the lead bank strong incentives to develop a reasonable plan.

This chapter examines the bank conciliation procedure in action by looking at how it operated in a sample of sixty-two firms. These firms form part of the larger stratified sample of 139 firms described in chapter 7. The 787 firms in the base portfolio of the seven state-owned banks and the final sample of 139 firms are broken down by resolution path in table 7.1 in chapter 7. The breakdown of the 139-firm sample by bank is shown in table 7.2 in chapter 7, and the breakdown of the sixty-two conciliation cases by bank is shown in table 8.1 below.

Table 8.1
Distribution of Bank Conciliation Cases (62) over Nine Banks

	Financial condition	Number of bank conciliation agreements signed as of April 1994	Number of bank conciliation agreements in sample	Share of bank's total in sample	Bank's share in total sample
Bank 1	weak	41	7	17%	11%
Bank 2	weak	28	11	39%	18%
Bank 3	weak/adequate	20	8	40%	13%
Bank 4	adequate/strong	38	18	47%	29%
Bank 5	strong	13	5	38%	8%
Bank 6	strong	N.A.	8	N.A.	13%
Bank 7	strong	20	2	10%	3%
Bank 8	strong	20	3	15%	5%
Bank 9	strong	N.A.	0	0%	0%
Total		180	62	30%	100%

Source: Authors' calculations.

Structure of Enterprise Debt

EBRP provided numerous avenues through which banks and problem debtors could tackle their bad-debt problems. In theory, the firms in the worst financial state—that is, those with debts exceeding assets and with a liquidation value higher than their value as a going concern—should have entered either bankruptcy or state enterprise liquidation. Other firms, in contrast, should have resolved their debt problems through means that would keep them alive—either paying back debts, becoming current on their debt-servicing obligations, entering into one of the two work-out processes (bank or court conciliation), or having their debt sold on the secondary market. As noted in Chapter 7, firms entering bank conciliation came from many sectors, were generally large, and had high levels of bank debt. As expected, they were on average more profitable than firms entering liquidation or bankruptcy.

The change from 1991 to 1994 in the structure of outstanding debt reported on the balance sheets gives a rough snapshot of financial developments in our sample of sixty-two firms.[8] Although the nominal value of total reported debt rose substantially from 1991 to 1993, its real value, after indexing for inflation, rose only slightly during that period and fell sharply in 1994 as a result of the conciliation process (table 8.2). The balance sheets changed dramatically over the period. As a share of

Table 8.2
Average Debt per Firm to Various Creditors
(billion 1991 Zl, indexed for inflation[a])

Debt owed to:	1991	1992	1993	1994 (post-conciliation)
Banks	42.5	34.7	29.9	13.2
Suppliers	40.6	35.8	36.5	22.9
Tax and ZUS	15.8	24.8	35.5	30.9
Other payables[b]	9.9	10.1	12.7	10.6
Other liabilities[c]	9.1	8.2	7.7	16.4
TOTAL	118.0	114.1	123.4	96.1

[a] Using the producer price index.
[b] Includes in some cases accrued interest on overdue debt; payables to workers are small throughout the period.
[c] Includes workers' capital, obligations to housing and other funds, and some debt write-offs (particularly of government debt) in conciliation agreements that remained on the balance sheet to be slowly written off as the agreements were implemented.

Source: Authors' calculations.

total assets, total reported debt rose on average from 54 percent in 1991 to 101 percent in 1993, before falling back to 79 percent in 1994 (figure 8.1). Most of this increase reflected a decline in the real value of assets, due both to the shedding of assets and to inadequate indexing for inflation.[9] With regard to the structure of reported debt, bank debt and

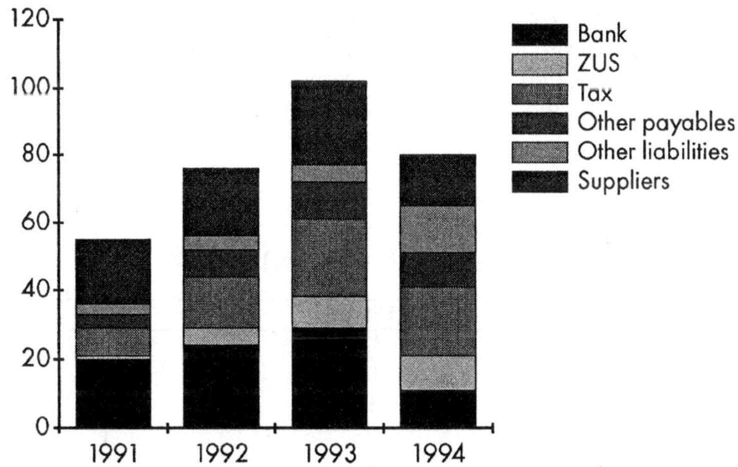

Figure 8.1: Debt as a Share of Total Assets

Source: Authors' calculations.

Table 8.3
Debt to Various Creditor Groups as a Share of Total Debt[a]

	1991	1992	1993	1994 (post conciliation)
Banks	38%	31%	27%	15%
Suppliers	35%	28%	26%	22%
Tax	12%	19%	22%	23%
ZUS	2%	6%	8%	10%
Other payables	7%	10%	11%	12%
Other liabilities	6%	6%	6%	16%
TOTAL	100%	100%	100%	100%

[a] N=48 in 1989, N=62 in other years;
Note that these proportions differ from those implicit in Table 8.2, because in this calculation each firm is weighted equally.

Source: Authors' calculations.

payables to suppliers fell significantly both in real terms and as a share of total debt (table 8.3), while government debt increased by both measures. Taxes and social insurance payables to the government more than doubled in real terms from 1991 to 1993. At least 70 percent of these payables consisted of overdue tax and social insurance arrears.[10] As a share of total assets, they increased from 7 percent in 1991 to 31 percent in 1993. In thirteen cases the government (the tax office and ZUS) replaced banks or suppliers as the largest creditor (table 8.4). It is interesting to note that debt to workers (that is, wage arrears) was negligible throughout the period, in contrast to the situation in distressed firms in Russia.

Table 8.4
Identity of Largest Creditor (number of cases)

	1991	1993
Banks	31	21
Suppliers	27	18
Tax	3	15
ZUS	0	1
Other	1	7

Source: Authors' calculations.

The Conciliation Process in Action

Initiating Debt Collection

EBRP was designed in large part to force large creditors to bear down on bad debtors and attempt to collect their debts. From our sample it is clear that creditors were indeed relatively passive in the early years of reform, and that EBRP was a catalyst for action.

Table 8.5 shows the average number of days between events (for those events completed by mid-1995) for our sample of sixty-two firms in the bank conciliation process. The base portfolio was intended to include loans classified as doubtful or loss as of December 1991. Thus, we start our timetable on September 30, 1991, the approximate date that banks should have realized that a given loan was in trouble.

Table 8.5
Timetable for the Bank Conciliation Process

	Average number of days	Number of Cases
Sept. 30, 1991 until date of first debt collection action	679	62
Sept. 30, 1991 until initiation of bank conciliation proceedings	800	61
Initiation of conciliation proceedings to final vote on draft agreement	118	61
In case of no appeal: final vote to date conciliation agreement took effect	49	36
In case of appeal: final vote to date conciliation agreement took effect	124	23
Overall length of bank conciliation procedure: initiation of conciliation proceedings to date conciliation agreement took effect	198	59
In case of a debt-equity swap: Date conciliation agreement took effect to issuance of shares	298	14(as of mid-1995)

Source: Author's calculations

Table 8.6
What Triggered Bank Conciliation? (in percent of firms)

	Most important reason	One of three most important reasons
Attempts or threats by creditors to foreclose on collateral	16	29
Inability of debtor to obtain additional working capital	36	82
Pressure by founding organ to deal with creditors	0	13
Threat by creditor to sell their debt	21	52
Other[a]	27	47

[a] Because "other" was such a high percentage, we analyzed these answers in detail. Half of the answers listed under "other" point out that the BPU procedure gave a possibility of obtaining a reduction in debt, another group of answers indicate increased pressure from creditors (37 percent of "other"), while the rest is difficult to categorize.

The first step noted on the timetable is the initiation of debt collection. EBRP was clearly an important catalyst for the banks. Only twenty-four of the sixty-two firms in our sample were subject to any debt collection whatsoever before they applied for bank conciliation. Even for those twenty-four firms, an average of about fifteen months elapsed between when the loan should have been recognized as bad and when debt collection began. In only eleven cases was action taken before the passage of the law. The conciliation procedure began on average ten months after passage of the law and a full 800 days after banks should have known that the loans were in trouble.

What triggered the initiation of bank conciliation proceedings? Table 8.6 shows the answers that our sample enterprises gave to this question. In very few cases was it aggressive action by creditors to collect their money that triggered the specific timing of conciliation discussions, although some form of creditor pressure may have figured prominently in up to one-half of our cases. In the other half, it appears that enterprises sought bank conciliation agreements to obtain additional working capital or to obtain a debt write-off (the major subcategory of "other"). Enterprises would not normally need additional working capital if their operating profitability was satisfactory. Therefore, it is safe to conclude that conciliation—from the enterprise's viewpoint—was triggered more often by the desire of managers to continue covering weak performance than by decisive actions by creditors to collect the money they were owed.

Forming Creditor Groups

The rules for bank conciliation allowed creditors to be divided into different groups for purposes of negotiating the conditions in the conciliation agreement. Creditors in the same group would receive the same treatment, and creditors in groups not including the main bank, generally small creditors, could not receive worse treatment than creditors in the group with the main bank, generally large creditors. In this way, creditors—particularly small creditors—were protected from being disadvantaged by other creditors, particularly the bank leading the negotiations. Another protection was included in the rules to prevent the lead bank from protecting its interests at the expense of other creditors: each bank was charged with monitoring the implementation of the conciliation agreements it led and was responsible to other creditors if the conditions of the agreements were not fulfilled by the debtors.

Because of these nondiscrimination requirements, it was clearly in the interests of the main bank to differentiate as little as possible among creditors: that is, to include as many creditors as possible in the same group. However, to obtain a 50 percent voting majority and to reduce the likelihood of appeals brought by disgruntled creditors, it might still be necessary to provide better treatment for some creditors—particularly small creditors whose full payback would not "cost" too much for other creditors. Indeed, analysis of our sample confirms that these incentives were prominent. In fifty-three of the sixy-two cases, different creditor groups were formed, while in nine cases all creditors were grouped together.[11] Where different groups were formed, the second group (that is, the one not including the lead bank) contained only creditors holding small claims.[12] The first group tended to have quite a large number of creditors (fifty-seven on average) and held the overwhelming majority (87 percent on average) of the debt subject to conciliation. The small creditors, even though there were many (ninety-five on average) held relatively little debt and thus could be given better treatment without severely damaging larger creditors.

Negotiating and Monitoring Agreements

Once initiated, the conciliation process could last as long as a year or could be completed within the course of a week. On average, it took four months, although in many cases the agreement had in effect been negotiated before the process officially began.[13] In the case of the seven state-owned banks, 15 percent of the agreements in our sample were concluded after the deadline of April 30, 1994 imposed by the Ministry of Finance.[14] Nevertheless, the existence of a deadline was very important as a spur to banks to finish the process (figure 8.2).

Even though smaller creditors were legally entitled to equal or better treatment, they tended to be less inclined to approve conciliation agreements. The majority of large creditors favored the agreement in 85 percent of cases,[15] while the majority of small creditors favored the agreement in only 38 percent of cases, even though small creditors received much more favorable treatment.

EBRP provided that a conciliation agreement should take effect within thirty days of its signing. In practice, agreements that were not appealed took effect on average forty-nine days after the final vote.[16] About 40 percent of the agreements in our sample were appealed, over four-fifths of the time by a supplier. Nevertheless, not a single conciliation agreement was nullified or modified by a court. Twenty-three appeals were rejected, and one was still pending as of mid-1995. If there was an appeal, the duration of the overall procedure lengthened considerably, but even agreements that were appealed came into effect on average three months after signing.

A creditors' council was formed in most cases (fifty-one out of sixty-two) to monitor the agreements, but its importance appears to have been small.[17] In eleven cases, the creditors' council had not even met once when the company was interviewed in the summer of 1995, although the agreement had on average been signed for more than a year. In the other cases, the period from the date the conciliation agreement took effect until the creditors' council first met was on average about four months and in some cases up to eleven months.

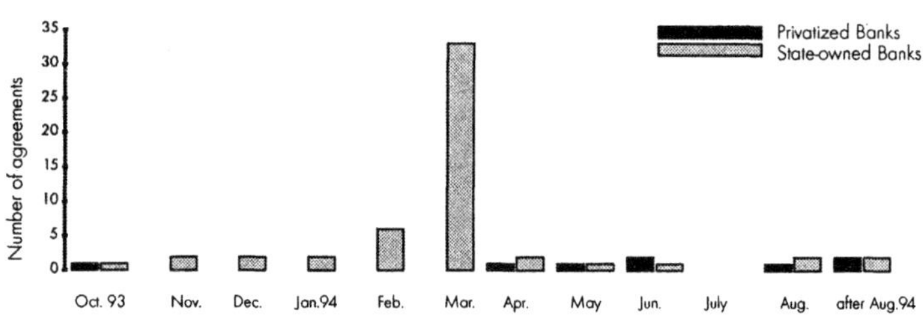

Figure 8.2: Timing of Conclusion of Conciliation Agreements
Source: Authors' calculations.

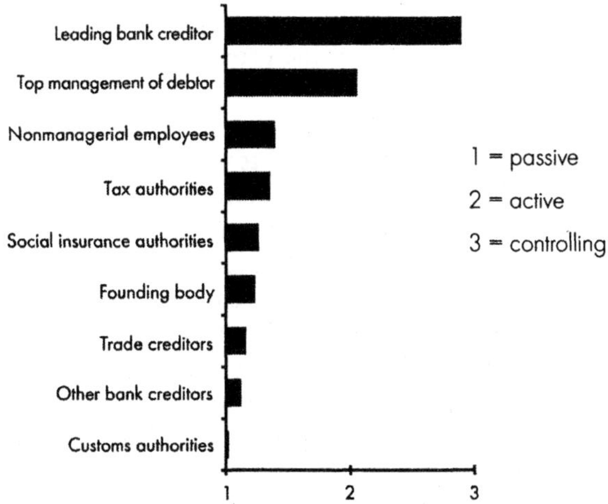

Figure 8.3: Average Involvement of Various Creditor Groups
Source: Authors' calculations.

Rather than a group of creditors, our data indicate that the lead bank was generally in control of the bank conciliation process (see figure 8.3). The top management of the creditor was also actively involved. Nonmanagerial employees in the firm were much less involved, despite the traditional role of labor in the management of Poland's state-owned firms. Creditors other than the lead bank were generally passive, although among these other creditors, the tax and social insurance authorities appear to be somewhat more involved than trade creditors or other bank creditors. Although this general pattern is not uncommon in work-out processes in advanced market economies, the passivity of creditors is more marked in transition settings. Such passivity potentially compromises the effectiveness and fairness of work-out processes.

Outcomes of Bank Conciliation to Date

The most important question surrounding the bank conciliation process, and EBRP more generally, is its impact on enterprise restructuring. Did the process allow viable firms to survive that might otherwise have been forced to close? Did it lead firms to improve their efficiency? Did it result in changes in ownership or management? While our data do not provide answers to all of these questions, they offer interesting clues on the likely impact of the process.

Financial Restructuring

The law of February 3, 1993 allowed debtors and creditors to use a wide variety of techniques to adjust debt obligations and reduce debt-service burdens. They could write off, in full or in part, principal and/or accumulated interest, extend due dates or payment periods, reduce the interest rate charged on outstanding loans, increase the collateral attached to loans, or swap debt for equity. Banks were also allowed to extend additional credit as part of the restructuring agreement.

Our survey indicates that the two universal provisions in conciliation agreements were debt write-offs and extensions in the payment period (table 8.7). It also shows that the second category of creditors, typically small creditors, received more favorable treatment than the first category. For the fifty-three cases with two classes of creditors, large creditors wrote off an average of 54 percent of the debt owed to them, while small creditors wrote off only 4 percent. For the nine cases with only

Table 8.7
Financial Conditions in Conciliation Agreements

Condition	Weak banks		Strong banks		All banks	
	No. of cases	% of debt in conciliation in those cases	No. of cases	% of debt in conciliation in those cases	No. of cases	% of debt in conciliation in those cases
Write-off						
—large creditors	25	53%	28	55%	53	54%
—small creditors	25	5%	28	4%	53	4%
—one category	1	80%	8	65%	9	66%
Immediate partial repayment						
—large creditors	0	0	0	0	0	0
—small creditors	2	1%	4	.5%	6	.6%
—one category	0	0	0	0	0	0
Debt–equity swap						
—large creditors	18	30%	6	36%	24	32%
—small creditors	0	0	0	0	0	0
—one category	0	0	1	37%	1	37%
New equity	1	.1%	1	11%	2	6%
New bank credit	9	9%	10	10%	19	10%

Source: Authors' calculations.

one class of creditor, the average write-off was 66 percent. The maximum write-off for large creditors was 89 percent. In no case was there no write-off of debt.

Banks had consistently been capitalizing interest not paid in the past, while other creditors had not.[18] Because equal treatment was by law required for all creditors, there tended to be a greater percentage of write-offs of accrued interest than of principal. Other than this, our analysis could find no significant relationships between the size of the write-off given to individual firms and any other variables—whether the extent of firm indebtedness, the size of the firm, the profitability of the firm, the date negotiations on the agreement began or ended, or the identity of the bank.

A renegotiation of the maturity of the remaining loans was of course necessary in virtually all cases. The new maturity structures were also more favorable for small creditors. On average, the first payment was due to them 107 days after the agreement took effect, and the last payment was due 241 days later. In contrast, the first payment was not due to large creditors until 205 days after the agreement took effect, and the last payment was not due until 894 days later. In other words, small creditors could on average expect to have their loans entirely repaid within a year, while on average large creditors had to wait until early 1995 for their first payment and could expect to see the final payment during the summer of 1997. Clearly the large creditors, led by the main bank, took the brunt of the financial burden for these agreements. While nondiscrimination against small creditors was written into the design of the process, this extent of preference to small creditors was perhaps not anticipated.

Other financial restructuring tools were less common. Immediate partial payback of outstanding debt was required in only six cases, and even in these cases the amount was miniscule—on average less than 1 percent of outstanding claims. In only two cases did creditors move to increase their collateral, which may be in part explained by the weakness of collateral systems in Poland.[19] Finally, our survey saw no evidence of any reduction in interest rates. Rather than adjust interest rates on outstanding balances, the agreements essentially pooled all remaining principal and accrued interest obligations (after write-offs), and assigned schedules for their repayment—without additional interest.

The design of EBRP was to a large extent predicated on the hope that debt would be swapped for equity on a large scale, and thus the process would result in a change in ownership (and privatization once

Table 8.8
Expected Ownership Structure in 25 Cases with Debt–Equity Swaps

	Average share of debt, end-1993	**Average post-swap equity stake**	**Maximum post-swap equity stake**
Government	23%	47%	100%
Bank(s)	29%	23%	58%
Suppliers	26%	20%	55%
Managers/employees	1%	6%	37%
Other	21%	4%	36%

Source: Authors' calculations.

the banks were themselves privatized) as well as furthering enterprise restructuring. In practice, debt–equity swaps occurred in twenty-five of our sixty-two cases and covered on average 33 percent of the debt in those cases. The swaps involved almost exclusively large creditors; small creditors took equity in only one case—where all creditors were classified in only one group.

It is interesting to note that the weakest banks (as defined in chapter 7) were the most active in swapping debt for equity, while they more or less matched the stronger banks in the amount of loans they agreed to write off. Other research has indicated that Polish banks are in general not eager to own equity because of the extra risks and monitoring burdens associated with it.[20] Our sample provides additional evidence that the stronger banks were indeed more cautious. The fact that weaker banks were the primary ones to use this restructuring tool may reflect the fact that they had worse clients and fewer options. But even so it does not augur particularly well for the central role originally envisioned for debt-equity swaps in the work-out process.

Because debt–equity swaps were limited and because the provision of the law regarding the forced debt-equity conversion did not work, the privatization goals of the program were not met.[21] The Polish government originally set minimum targets whereby conciliation agreements would result in a reduction in government ownership to below 50 percent of shares in at least 30 percent of all cases. The average expected post-swap pattern of enterprise ownership for the twenty-five cases with debt–equity swaps is shown in table 8.8. The government retained on average a 47 percent stake; it kept an absolute majority in twelve cases. When added to the thirty-seven cases that did not feature a debt–equity swap, the government maintained majority ownership in forty-nine cases, or 79 percent of the sixty-two firms in the sample. The main bank obtained a majority stake in only one case, and in twelve cases no one party obtained a majority, although banks, suppliers, managers, and employees together had a majority. At best, one could argue that the conciliation process would eventually result in privatization of thirteen of the sixty-two firms in our sample, or 21 percent, once the banks and and state-owned suppliers were themselves privatized.

Finally, new loans were—perhaps not surprisingly—relatively uncommon. The two privatized banks did not give new money in any of the cases in our sample. The state-owned banks gave new loans in nineteen cases and new equity in two cases. The new loans equalled on average 10 percent of the outstanding debt covered by the conciliation process.

It is interesting to note that ZUS, although not a party to these agreements, did negotiate separate agreements with fifty of the sixty-two firms in our sample. The debt covered by these agreements with ZUS was on average one-fifth as large as the debt covered by the conciliation agreements. On average, the ZUS agreement was concluded twenty-four days after the conciliation agreement was signed. This average masks wide variability, with some ZUS agreements being finalized more than one year either before or after the conciliation agreement. In contrast to other creditors, ZUS did not agree to any write-offs in 1994 but only to reschedulings of debt. Renegotiated payback periods were quite tight, beginning on average two and a half months after signing and ending on average twenty-three months later. Some immediate repayment was required in thirteen of the fifty cases, but in all thirteen cases, the amount was very small, generally less than 1 percent of the debt.

Commercialization

According to the Law of February 3, 1993, application for a bank conciliation procedure by a state-owned enterprise was equivalent to consent by its governing bodies (management and the workers' council) to be commercialized; i.e., transformed into a joint-stock company, 100 percent owned by the treasury and represented by the Ministry of Privatization.[22] The donor-community believed that the "program... seeks the commercialization...of virtually all troubled SOEs,"[23] with the goal of improving corporate governance, and the "Government [of Poland] has...agreed to minimum targets whereby conciliation agreements would result, in at least...70 percent of the cases in...commercialization."[24] If our sample is representative, this objective was fulfilled (see table 8.9), assuming one includes those companies commercialized

Table 8.9
Year of Commercialization[a]

1991	1992	1993	1994	1995	1996	Total	Not transformed
3	10	2	23	7	1	46 (75%)	15 (25%)

[a] 61 enterprises; one firm was already a limited liability company.

Source: Authors' calculations.

before the law was passed in 1993 or long after all agreements took effect (i.e., in 1995 and 1996).

Commercialization occurred in forty-six of our sixty-two cases. Fifteen companies were transformed before signing a bank conciliation agreement, including those already commercialized before conciliation began; thirty-one companies were transformed after going through the process. On average, these thirty-one enterprises were transformed into 100 percent state-owned joint-stock companies 200 days after the final vote on the agreement, despite the stipulation in the law that transformation has to occur within thirty days.[28] No transformation had occured in fifteen firms by the summer of 1996, including three cases with debt–equity swaps. It is unclear why some firms in bank conciliation escaped commercialization given the automatic consent implied by the application process.

Restructuring Plans

Firms entering into bank conciliation were supposed to present restructuring plans, and of our sixty-two sample firms, fifty-two presented plans that were still accessible when the survey was undertaken.[26] But the contents of many of these plans were vague or unrealistic, based more on hopes than on actual analysis. On the financial side, most of the plans were optimistic. Forty-eight forecast profits in 1994 and fifty-one in 1995. The plans generally contained little detail on operational restructuring, with half or fewer committing to specific changes such as sales of assets (ten firms) or changes in staffing levels (twenty-eight firms); five plans included sales of parts of the firm as a going concern. The plans that projected employment levels expected the average number of employees to grow. No management changes were envisaged in any restructuring plan.

The conclusion that the plans were more fantasy than fact is evidenced by a comparison of actual performance with planned performance. Table 8.10 shows actual and projected operating profits—that is, operating

Table 8.10:
Actual vs. Planned Operating Profits, 1994 (40 firms, in percentage)

	Average actual operating profit		Average planned operating profit		Average difference (planned minus actual)	
	1994	1995	1994	1995	1994	1995
All banks	0.4	-3.1	9.0	12.0	8.8	15.0
Strong banks	3.8	0.3	8.0	11.5	4.4	11.0
Weak banks	-3.0	-6.4	10.2	12.0	13.2	18.0

Source: Authors' calculations; numbers do not add exactly due to rounding.

earnings before interest and taxes (EBIT)[27] as a share of operating revenues—for 1994 and 1995 for the forty cases in which detailed financial plans were presented for both years. Because in almost all cases 1994 was the first year of implementation, one would expect the plans to be reasonably accurate. However, the plans projected an average operating profit of 9 percent, while the firms realized an average operating profit of less than 1 percent.[28] When divided between strong and weak banks, the average difference between plan and actuality was 4.4 percent for the former, compared with 13.2 percent for the latter.[29] Differences between planned and actuality were even larger in 1995, with the divergences being again more marked in the case of weaker banks.

Operating Performance

With regard to actual performance, the financial operating performance of most of the sixty-two firms in our sample deteriorated rather than improved in the first two years after the conciliation agreements were concluded. Average operating profit for the fifty-seven firms in our sample with data throughout the period was 4 percent in 1991. It fell to 3.5 percent in 1992, rose back to 0 percent in 1993, fell slightly to 1 percent in 1994, and fell further to -3 percent in 1995 (figure 8.4). Operating profits in market economies are generally on the order of 5 to 13 percent. The number of firms in our sample with operating profits over 5 percent fell consistently over the period (table 8.11). This operating performance is not impressive, especially given the robust growth in the Polish economy of over 6 percent per year in both 1994 and 1995.

Table 8.11
Break-down of 57 Firms by Operating Profitability, 1991–95
(number of firms)

	1991	1992	1993	1994	1995
Greater than 5%	32	20	22	16	14
0 to 5%	10	7	11	16	16
-5% to 0	5	7	5	10	8
Less than 5%	10	23	19	15	19
Total	57	57	57	57	57

Source: Authors' calculations.

Before- and after-tax profit figures reported by firms in 1994 were much higher than these figures for operating profit and seem to show major improvements in financial performance. But all suffer from a major distortion: the firms booked debt write-offs as profits. This raised 1994 gross and net profit figures (over 1993 amounts) by 40 to 50 percent of total revenue on average, as shown in figure 8.4, and put them at over 10 percentage points above operating profits.

The fact that operating profit hardly changed in 1994 and 1995 is explained by the behavior of operating revenues (figure 8.5) and operating costs (figure 8.6). These figures show average changes in the level and structure of revenues and costs in fifty-four firms (i.e., those with

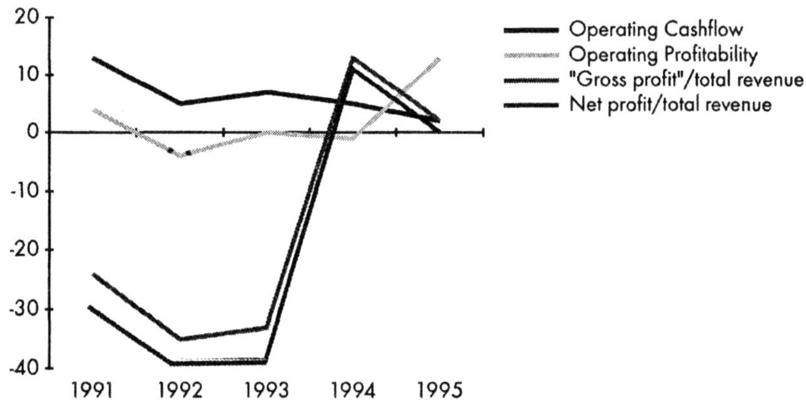

Figure 8.4: Profit Measures for Firms in Bank Conciliation (57 firms)

Source: Authors' calculations.

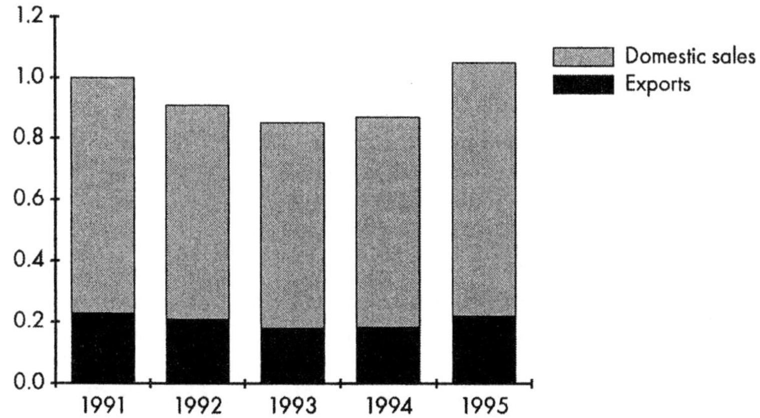

Figure 8.5: Operating Revenue (in real terms, 54 firms)

Source: Authors' calculations.

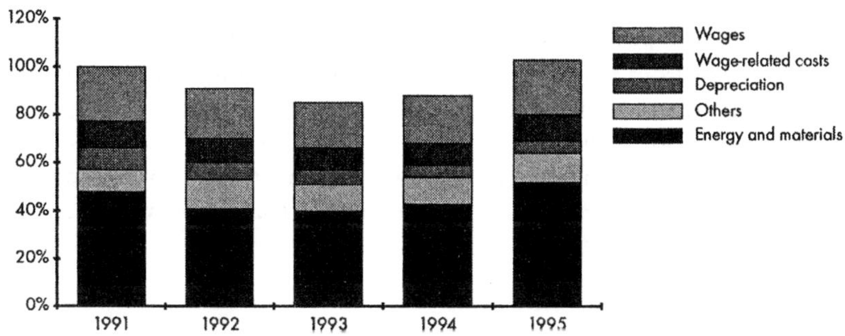

Figure 8.6: Operating Costs (in real terms, 54 firms)

Source: Authors' calculations.

adequate data) from 1991 to 1995, using 1991 as an index and giving each firm an equal weight. Both revenues and costs rose slightly from 1993 to 1994 and much more from 1994 to 1995. However, the patterns of change give little evidence of significant restructuring in 1994. On the revenue side, domestic sales increased significantly, as would be expected given the strong recovery in the Polish economy in 1994 and 1995, but exports increased only slightly. On the cost side, costs for energy and materials rose in both 1994 and 1995—probably in part a reflection of increases in regulated energy prices. Other costs stayed roughly level, with a slight fall in depreciation expense being compensated by a slight rise in other costs.

Financial performance is only one measure of restructuring. Employment and wages are another. Our sample of sixty-two firms had been reducing employment about 10 percent per year on average from 1990 to 1993. In both 1994 and 1995 the layoff rate slowed to about one-half that level. The average wage rose roughly in line with inflation in 1994 and rose even faster—by 18 percent in real terms—in 1995. It had fallen by over 10 percent in real terms between 1991 and 1993. As seen in figure 8.6, the wage bill and wage-related costs declined steadily from 1991 to 1993 but stayed level in 1994 and rose in 1995. These trends are difficult to interpret in the abstract. They could indicate that conciliation agreements provided breathing room that allowed firms to slow down painful restructuring. Alternatively, they could signal that staffing levels and wages had already been reduced sufficiently. The former is arguably the more likely explanation, given the weak operating profits of these firms in 1994 and 1995. With regard to other indicators, numerous firms reported some changes in the membership of management boards, some discontinuation of unprofitable products, and some sale or leasing of assets, but in no case did these indicators alter significantly in 1994 from what they had consistently been in 1992 and 1993. In sum, our data do not provide evidence of a significant change in either the methods or the rate of firm restructuring in 1994 as compared to earlier years, and financial performance in most firms in our sample appears to have stayed even or weakened rather than improved after the conciliation agreements were signed.

Conclusions

Since 1992, Poland has been considered a model of commercial banking reform among transition countries. Its Enterprise and Bank Restructuring Program, adopted by parliament in early 1993, aimed to build institutional capacity in state-owned commercial banks and to take concrete steps to resolve their problem loans, through work-outs, liquidation processes, or loan sales. This chapter has reviewed in detail the process and initial impact of Poland's bank-led work-out (conciliation) process in a sample of sixty-two enterprises, part of a larger sample of 139 firms following one of the five paths of loan resolution under EBRP.

How effective was the conciliation process? Although our assessment was somewhat preliminary, experience though 1995 suggests some outcomes. First, many aspects of EBRP in general and the conciliation process in particular appear quite positive, as noted in chapter 7.[30] The reform program was clearly innovative and well designed. In general, banks and enterprises took the program seriously, and it appears to have been free of fraud or corruption. Compliance with the program's prescriptions was high but not perfect.

EBRP was clearly very useful as a catalyst in forcing otherwise passive creditors to take action against bad debtors. Although the debts in question turned bad in 1991, creditors took no action at all in over 80 percent of our sixty-two conciliation cases until the law was passed in early 1993. Even after the law was adopted, in over 60 percent of cases nothing happened until bank conciliation was initiated, an average of ten months afterwards. By then the debt had been in arrears for well over two years. The signing dates of most agreements cluster closely around March 1994, the original deadline under the law.

Not only was the law an important catalyst, but the process was reasonably rapid once initiated. On average, the conciliation process took between six and seven months from the date it was initiated until the date it finally took effect. Creditors reached an agreement on restructuring plans quite quickly—in about an average of four months. After an agreement was reached, it generally took somewhat longer than the law anticipated actually to take effect. But major slowdowns occurred only in cases of debt–equity swaps; for the fourteen cases in which swaps had been completed by mid-1995, it took some ten months on average for shares to be issued after agreeing on swaps, largely because of delays by the Ministry of Privatization in giving approval. For the other cases it took even longer.

Finally, the division of firms among resolution paths appears to have followed some economic logic (see chapter 7). Better-off firms tended to enter conciliation, while weaker performers tended to go into bankruptcy or liquidation. Profitability was not all that mattered, however; size also appears to have been important, with larger firms tending to enter conciliation regardless of profitability. This is not surprising: these firms are politically more difficult to close.

Despite these strengths, the data suggest that the conciliation process may have had limited power to promote needed restructuring in firms. The agreements themselves were relatively unsophisticated, perhaps one reason they could be concluded so rapidly. They dealt primarily with financial conditions—mostly large debt write-offs and renegotiation of payment dates—and included very few tangible requirements for operational or managerial change. Only weaker banks were willing to undertake significant debt–equity swaps; the stronger banks undertook very few. To the extent that restructuring plans were actually prepared for firms, they appear to have greatly overestimated future profitability, particularly when the weaker banks were in the lead.

Given these features, it is perhaps not surprising that the agreements appear to have resulted in little restructuring. The first two years of the agreements' implementation saw a slowdown in the rate of layoffs from previous years, an increase in the average wage rate (after adjusting for inflation), and a decline in average operating profitability and cash flow. (Reported net profits soared, but this was because loan write-offs were booked as income.) The main impact of the conciliation process was probably to provide firms with breathing space. The weak operating performance in 1994 and 1995 suggests that many firms continued to have problems and that financial discipline was perhaps still somewhat soft. Indeed, the practice of firms booking write-offs as profit may have given a misleading impression of higher postconciliation profitability—and may possibly lead to further pressure for wage increases or more debt forgiveness.

Debt–equity swaps were not used as widely as originally hoped, and the conciliation process did not lead to extensive ownership change. Of the sixty-two state-owned enterprises in our sample, majority stakes in at most one-fifth of the enterprises would eventually be in private hands as a result of the process, if the banks themselves were privatized. The fact that most debt–equity swaps were concluded by the weaker banks (i.e., those last to be privatized) and that the equity also went proportionately to other, often passive, creditors (including government) heightens the concern that it may be a long time before these swaps translate into effective private ownership and governance.

Initial evidence therefore suggests that the outcome of Poland's first experiment with bank-led work-outs is decidedly mixed. The conciliation process forced banks to confront their problems, helped them build institutional capacity in their work-out units (but not necessarily in their credit units), and furthered the difficult task of weeding out and closing clearly unviable firms. Loans could be written down without creating an environment of general debt forgiveness. These are important achievements in transition, and the Polish approach serves in many ways as a model for other transition economies. The process does not, however, seem to have rapidly imposed strong restructuring mandates on problem debtors, and its success in privatizing them was limited. EBRP was a good start, but continued work is needed to build strong banks that can impose effective corporate governance on enterprises in times of financial distress.

References

Baer, Herbert and Cheryl Gray. 1996. Debt as a control device in transition economies: Evidence from Hungary and Poland. In *Corporate Governance in Central Europe and Russia*, edited by Roman Frydman, Cheryl W. Gray, and Andrzej Rapaczynski. Budapest: Central European University Press.

Belka, Marek. 1994. Financial restructuring of banks and enterprises: The Polish solution. Paper presented at International Conference, Bad Enterprise Debts in Central and Eastern Europe, June, Budapest.

Belka, Marek, et al. 1995. Enterprise adjustment in Poland: Evidence from a survey of 200 private, privatized, and state-owned firms. Discussion paper no. 233, CEPR.

Dittus, Peter and Stephen Prowse. 1996. Corporate governance in Eastern Europe: Should banks own shares? In *Corporate Governance in Central Europe and Russia*, edited by Roman Frydman, Cheryl W. Gray, and Andrzej Rapaczynski, Budapest: Central European University Press.

Estrin, Saul, Alan Gelb, and Inderjit Singh. 1996. Shocks and adjustment by firms in transition: A comparative study. In *Firms in Transition: Cases from Poland, Czechoslovakia and Hungary*, edited by Saul Estrin, Joe Brada, and Inderjit Singh. Armonk and London: M.E. Sharpe.

Fan, Qimiao and Mark Schaffer. 1993. Government financial transfers and enterprise adjustments in Russia, with comparisons to Central and Eastern Europe. Working paper no. 394, CEPR.

Groszek, Mieczyslaw et al. 1993. *Restrukturyzacja Finansowa Przedsiebiorstw i Bankow* Warsaw: Komentarz, Elinex.

Kawalec, Stefan, Slawomir Sikora, and Piotr Rymaszewski. 1994. Dealing with bad debts: The case of Poland. In *Building Sound Finance in Emerging Market Economies*, edited by Gerard Caprio, David Folkerts-Landau, and Timothy D. Lane, Proceedings of a Conference held in Washington, D.C., June 10–11, 1993.

Pawlowicz, Leszek, ed. 1994. *Restrukturyzacja Finansowa Przedsiebiorstw i Bankow*, Gdansk: I raport z badan, Instytut Badan nad Gospodarka Rynkowa.

Pawlowicz, Leszek, ed., 1995. *Restrukturyzacja Finansowa Przedsiebiorstw i Bankow*, II raport z badan, Gdansk, Instytut Badan nad Gospodarka Rynkowa.

Pinto, Brian, Marek Belka, and Stefan Krajewski. 1993. Transforming state enterprises in Poland: Evidence on adjustment by manufacturing firms. *Brookings Papers on Economic Activity*, no. 1.

Polanski, Zbigniew. 1995. The role of the financial system in supporting economic development. In *Monitoring Economic Transition*, edited by G. Blazyca and J.M. Dabrowski. England: Avebury Ashgate Publishing Ltd.

van Wijnbergen, Sweder. 1995. On the role of banks in enterprise restructuring: The Polish example. In *Bank Rehabilitation and Enterprise Restructuring*, edited by M. Simoneti and S. Kawalec.

World Bank. 1993. Report and recommendation of the president of the International Bank for Reconstruction and Development to the executive directors on a proposed enterprise and financial sector adjustment loan, April 8.

World Bank. 1996. *World Development Report 1996: From plan to market*, Oxford: Oxford University Press.

Wyczanski, Pawel. 1993. The Polish banking system 1990–1992, Economic and Social Policy Series, no. 32, Warsaw: Friedrich-Ebert Stiftung Polen.

Notes

1. Polish government subsidies to enterprises shrank from more than 16 percent of GDP in 1986 to 3.3 percent in 1992 (World Bank, 1996).

2. Pinto et al. (1993).

3. Kawalec et al (1994); Belka (1994); van Wijnbergen (1995).

4. For an analysis of other debt-resolution paths included in the reform program, including bankruptcy and state enterprise liquidation, see chapter 7.

5. Pawlowicz (1994) and (1995).

6. Secured creditors can choose to forego their security and become part of the process, as most indeed did—due to the virtual impossibility of collecting debts by foreclosing on collateral in Poland (see Baer and Gray, 1996). The social security office (ZUS) can and typically does negotiate a separate agreement with the problem debtor.

7. The Ministry of Privatization was required by the law to give consent to debt–equity swaps contained in conciliation agreements. In practice the process of obtaining such consent was very slow.

8. Several words of caution are in order concerning this data, which were taken from the balance sheets of the surveyed firms. First, accrued interest on debt to suppliers is not typically included in enterprise accounts, while accrued interest on debt to government and ZUS is always included and that on debt to banks is sometimes included. Second, the 1994 figures overstate debt burdens, because many write-offs (particularly of government debt) were not reflected immediately in firms' balance sheets.

9. Revaluation of assets during this period was allowed several times, with the extent of revaluation being largely at the discretion of firm management.

10. We do not know the exact break-down between current and overdue payables for all categories of taxes for all years. Of debts to the tax office and the social insurance agency at year-end 1993, 28 percent of payables were current and 72 percent were overdue (43 percent for more than one year). Because payments to ZUS were in general more likely to be made than payments to other tax agencies, an estimate of three-quarters of tax liabilities in arrears appears reasonable.

11. Of the nine cases with only one creditor group, eight were from the stronger banks.

12. In 51 of the 53 cases, the groups were distinguished by the size of debt that the creditor was holding. In 46 of these, two groups were

formed, large and small creditors, the cut-off between the two being anywhere between Zl 5 million (US$238) and Zl 5 billion (US$238,000). The average cut-off between the two groups in our sample was roughly Zl 255 million (US$12,140). In the five cases where three groups were formed, the average cut-off between "medium" and "small" creditors was also at that mark. In the other two cases, the groups were distinguished by type of creditor, which is in fact highly correlated with size of debt (because trade creditors tend to have smaller debt claims than banks).

13. There does not seem to be a clear correlation between length of the process and the size or number of creditors of the firm. The process does appear to have gone somewhat faster for firms with higher debt burdens (debt/asset ratios), perhaps because more attention was paid to those cases.

14. Initially, the deadline was March 31, 1994, but was subsequently moved by one month to April 30, 1994.

15. In all but one of the cases approved by large creditors, their vote alone was sufficient to carry the total vote over the required 50 percent threshold.

16. A "waiting" period of one-month was provided in the law to allow time for appeals. The forty-nine days in practice reflected delays by the Ministry of Privatization, which had to approve all agreements.

17. The functions of the creditor council provided for by the EBRP law and those of a creditor council in Western economies are somewhat different. In the EBRP the creditor council serves primarily to monitor the bank conciliation agreement once it is concluded.

18. Approximately 44 percent of the total debt subject to conciliation agreements was accrued interest.

19. For further discussion of Poland's collateral system, see Baer and Gray (1996).

20. Dittus and Prowse (1996).

21. To facilitate privatization, the law allowed any creditor with at least 30 percent of the debt of a firm in default to apply to the Ministry of Privatization for a debt–equity swap (preceded by compulsory commercialization), even outside the bank conciliation procedure. The swap was supposed to be approved by the Ministry within 30 days. That provision of the law was not used in practice, mainly because in practice it was blocked by the Ministry of Privatization.

22. At year-end 1991, 54 of 62 firms that would later enter bank conciliation in our sample were state enterprises. Four were already

commercialized joint-stock companies, two were fully owned by another state enterprise, and two were partially privatized (with a majority stake still in state hands).

23. World Bank (1993), p. 30

24. World Bank (1993), p. 31 and annex 2: "Letter of Development Policy" from the Polish Government, p. 60. The latter mentions 75 percent as a goal.

25. The standard deviation was 78, indicating quite a wide distribution of answers. The quickest registration in the sample occured 36 days after the final vote, while one company was converted only after 387 days—a year more than required by the law.

26. Sixteen percent of the firms surveyed were not able to find a copy of any restructuring plan. Such a plan was required under the law.

27. In Polish terminology, operating profits as we use them here equal "operating revenues" plus "revenues from the sale of products not produced inside the company" minus "costs of products produced inside the company and sold during the period" minus "costs of purchase of products not produced inside the company but sold during the period." There is no addition of income from stocks nor deduction for interest payments.

28. If one adds depreciation back in, operating profit becomes operating cash flow. The average difference between actual and projected operating cash flow was also 9 percent.

29. Statistical analysis confirmed the lack of any significant correllation between planned and actual operating profits as well as the fact that the difference between these two figures was significantly higher for weak banks than for strong banks.

30. But large segments of the financial system, representing well over one-half of the total bad debts in the banking system, were not covered by the program and were in even worse shape.

9 Why Does Exit Matter? Exit, Growth, and Other Economic Processes in Transition Economies

Irena Grosfeld

Enterprises in centrally planned economies were not concerned with survival. Central planners decided which enterprises should be created, enlarged, and contracted. Enterprise failures were treated through various subsidies and mergers. The break with the old regime necessitated a central change in the paradigm: in a market economy no central institution is supposed to know what is the comparative advantage of a particular firm, of a particular industry or of a particular sector. The fundamental uncertainty about what should be produced and how is magnified in Central and Eastern European (CEE) countries by the need to deal with the heavy legacy of central planning. The countries of Central and Eastern Europe are not in the process of industrialization: rather these countries have to channel resources from the industrial sector to services, deconcentrate their industrial structure, and unbundle irrationally bundled assets. In other words, an unusually large amount of resources must be liberated from their entrenched uses and moved to places where they can be of the highest value. The difficulty in identifying the directions of such reorientation can be alleviated by initiating a process of selection—indeed a hallmark of a market economy. Such a process is based on the existence of exit mechanisms for individual enterprises, allowing unprofitable firms to decline and fail.

This chapter discusses the reintroduction and application of various classical and nonclassical exit processes in Central and Eastern Europe. There are obviously multiple direct and indirect relationships between exit processes and economic performance, and in attempting to disentangle these relationships we come up against the great complexity of causalities involved. Among the various factors and mechanisms that are affected by downsizing and the threat of exit, we shall focus on the following: expectations, economy-wide and enterprise restructuring, allocation of managerial skills, market structure, financial systems, and privatization. Although these variables are strongly interrelated and influence the process of exit, this analysis largely considers their influence as exogenous. Looking at linkages between exit processes and other variables may help to identify potential trade-offs and contribute to the debate about the design of bankruptcy law and, more generally, about the place of exit in transformation strategy.

Classical Exit Mechanisms and the Credibility of Regime Change

Several policy measures contribute to the transformation of the environment which modify the expectations of economic agents and increase the credibility of regime change. These measures include demonopolization and trade liberalization, restrictive monetary and fiscal policies, and the hardening of bank and interfirm credit. The introduction of properly functioning bankruptcy procedures is also an important signal of regime change. Such a signal may be a crucial element in the process of adjustment of informal institutions (such as attitudes, conventions, and norms of behavior), the evolution of which will determine, in the long term, the success of transformation. Flexible exit routes, including formal bankruptcy procedures and informal workouts, convince economic agents that the survival of lossmakers will not be guaranteed any more and that the rights of various creditors will be respected.

Although the importance of classical exit mechanisms in shaping expectations is commonly accepted, both the place of bankruptcy reform in the global sequence of reform and the commitment to enforce exit vary across countries. The place of and commitment to bankruptcy reform seem to depend on each country's understanding of the priorities of transition and the working of a market economy. Some countries change their legal and regulatory framework in a very gradual way—in particular, delaying the enforcement of bankruptcy law and relying instead on rapid privatization as a prerequisite of credible regime change (as in the Czech Republic). The underlying assumption of such sequencing is that a rapid transfer of property from the state to the private sector can have important externalities—in other words, a positive correlation exists between the speed of adjustment of attitudes and behavior and the size of the private sector. Thus various behavioral legacies will be easier to overcome once the private sector has become sufficiently large.

Other countries (like Hungary) in which privatization has been much slower have chosen to impose radical bankruptcy legislation. Such a decision was probably based more on pragmatic considerations, such as the need to deal with accumulated debts, than a global view of transformation. (Poland appears to be a case that falls somewhere in between.) It is not clear which strategy is more efficient in terms of changing standards of behavior and attitudes. The learning-by-doing process obviously depends on the capacity of the government to commit to nonintervention in massive waves of bankruptcy or in insolvencies of large and politically sensitive state-owned enterprises. The mere existence of a bankruptcy law does not guarantee its effective enforcement. The radical Hungarian approach has been partly reversed, creating a strong potential for moral hazard, reinforced by the successive programes of bank recapitalization. The Czech authorities, concerned with the credibility and irreversibility of their privatization strategy, preferred to weaken the bankruptcy threat until the transfer of assets to the private sector had been completed.

How exit processes are introduced and managed plays a key role in shaping expectations. Although the effects of these processes may be diffused and hence difficult to capture, they may prove to have the strongest long-lasting consequences for the whole economy. The experiences of the Czech Republic, Hungary, and Poland suggest that a lack of enforcement of classical exit mechanisms may be partly compensated in the short run by the commitment to privatize rapidly. Such a commitment provides a convincing signal that some forms of exit will become unavoidable in the future. Indeed, despite significant differences in national strategies of transition, downsizing and cost-cutting activities have been undertaken on a massive scale by existing management in all three countries (see the next section). On the one hand, the progressive enforcement of bankruptcy law in the Czech Republic acted as an indirect constraint on managers' behavior, threatening them with the potential penalties. On the other hand, credible prospects for privatization created positive incentives for managers: by adjusting their enterprises, managers hoped to signal their managerial skills and to position themselves well during the process of privatization (Grosfeld and Roland, 1995). Because of the postponement of the enforcement of the bankruptcy law, they were probably compensated by the positive incentives created by the very rapid and credible privatization process.

Hungarian and Polish managers, less convinced about the unavoidability of privatization, were more constrained by negative incentives and by the higher risks of bankruptcy and liquidation.

Exit Mechanisms and Restructuring

The need for a comprehensive redeployment of assets implies that restructuring in transition economies has two dimensions (Grosfeld and Roland, 1996). On the economy-wide level, this restructering entails a drastic reallocation of resources among sectors, industries and firms, and from the state to the private sector. On the microeconomic level, restructuring means the adjustment of firms to market conditions. Exit processes may have an important impact on both levels.

Economy-Wide Restructuring

Radical changes in relative prices alter the comparative advantage of industries and sectors and bring about interindustry, intersectoral reallocation of resources. Some sectors shrink and others develop. An important part of output expansion in developing sectors comes from the entry of new firms. Classical and nonclassical forms of exit—in particular, the process of liquidation and downsizing of state-owned enterprises—give an additional impetus to such expansion. A significant retrenchment of output and employment seems to be the common reaction of most enterprises in the Czech Republic, Hungary, and Poland. According to Bouin and Grosfeld (1995), employment in 400 large industrial firms in Poland and the Czech Republic fell 37 and 32 percent, respectively, between 1989 and 1993; sales decreased from 41 to 42 percent in both countries. Similar results are obtained by Hoshi et al. (see chapter 4) on the basis of a slightly different sample of manufacturing firms. The decline in employment is identical, and sales fell by 46 percent in the Czech Republic and by 38 percent in Poland. The study also provides an estimate for downsizing in 150 large industrial firms in Hungary which is the most spectacular of all: between 1989 and 1993 sales declined by 60 percent and employment by 47 percent.

The question remains to what extent downsizing or liquidation of existing enterprises leads to the reallocation of assets to entirely new uses. It is not possible to give an aggregate quantitative assessment of such a process. The only available information comes from case studies and surveys and is obviously incomplete. In Poland, in the case of liquidation in the form of the sale of firms, bids often come from outside the given sector of industry (Szomburg, 1994). Also in the case of enterprises liquidated according to Article 19 of the law on state enterprises, Dabrowski and Kaminski (1994) reported that almost half of all assets sold to new buyers in their sample were used in a completely different way, from productive to nonproductive uses or vice versa. Clearly, the opportunity of exit via a piecemeal sale of assets is less for enterprises with highly specific assets. But if assets are not very specific, straight exit may stimulate the intersectoral, interbranch movement of assets. It seems, therefore, that no constraints should be imposed on the utilization of assets sold by insolvent firms.

A particular dimension of the downsizing or liquidation of state-owned enterprises concerns the enterprises effort to get rid of so-called "social assets," often considered an obstacle to restructuring. This process, usually motivated by the survival-oriented strategies of enterprise managers, contributes to the redefinition of the boundaries of firms and transforms the function of enterprises which previously were supposed to provide social protection to the employees.

Enterprise Restructuring

What is the role of classical and nonclassical forms of exit in restructuring existing firms? In transition economies, enterprises must take measures to reduce costs and scale down enterprise activity, such as cutting obsolete product lines, shedding labor, writing off debts, or getting rid of nonproductive assets. We have qualified such measures as "defensive" (Grosfeld and Roland, 1995) in the sense that their primary goal is the immediate survival of the enterprise. Another aspect of restructuring is strategic, and this must also be based on a thoughtful business strategy. This implies the transformation of the enterprise product mix and withdrawing capital from some lines of production and investing it in new ventures. The extent of the necessary disbanding of irrationally bundled assets distinguishes enterprise restructuring in CEEs from structural adjustment in developing countries. How much do exit processes help such a transformation?

Exit processes may have both indirect and direct impacts on enterprise restructuring. On the one hand, the mere threat of bankruptcy may change the expectations of managers and employees and encourage them to adopt various restructuring measures, including scaling down production and employment, to avoid insolvency. On the other hand, the actual implementation of bankruptcy procedures is often dependent on and may bring about specific restructuring measures.

In discussions concerning the role of exit in transition, in particular the effect of bankruptcy on the strengthening of financial discipline in large enterprises, it is typically assumed that classical exit mechanisms are not effectively enforced and that the stronger financial discipline observed is due rather to increased macroeconomic discipline. In large enterprises various complementary mechanisms motivate managers to restructure. These mechanisms include competition in the product market; internal corporate control by boards of directors or supervisory boards; remuneration tied to corporate performance, as measured by prices in the stock market; competition in the capital and managerial labor markets; and the regulatory system, including bankruptcy laws that transform creditors into owners and allow for reorganization of poorly performing borrowers under their supervision. Various combinations of these methods are used in different countries, depending upon their stage of development and regulatory history. Clearly, a sudden surge in product market competition played the key role in the first stage of transition. The initially weakly developed capital and managerial labor markets could hardly correct for the imperfections in managerial incentive systems. Agency costs were large in state-owned firms, in firms privatized to insiders, and in large widely-held corporations emerging from mass privatization programmes.

Did bankruptcy procedures for both private and state-owned enterprises prove to be important in enforcing market discipline and in providing incentives for managers to adjust and innovate? To be sure, bankruptcy procedures were not smoothly implemented in any CEE country. Many state-owned enterprises qualified for liquidation. Various attempts in each country to address the high indebtedness of state-owned enterprises to banks, suppliers, and the treasury have only been partially successful. All CEEs have had government bail-outs of large insolvent firms. However, we conclude, after looking at various case studies and surveys of enterprise restructuring, that liquidation has come to be considered by enterprise managers as a real threat. In Hungary and Poland, the fact that most downsizing was initiated by enterprise managers should be attributed partly to the progressive strengthening of financial discipline and notably to the enforcement of bankruptcies. These measures were certainly very threatening in Hungary in 1992–3, and in Poland various liquidation and bankruptcy routes contributed to harder budget constraints for illiquid firms. After years without bankruptcy, it was not necessary to have massive bankruptcies to make managers take them seriously: the limited number of firms going under could convincingly show that gambling on bailouts was becoming increasingly risky and potentially costly. In assessing the risks facing their firms, managers had to incorporate the possibility of closure. Such a change in perception has in some cases indirectly contributed not only to significant downsizing but also to the change in ownership structure. For instance, in the case of employee buy-outs (leasing) in Poland, the search for active outside investors has often been motivated by the fear of bankruptcy if the firm failed to restructure.

So the introduction of classical exit processes appears to have played an important role in changing the incentives of managers and indirectly influencing enterprise restructuring. But what was the direct impact of bankruptcy procedures as actually implemented on enterprise restructuring? Here it is useful to distinguish between reorganization and liquidation procedures. It has often been argued that bankruptcy laws in transition economies should be biased towards reorganization rather than liquidation in order to give necessary breathing space to enterprises facing unusually strong shocks. However, the available forms of reorganization do not seem to provide appropriate routes for restructuring. The reorganization plans usually include only measures of financial restructuring. What we have called strategic restructuring (Grosfeld and Roland 1996), i.e., programmes based on well-elaborated business plans and involving the introduction of new product lines, new processes, new technologies, and new forms of organization, occurs very rarely. According to Gray et al. and Gray and Holle (chapters 6, 7 and 8 of the volume), in Hungary and Poland the reorganization plans included financial terms (writing off debt principal, increasing the maturity of debt, and reducing interest rates) but little real operational restructuring. In Poland, the difficulty of working out a credible restructuring programme has been identified by banks as the key obstacle in the implementation of bank conciliation agreements (cf. Pawlowicz, 1994); typically, the quality of reorganization programs submitted by the debtor was rather poor, and about one-third of the programs that were agreed upon were not implemented (cf. Pawlowicz 1995).

From the point of view of the efficiency of restructuring, reorganization may unexpectedly prove to be less efficient than liquidation processes. First, most of the enterprises entering liquidation are not wound up and instead go through some kind of reorganization. According to chapter 6, firms entering liquidation in Hungary are rarely closed: most of the firms in the sample of fifty that filed for liquidation were still in operation two years later. Financial incentives provided to liquidators may hinder liquidations but stimulate restructuring. In Poland, up to the end of March 1995, only 25 percent (i.e., 318 out of 1,284) of firms in which liquidation had been initiated according to the law on state-owned enterprises were actually closed.[1] Moreover, the straight sale of a firm or the piecemeal sale of assets appears in some cases economically more efficient than reorganization. An important advantage of such exit mechanisms is that they reassign control over assets (see below).[2]

One set of costs usually associated with liquidation involves its negative impact on managerial behavior: managers expecting to be replaced in liquidation may act in a risk-averse manner. Such an effect should not be underestimated in transition economies, where efficient restructuring strongly depends on the implementation of innovative and risky projects. An increase in positive incentives for managers, including the development of managerial labor markets, may neutralize this effect. The concern that liquidation destroys contractual arrangements and contributes to the loss of organizational capital has also been expressed, and this point should be carefully analyzed.[3] Given the need for the rebundling of assets, the value of the existing arrangements may not be high compared to possible synergies that could be discovered outside the existing network.

Exit and the Allocation of Managerial Skills

Various surveys and case studies of enterprise restructuring show a great heterogeneity in the behavior of firms operating in the same sector and, in principle, subject to similar demand shocks. We find enterprises doing very well or doing very poorly, expanding or contracting, burdened with debt or financially strong, passively waiting for rescue proposals or implementing imaginative restructuring solutions by themselves. The interpretation of these differences is not easy, and various attempts to identify factors determining the performance of firms in transition have not yet produced convincing results. A plausible although hardly testable hypothesis is that firm adjustment strongly hinges on the quality of managers. Some managers prove to be capable of independent judgement and initiative, but others are clearly unable to offer firms any prospects for survival and would rather engage in rent-seeking activities. Unusually large differences in the abilities of managers can be explained by the legacy of the previous regime: the establishment of a selection process which hinged on bureaucratic loyalty rather than entrepreneurial spirit. Management turnover in Central European enterprises is rather low. Most incumbent managers have retained their position. In Hungary, for instance, only 6 percent of 117 surveyed firms undertook steps to change management.[4] Zemplinerová (1995a) reports, however, that from 1992 to 1995 70 percent of 257 surveyed Czech enterprises replaced the majority of their managers. If we agree that an efficient matching of managers is crucial for effective restructuring, it seems important to look at the institution of bankruptcy from this perspective. In particular, the question is whether incumbent managers should retain control of the firm in bankruptcy and whether they should have an exclusive right to propose a reorganization plan.

The answer to the first question is usually positive, two arguments being advanced. First, it is argued that in the period of transition managers face a very high aggregate uncertainty, and a company failure may have a number of reasons external to the firm (for example, shocks, government policy, unresolved problem of indebtedness, etc.). Consequently, incumbent managers should not necessarily be considered responsible for the sickness of the firm. The second position argues that incumbent managers should remain in place because they have superior knowledge of their enterprise. They know the value of the firm's assets and its opportunities better than outsiders do.

Given the profound changes in the environment of firms, managers should obviously be given the right to make mistakes, and the penalty for failure should not discourage risk taking. But if the efficiency of restructuring strongly depends on the efficient allocation of highly competent and innovative managers, a firm in bankruptcy should not systematically be left with the same managerial team that has brought it to insolvency. The informational advantage of incumbent managers also seems to be overestimated. It is true that managers have privileged access to existing information about the firm. Such information is valuable in a routine situation when it is well known what should be produced and how, but choosing restructuring projects in transition economies is not a routine decision. The managers must look for organizational innovations, and they often have to redefine the firm's production profile and recombine assets in line with a thoughtful long-term business strategy. Many incumbent managers, lacking a fresh view of the company's potential in a completely different environment, may be unable to work out such a program.[5] As we suggested earlier, the quality of restructuring might be enhanced if some elements of contestability were introduced through, for instance, open bidding for the control of the firm. Various shareholders and outsiders should be encouraged to submit competing restructuring plans. An example of such a procedure is the so-called program of restructuring and privatization in Poland, according to which various management groups are invited to submit a proposal for restructuring and bid for the right to manage a particular company. The very limited success of this program (as evidenced by the fact that only four contracts were signed in the first three years) suggests, however, that in a very uncertain environment, potential managers are reluctant to take the risks that the scheme imposes on them.[6]

The importance of stimulating competition among potential investors and managers has apparently been well understood by the architects of the Czech large-scale privatization program. Outsiders were encouraged to submit privatization projects. Unfortunately, probably because of the program's conflicting objectives, the privatization projects actually accepted were rarely those submitted by outsiders: 85 percent of the privatization projects approved by the Ministry of Privatization in the first wave of the voucher scheme were submitted by incumbent managers.

Different exit routes offer different possibilities for replacing incompetent managers. In mature economies, with strong capital and financial markets, badly performing firms can be liquidated or taken over. The new boards of directors may appoint new managers and begin reorganization. In transition economies, however, shareholders cannot use the market for corporate control to replace managers pursuing their own objectives, and other exit mechanisms should be available in order to provide such an opportunity. In Poland, only under the bankruptcy law do enterprises cease to be controlled by incumbent managers. Under court reorganization (the Arrangement Proceedings Law discussed in chapter 7), bank-led conciliation (chapter 8) and liquidation through the Law on State Enterprises (chapter 7), the appointed liquidators or trustees are usually former managers or trade union activists (as in the latter case, with URSUS and WIFAMA). In Hungary, top managers remain active in both liquidation and reorganization procedures (chapter 6).

A good example of contestability is provided in Poland by the so-called "privatization through rapid sale." Applied to firms in weak financial condition, this process may be considered as a form of reorganization which, through the sale of the firm on the open market, lets various investors bid for the firm. Such an open contest brings about multiple external assessments of a firm's value and of its expected future performance.[7] Efforts to promote the privatization of medium enterprises through auction should be welcome in this context.

Exit and Market Structure

The market structure typically inherited from the regime of central planning was dominated by highly capital intensive and concentrated industries and by excessive development of industry as compared to services. Vertical concentration was motivated by the attempts of enterprises to become self-sufficient and to limit uncertainties of supply. Horizontal concentration occurred because of the willingness of planners to exploit economies of scale and to ease coordination and the tendency of planners to merge weakly performing firms with strong ones. The introduction of exit processes affects market structure directly by changing the number and the size of firms and indirectly by stimulating the entry of new firms.

Entry

Progressively removing barriers to entry by domestic and foreign firms, breaking up existing monopolies and oligopolies,[8] and making anti-monopoly offices responsible for the control of monopolistic behavior were recognized as key steps at the beginning of transition. It also quickly became apparent that no reasonable degree of competition could be injected in an economy without putting in place flexible mechanisms through which inefficient firms could exit the market. Eliminating barriers to exit may temporarily reduce the number of existing firms and therefore reduce the degree of competition. However, if barriers to entry are low, price increases brought about by closures stimulate new entry. New firms with good investment ideas have more chance to succeed if inefficient firms are eliminated or forced to downsize. New entry enhances competition, which in turn puts pressure on existing firms and forces losers to go bust. But if existing firms are subsidized and sheltered from competition—especially in the case of large state-owned enterprises in the nontraded goods market and in markets protected by tariffs—dynamic firms with some advantages over established enterprises will fail to enter.

In Central and Eastern Europe, the weakening of barriers to the entry of new firms gave an impetus to the development of the new private sector. The spectacular increase in the number of economic organizations is, however, only a partial indicator of the number of new entries, as it should also take into account the important process of break-ups, spin-offs, and split-ups (see table 9.1).

Table 9.1
Number of Economic Organizations by Legal Status

	1989	1990	1991	1992	1993	1994
Czech Republic (a)						
SOEs (b)		1576	3505	3737	3272	1827(e)
companies (c)		46	658	2541	4076	5847(e)
Hungary (d)						
SOEs (b)	2400	2363	2233	1733	1130	821
companies (c)	4792	18963	42276	58274	75272	90853
cooperatives	7076	7641	7766	8229	8668	8252
Poland (d)						
SOEs (b)		8454	8228	7245	5924	4955
companies (c)		36267	53771	69907	83283	95017
cooperatives		18575	18949	19372	19746	19816

(a) beginning of the year, (b) state-owned enterprises, (c) limited liability and joint-stock companies, (d) end of the year, (e) october

Source: *Rocznik Statystyczny*, GUS 1994; *Statistical Yearbook of Hungary*, 1994; *The Privatization Newsletter of the Czech Republic and Slovakia*, N° 32, March 1995; Rzeczpospolita, 1995.

The link between exit and entry is, however, very indirect. If it were not, the countries that adopted more stringent bankruptcy laws would see more entries, assuming the extent of downsizing in the existing firms was similar. Taking one of the available measures of entry, i.e., the number of individual entrepreneurs (see table 9.2), we can see that their share in total employment is the biggest in the Czech Republic, the country that delayed in a spectacular way the implementation of the bankruptcy law. In 1993 the share of private entrepreneurs in total employment reached 16.6 percent in the Czech Republic, 12.1 percent

Table 9.2
Number of Private Entrepreneurs (thousands)

	1989	1990	1991	1992	1993	1994
Poland(a)	81.1	1135.5	1420.1	1630.6	1783.9	1876.6
Hungary(a)	320.0	393.5	510.5	606.2	688.9	778.0
Czech Republic(b)		124.5	891.9	982.1	785.7	911.3(c)

Notes: (a) end of the year; (b) beginning of the year; (c) october.

Source: *Rocznik Statystyczny*, GUS, 1994; *Statistical Yearbook of Hungary*, KSH, 1994; *The Privatization Newsletter of the Czech Republic and Slovakia*, N° 32, March 1995

in Poland, and 15.8 percent in Hungary. In the long term, however, the complex relationship between exit and entry can be expected to lead to a positive correlation between the intensity of exit and the intensity of entry.

Industrial Structure

Letting firms exit and enter may help lower the degree of concentration of the industrial structure. Under the combined effects of breaking up, spinning off, and downsizing existing firms and new entries, the size distribution of enterprises quickly showed signs of deconcentration (see table 9.3). In Poland, the share of small enterprises employing between fifty and 100 people increased from 14 percent in 1990 to 37 percent in 1993; in the same period the share of large enterprises employing over 500 people decreased from 31 percent to 17 percent. In the Czech Republic, small and medium-size enterprises employing between 100 and 300 people increased their share in the total number of enterprises from 25 percent in 1990 to 56 percent in 1993. Again, however, this evolution was the combined effect of a number of complex and interrelated forces and not only the result of various exit processes.

The spectacular increase in the number of small and medium-sized enterprises was not accompanied, however, by significant deconcentration in terms of the share of the largest firms in total sales. In Poland,

Table 9.3
Poland and the Czech Republic: The Share of Industrial Enterprises by the Number of Employees (in percentage)

	1990	1991	1992	1993
Poland				
< 100	14	30	35	37
101–500	55	49	47	46
501–2000	24	17	14	15
> 2001	7	4	4	2
Total	100	100	100	100
Czech Republic				
100–299	25	33	45	56
300–2499	59	47	49	41
2500+	16	11	6	3
Total	100	100	100	100

Sources: Poland: Own calculations based on *Rocznik Statystyczny*, GUS, 1991, 1992, 1993, 1994. The data concern enterprises over fifty employees, except for 1993 when the numbers for energy, gas and some other sectors include enterprises with over twenty employees; The Czech Republic: Bouin (1995), p. 136.

the share of the largest 500 manufacturing firms in total manufacturing sales decreased from 56 percent in 1989 to 52 percent in 1994, but the share of the 100 largest firms increased in the same period from 32 to 35 percent.[9]

The first signs of deconcentration may be considered encouraging because a less concentrated industrial structure is less vulnerable to liquidation. However, when considering the relationship between exit and industrial structure we cannot omit the possible effects of the evolving industrial structure on the probability and intensity of exit. Although the aim of this work is to assess the impact of exit on different dimensions of the economies in transition, we would like to mention this reverse connection because it appears potentially very damaging. The emergence of new types of large and strong organizations, such as financial-industrial groups, holdings and conglomerates, should be a matter of concern.The large financial-industrial groups can undermine competition and practice collusive and rent-seeking behavior. Such groups can more easily lobby the government for protection, subsidies and privileged credits. They can make policy makers representatives of their own interests (regulatory capture). As they grow, these financial-industrial groups may become too big to fail. Company failure within such groups is less apparent and can be masked through cross-subsidization. Consequently, the mechanisms of exit may be blocked.

Attempts to form large groupings of state-owned enterprises in the same industry may recreate the familiar relationships of the old regime (Joskow et al., 1994). It is less clear, however, whether and under what conditions the integration of firms after privatization or in the process of transformation of their legal status can have positive effects on efficiency. Obviously, vertical integration can increase efficiency if, other things being equal, it allows firms to take advantage of economies of scale: an increase in output or the production by multi-product firms may bring about a less than proportionate rise in total costs.[10] However, to the extent that integration means transferring residual rights of control, its benefits should be carefully compared with its costs. Integration "shifts the incentives for opportunistic and distortionary behavior but it does not remove these incentives" (Grossman and Hart, 1986). In particular, the decision about integration should be based on a good understanding of firms' prospects. Mergers in countries in transition and the strengthening of links between firms, their suppliers and customers, or between banks and industry, seem to be based on short-term considerations and are usually motivated by a willingness to shelter the individual firms from market uncertainties. Uncertainty about contract enforcement, including the weak credibility of exit, provides part of the rationale for concentration, which allows firms to internalize more transactions. Such uncertainty clearly appears to be the motivation behind the creation of capital groups in Poland which are being built around banks and foreign trade companies having accumulated large foreign-currency receipts. These cash cows are merged with enterprises that have attractive investment projects but are unable to finance them because of the underdevelopment of financial markets. Less convincing are arguments in favor of the creation of holding companies that link, vertically or horizontally, enterprises in the same industry. Ensuring timely supplies is a weak rationale for concentration.

To be sure, we do not suggest that the creation of large nonstate groups should be forbidden, as long as they are subject to antimonopoly laws and can reasonably claim that the proposed structures would bring about substantial gains in efficiency (Joskow et al., 1994). But these groups certainly should not be created as a result of an administrative decision or encouraged by special fiscal advantages. The negative effects of concentration can be weakened if various forms of divestiture—sell-offs, spin-offs, and demergers—remain available. The impediments to exit could also be alleviated if the loss-making divisions of a conglomerate could be wound up without a formal procedure.

Classical Exit Mechanisms and Financial Systems

Properly functioning exit processes that provide safeguards for potential creditors make lending less risky and stimulate the development of the credit market. Creditors need clear mechanisms that allow them to enforce their claims in the case of default. Less formal mechanisms can be satisfactory in the case of short-term contracts, but long-term, large-scale investment may suffer from a lack of formal enforcement mechanisms (Rubin, 1994). In other words, the enforcement of bankruptcy procedures may be one of the prerequisites for the availability of credit.

On the other hand, in order for bankruptcy proceedings to function smoothly, well-developed financial markets are needed. This sequencing dilemma has been addressed differently in different countries. The originality of the Czech case in this context lies in its favoring the development of the capital market and only then enforcing the bankruptcy law.[11]

The question has often been asked whether the design of bankruptcy laws in transition countries should aim at protecting creditors' rights or favor the survival of illiquid or even insolvent firms and fostering employment protection at the cost of delaying the satisfaction of creditors' claims. The usual suggestion is that because these economies need to be profoundly restructured, and indicators of insolvency may be misleading, priority should be given to reorganization. The trade-off between the protection of creditors and the survival of enterprises may prove to be less sharp than suggested. If creditors' expectations can be changed, i.e., if they become sure that their rights will be protected in bankruptcy, they will be motivated to gather information about their borrowers and to exercise their voice in the case of default, which may eventually contribute to the revival of troubled firms. Avoiding exit and bailing out bad firms may perpetuate the passivity of creditors and fuel self-fulfilling expectations of inertia.

In fact, most of the existing exit processes seem to be unfavorable to creditors. Debt holders in the countries under study do not really have the possibility of exit via the capital market for debt. The secondary market for debt is developing very slowly. In Poland, it has been fueled by the programe of financial restructuring of enterprises and banks.[12] Recent experience in Hungary shows that creditors have very little influence during the liquidation process (chapter 6); the balance seems to be in favor of troubled firms. Creditors' interests are better protected in Poland, especially within the framework of the law on the financial restructuring of enterprises and banks. The greatest advantage of this law might actually be in providing creditors with the possibility of protecting their interests in the bankruptcy process. Banks have been forced to learn and to become involved in working out restructuring programs.

The weak enforceability of bankruptcy laws may be partly responsible for the prohibitively high cost of credit in transition economies. The reluctance of Czech banks to lend in the 1991–3 period may reflect the fact that the implementation of the bankruptcy proceedings was delayed.

Exit processes are also one of the factors determining the emergence and the proper functioning of financial intermediaries. Properly designed and implemented bankruptcy laws may help to improve the quality of bank assets which is a precondition for their restructuring and privatization. Financial intermediaries not only provide finance to firms but also play an important role in corporate governance, especially if there is a free-rider problem in the monitoring of managers by shareholders (due to dispersed ownership). It has been argued elsewhere (Grosfeld and Roland, 1996) that venture capital funds might be the most beneficial form of financial intermediary under the conditions of transforming economies. Managers of such funds usually have skills that go beyond purely financial analysis: the provision of capital is accompanied by strategic guidance, business and managerial expertise, and monitoring. This is notably the case in independent venture capital companies not owned by banks or other financial intermediaries, as opposed to "captive finds" that are usually bank subsidiaries.[13] But an important condition for the development of venture capital firms seems to be the existence of divestment options. If exit routes are not flexible enough, the returns required by the venture capital companies will be prohibitively high. Among these exit routes, the development of the stock market seems to be particularly important. Sagari and Guidotti (1992) show that venture capital firms were established in those developing countries that had an active stock market, i.e., in Taiwan, Korea, Malaysia, and India.

Exit and Privatization

In transition economies undertaking large-scale privatization, various routes of exit lead to the transfer of assets from the state to the private sector. Some routes are straightforward and have even been designed to allow such transfer. In the case of piecemeal liquidation, assets are sold in order to satisfy creditors, and buyers are more often than not private entrepreneurs or private companies; firms are also often bought by private investors. Some other routes of exit have emerged somewhat unexpectedly and seem to offer an interesting alternative to classic privatization methods.

In Poland, one of the objectives of the law on financial restructuring of enterprises and banks was to accelerate privatization: swapping debt for equity was considered one of the mechanisms of solving the problem of bad debts. It appears that in sixty-six cases out of the total of 419 conciliatory agreements, debts have indeed been converted into equity (Pawlowicz 1995). However, it is not clear how far this can be considered as privatization, given that most shares have been taken over by firms and banks that are also still state-owned (Pawlowicz, 1995 and chapter 8).

Another privatization option could be swaps of debt bought on the secondary market for equity. It was argued in Grosfeld (1997) that banks do not necessarily have a comparative advantage in working out corporate restructuring programs and being at the same time creditors and shareholders. The responsibility of reorganization and ownership should rather be left to those who give the highest value to the debt of the firm. Therefore, the sale of bank debt on the secondary market could increase the efficiency of privatization and of enterprise restructuring. The recent experience in Poland shows some development of the secondary market for debt, which has been fueled by the implementation of the law on the financial restructuring of banks and enterprises (but see chapter 8 for a discussion of problems with the procedure). Some swaps for equity of nonbank debt bought on the secondary market have already occurred and appear to be a promising privatization route.

Conclusions

The design and implementation of exit mechanisms in transition economies is often discussed in terms of their expected impact on the labor market. The argument for postponing or gradually introducing bankruptcy procedures often relies on the assumption that they will bring about a large number of liquidations and, consequently, may provoke a massive, politically unsustainable wave of lay-offs. On the other hand, it is argued that the bankruptcy law itself should be biased in favor of reorganization rather than liquidation, because the former saves jobs.

We have seen, however, that even outside formal bankruptcies, enterprises in Central European countries are forced to adjust. Under the combined effects of increased competitive market pressure and changes in managerial incentives, firms often react by downsizing and laying off workers. These reductions in employment, which are survival-oriented measures of adjustment, might have been influenced, however, by increases in the threat of foreclosure. Firms entering bankruptcy and continuing to operate are also forced to reduce employment. But the dynamic effect of liquidations on employment may be positive: the piecemeal sale of assets or of parts of firms facilitates the transfer of assets to more productive uses and may therefore contribute to an increased demand for labor.

The functioning of the labor market may also be indirectly influenced by the existence of a system of bankruptcy. Employees may accept reductions in employment and foreclosures more easily if they know that their claims for unpaid wages and pension benefits will be satisfied according to a transparent rule. The mere existence of exit processes can play a key role in anchoring the expectations of employees, managers, creditors, and shareholders. The actual intensity of exit can be decisive for enterprise restructuring and the evolution of market structure.

The needs of economies in transition put specific requirements on the design of bankruptcy law. The initial concern regarding the negative effects of excessive piecemeal liquidation should give way to the notion that promoting reorganization by insiders may perpetuate inertia and postpone real restructuring. Outsiders should be allowed to take their chances.

Physical capital may be more easily redeployable than human and organizational capital. But if an economy needs to profoundly reorient its productive structure, as we think transition economies must do, it should also look for a new bundling of assets, including managerial skills, contacts, and information. Therefore, liquidation may be less damaging than is usually assumed.

References

Aghion, Ph., O. Hart, and J. Moore. 1992. The economics of bankruptcy reform. *The Journal of Law, Economics and Organization,* 8, no. 3: 523–46.

Audretsch, D. B. et al. 1995. Sub-optimal scale firms and compensating factor differentials in Dutch manufacturing. Centre for Economic Policy Research, London, Discussion Paper, no 1162.

Beecroft, A. 1994. The role of the venture capital industry. In *Capital Markets and Corporate Governance,* edited by N. Dimsdale and M. Prevezer. Oxford: Clarendon Press.

Bouin, O. 1995. Privatization et transformation économique en Europe Centrale et Orientale: L'example de la République Tchèque. (Privatization and Economic transformation in Central and Eastern Europe: The Czech exemple), PhD Dissertation, Ecole des Hautes Etudes en Sciences Sociales, Paris.

Bouin, O. and I. Grosfeld. 1995. Crédibilité des réformes et ajustement des entreprises en Pologne et en République Tchèque, Revue Economique, (Reform credibility and enterprise adjustment in Poland and in the Czech Republic) 46, no. 3.

Dabrowski, J.M. and T. Kaminski. 1994. Likwidacja upadlosciowa (Liquidation of insolvent enterprises) In Szomburg et al. (1994).

Glowna Urzad Statystyczny, Prywatyzacja Przedsiebiorstw Panstwowych, wedlug stanu na 31.03.1995 (Privatization of state-owned enterprises as of 31 March 1995) 1995, (Warsaw, GUS.)

Grosfeld, I. and G. Roland. 1996. Defensive and strategic restructuring in Central European enterprises. *Journal of Transforming Economies* 3, no. 4.

Grosfeld, I. 1997. Financial systems in transition: The role of banks in corporate governance, in *Experiences with Financial Liberalization* edited by K.L. Gupta (Kluwer Academic Publishers, Dodrecht, Holland).

Grossman, S. J. and O. Hart. 1986. The costs and benefits of ownership: A theory of vertical and lateral integration. *Journal of Political Economy* 94, no. 41.

Joskow, P., R. Schmalensee, and N. Tsukanova. 1994. Competition policy in Russia during and after privatization. In *Brookings Papers on Economic Activity, Microeconomics,* edited by M.N. Baily, P.C. Reiss and C. Winston.

Novak, T. and M. Sazanyi (1995). Downsizing in Hungarian Manufacturing. mimeo.

Pawlowicz, L., (ed.) 1995. *Restrukturyzacja Finansowa Przedsiebiorstw i Bankow*. (Financial restructuring of enterprises and banks. The first report) *Pierwszy Raport z Badan,* Gdansk: Instytut Badan nad Gospodarka Rynkowa.

Pawlowicz, L., (ed.) 1995. *Restrukturyzacja Finansowa Przedsiebiorstw i Bankow*. (Financial restructuring of enterprises and banks. The second report) *Drugi Raport z Badan*, Gdansk: Instytut Badan nad Gospodarka Rynkowa.

Roe, M. J. 1983. Bankruptcy and debt: A new model for corporate reorganization, *Columbia Law Review* 83, no. 3.

Sagari, A. B. and G. Guidotti. 1992. Venture Capital: Lessons from the developed world for developing markets. International Finance Corporation Discussion Paper no. 13 (IFC, Washington).

Schwalb Hotchkiss, E. 1995. Postbankruptcy performance and management turnover. *The Journal of Finance* 50, no 1.

Stark, D. 1996. Recombinant property in East European capitalism. *American Journal of Sociology,* 101, no. 4.

Szomburg, J. 1994 "Szybka sprzedaz", (Rapid sale) in Szomburg et al. (1994).

Szomburg, J., J.M. Dabrowski, and T. Kaminski. 1994. *Monitoring przedsiebiorstw sprywatyzowanych*, (Monitoring of privatized enterprises) Gdansk: Instytut Badan nad Gospodarka Rynkowa,

White, M. 1989. The corporate bankruptcy decision. *The Journal of Economic Perspectives* 3, no. 2, 129–51.

Zemplinerová, A. 1995a. Restructuring of firms in Czech manufacturing in the context of privatization: Results of the enterprise survey. *Privatization Newsletter of the Czech Republic and Slovakia,* no. 31, February.

Zemplinerová, A. 1995b. Market structure adjustment during privatization. *Privatization Newsletter of the Czech Republic and Slovakia,* no. 35, June.

Notes

1. Cf. Prywatyzacja Przedsiebiorstw Panstwowych (1995). According to the same source, 30 percent of enterprises (380 cases) have left the process and are to be treated according to the general bankruptcy law.

2. The weakness of reorganization procedures has also been stressed in the case of developed market economies: several authors (cf. Roe, 1983, Bebchuk, 1986, Aghion et al.,1992) have suggested that instead of a reorganization procedure (chapter 11), a more market-based mechanism could be used to increase the efficiency of the bankruptcy process. A main motivation of these proposals is to give decisions about the prospects for a firm to those who put up their own money. The separation of debt restructuring into liquidation and reorganization creates an opportunity for voluntary filing for bankruptcy (reorganization) by inefficient firms. White (1989) underlines, however, the trade-off between efficiency of restructuring in bankruptcy and outside bankruptcy.

3. Stark (1996) argues forcefully that close interenterprise links should be preserved, even at the expense of allocative efficiency, because they allow risk-sharing.

4. Cf. chapter 6. However, 30 percent of firms that agreed on reorganization plans did in fact change top management.

5. Economic journals in different countries provide us with a lot of anecdotal evidence and complaints about the weakness of reorganization proposals submitted by incumbent managers. Even in developed countries, where the allocation of managerial talent is supposed to be more efficient, there is evidence that the continued involvement of original management in the restructuring process is strongly associated with poor postbankruptcy performance. See Schwalb Hotchkiss (1995)

6. Management groups are invited to bid for a particular company and submit proposals for restructuring before privatization. The winner, who gives the highest initial value of the enterprise, has to make a security deposit according to some predetermined scheme (e.g. 5 percent of the value up to 10 billion zlotys). New management is offered financial incentives in order to increase the value of the firm—a monthly salary, annual bonus based on net profits of the firm, and or capital gain premium payable in shares of the company. If a management group realizes a sale of at least 51 percent of the equity, it gets 70 percent of the real capital gain on the sale, i.e. the difference between the sale price and the tender price, adjusted for inflation; 20 percent goes to the employees and 10 percent to the supervisory boards.

7. However, it seems that in most cases of "rapid sales" competition among bidders is rather weak and the number of actual offers small. See Szomburg (1994).

8. In 1990 the Polish Anti-Monopoly Office broke up almost 200 large enterprises, giving rise to 700 new independent units. In the Czech Republic there were two waves of break-ups. In 1990 the process of spontaneous break-ups contributed to a two- to three-fold increase in the number of enterprises in some industries. An intense division of firms continued during the implementation of the large-scale privatization programme; 1,179 enterprises before the approval of privatization projects were transformed into 3,293 after the approval (Zemplinerová, 1995b).

9. Calculated on the basis of Lista 500 (state-owned manufacturing enterprises), Zarzadzanie, no. 6–7, 1990 and Lista 500 (public and private manufacturing enterprises), Zycie Gospodarcze, no. 1, 1995. Although in 1989 the list of 500 included only state-owned enterprises, it seems safe to assume that in 1989 privatization and the development of the new private sector in manufacturing had hardly begun, and the largest firms were certainly stateowned.

10. However, according to Audretsch et al. (1995) the cost disadvantage of small firms may at least to some extent be offset by the strategy of compensating factors of production differently than large firms—reducing the wage paid to labor, increasing investment in R&D activity, etc.

11. Such sequencing has been explicitly suggested by Márton Tardos at a very early stage of transformation: "Markets need to be developed and connected within the economy before passage of a bankruptcy law makes sense."

12. Banks were encouraged to sell the loans of unviable firms on the open market. According to preliminary estimates, about 13 percent of the total value of loans put on sale have actually been sold (Pawlowicz, 1995).

13. According to Beecroft (1994), captive funds tend to have more financial than industrial expertise and are more likely to engage in short-term investment activity, while independent funds have long-term perspectives and are usually run by people with industrial and management background and expertise.

Index

Numbers in *italics* refer to tables

For Product Safety Concerns and Information please contact our EU representative GPSR@taylorandfrancis.com Taylor & Francis Verlag GmbH, Kaufingerstraße 24, 80331 München, Germany

Batch number: 10725853

Printed by Printforce, the Netherlands